JOURNAL FOR THE STUDY OF THE OLD TESTAMENT SUPPLEMENT SERIES

57

Editors
David J A Clines
Philip R Davies

JSOT Press
Sheffield

MOSES

Heroic Man, Man of God

George W. Coats

Journal for the Study of the Old Testament
Supplement Series 57

Copyright © 1988 Sheffield Academic Press

Published by JSOT Press
JSOT Press is an imprint of
Sheffield Academic Press Ltd
The University of Sheffield
343 Fulwood Road
Sheffield S10 3BP
England

Typeset by Sheffield Academic Press
and
printed in Great Britain
by Billing & Sons Ltd
Worcester

British Library Cataloguing in Publication Data

Coats, George W.
  Moses : heroic man, man of God.—
  (Journal for the study of the Old Testament
  supplement series, ISSN 0309-0787; 57).
  1. Moses. Prophet
  I. Title   II. Series
  222'.12'0924   BS580.M6

  ISBN 1-85075-096-3
  ISBN 1-85075-095-5 Pbk

CONTENTS

MOSES
Heroic Man, Man of God

Chapter 1

INTRODUCTION

According to Old Testament traditions, Moses led his people from the oppression of their slavery in Egypt to the edge of the promised land. Indeed, his stature dominates the entire collection of narratives from Exodus through Deuteronomy. In these narratives, the exodus event itself, the wanderings through the wilderness, the gift of the law at Sinai, and even the conquest of land in Transjordan stand in some measure under the shadow of his hand. Given the gigantic dimensions of his role in the Hexateuch, it is surprising that his position in the remaining parts of the Old Testament demands relatively little space. It is true, nonetheless, that despite the obvious dwarfing of Moses outside the Hexateuch, his figure still rises at key points, in both the Old Testament and the New. The following texts illustrate the point: Hos. 12.14 does not refer to Moses by name but nonetheless makes a clear allusion to his leadership: 'By a prophet the Lord brought Israel up from Egypt, and by a prophet he was preserved'. In Neh. 1.8, a prayer petitions God to 'remember the word which you commanded Moses your servant...' And in the Gospel of Matthew, 17.1-8, Jesus' transfiguration occurs in the presence of Moses and Elijah.[1]

The sheer magnitude of Moses' influence on the world cannot emerge, however, simply by reference to his role in biblical tradition. In ancient literature, Philo wrote a 'Life of Moses'. In the world of medieval art, Michelangelo made the strength of the horned Moses a masterpiece of intense beauty. And in the modern period, Karen Laub-Novak captured the twin roles of Moses' leadership and his dependency on God in a painting of perceptive quality. Moreover, as in the Old Testament, Ezra 7.6 for example, so in our time, the name of Moses has become a symbol for religious authority. The Torah has special authority for the life of both synagogue and church at least in part because tradition invests it with Mosaic origin.

Yet, why should Moses hold such a creative role in the history of the world's culture? The answer to that question resides in the biblical tradition itself, for no other source from the time of Moses to the time of the Babylonian exile tells us anything about this giant. The purpose for this book, then, is to explore the character of the Moses traditions in the Old Testament in order to see the more clearly why they have influenced the world as much as they have. Yet, caution must prevail. The task is, unfortunately, not as simple as would be suggested by this statement of purpose. In the allusions to Moses cited above, the image does not appear to be consistently formulated. In one text, he is labeled explicitly a prophet. But he does not deliver an oracle of God to the people, prefaced by a messenger formula, as we might expect from a prophet. Rather, he leads his people as a shepherd might lead his sheep. The image appears particularly strong in Hos. 12.14. The verb 'preserved', or better, 'kept', *nišmār*, suggests that the prophet leader of the people does the work of a shepherd (compare Gen. 30.31, where the same verb denotes the work of a shepherd). In the second text, Moses is lawgiver, the one who commands his people in the name of God, and they obey. In the Gospel text, where a primary facet of the tradition focuses on the issues of authority, Moses attends the transfiguration of Jesus. Thus, to explore the biblical tradition about Moses means to clarify the patterns of images associated with this figure. Who, according to the tradition, was Moses?

It would be presumptuous, however, to suggest that this task has never been undertaken. The artistic pieces representing Moses reach a wide section of the population. Moreover, in our own day, Hollywood and television movies project images of Moses into the intimate circles of many families. It cannot be surprising, then, that the bibliography for Mosaic studies is enormous. Artists of all generations reveal their fascination with this giant. And in like manner, so have Old Testament scholars. At least three different methods provide significant insight into the Moses traditions: (1) historical, (2) sociological, and (3) literary. I should emphasize here that while the three methods are distinct, they are by no means independent. Each contributes its own position of the question and its own perception to a total picture of the giant. And as each makes its distinctive contribution, the other two demand supportive hearing. In the following probe, I propose to explore the Moses traditions on the basis of a particular kind of literary analysis. But the literary analysis cannot afford to ignore the insights of historical or sociological studies.

But why should another study of the Moses traditions be necessary? And what kind of relationship does this one acknowledge with the contributions in each of the three fields of study? A critical assessment of some major items in each will demonstrate the perspective of this book.[2]

Historical Studies

A review of historical studies in the Moses traditions should begin with a famous observation by John Bright:

> Over all these events [exodus to the edge of the land] towers the figure of Moses. Though we know nothing of his career, save what the Bible tells us, the details of which we have no means of testing, there can be no doubt that he was, as the Bible portrays him, the great founder of Israel's faith. Attempts to reduce him are extremely unconvincing. The events of exodus and Sinai require a great personality behind them. And a faith as unique as Israel's demands a founder as surely as does Christianity—or Islam, for that matter. To deny that role to Moses would force us to posit another person of the same name.[3]

Bright's optimism about the historical Moses gains support from the work of W.F. Albright.[4] Like Bright, Albright carries out his historical studies of Moses under the assumption that Moses was a figure of historical importance and thus requires no historical verification. Albright's concern is rather to paint in the background of culture and national or international history for the period when Moses obviously lived and worked. His skill in composing such a background picture cannot be surpassed. Moses doubtlessly lived in the thirteenth century before the common era and, in fact, facilitated introduction of Egyptian influence into the traditions that became Israel's life blood. Under Albright's pen, the thirteenth century comes alive in great depth and variety. And he concludes, in a manner that supports Bright's assertion: 'Moses, probably born in the late fourteenth century BC and died about the middle of the thirteenth, was founder of ancient Israel'.[5]

But in none of these data, either archaeological or literary, does Moses himself appear as a figure in the process of history. Albright, like Bright, must simply assume that Moses was a historical figure whose influence affected the development of Egypt and Israel. We are left, then, with the accuracy of Bright's remark: 'We know nothing of his [Moses'] career, save what the Bible tells us, the details of which we have no means of testing. . . '[6] Historical analysis of the Moses traditions depends, therefore, on the data provided by the biblical text itself.

Dewey Beegle recognizes the impact of this point and thus grounds his investigation into questions about Moses and history on his understanding of the literature.[7] Yet, the text for Beegle appears to be only of secondary importance, submerged as it is under the dominating interest in reconstructing history. It is his intention 'to see Moses as he was and not what various periods of tradition attributed to him'.[8] Would this procedure not lose sight of the reality posed to any analysis of the Moses traditions by John Bright? Can we get to the historical Moses simply by cutting through the text and reconstructing the remainder as the subject of our interest? The text is itself the evidence. The points of view about Moses used in each stage in the 'various periods of tradition' are the only windows that offer us a vision of the figure we seek.

Beegle's work on Moses seems to me, therefore, to face two major problems.

1. If the historical Moses rises to our eyes only from the pages of the received text, under what circumstances can we reconstruct that text in order to win a more acceptable historical image? This question comes into focus especially in relationship to the structure of the plague narrative, Moses' negotiations with the Pharaoh, suggested by Greta Hort,[9] a reconstruction incorporated by Beegle substantially as his own position.[10] In Hort's picture, the plagues occurred in sequence as the consequence of certain natural events. For example, in excessively heavy rainfall, the Blue Nile would have picked up heavy silt washed off of the red earth in the walls of its valley. It would then have flowed, blood-red, into the White Nile, blocking introduction of any water that would change its color. Moreover, the silt and algae would have polluted the water, leaving it with a foul smell and denying the people in the valley its water for drinking and irrigation. In addition, the algae would have caused a fluctuation in the oxygen level of the water, weakening the fish and finally killing them. And so the sequence goes. But the problem is in the reconstruction of the received text. The text does not report that the water turned a blood-red because of silt and algae. It insists that the water turned to blood. How much liberty do we have, then, to

read a rational construction of historical events directly from the story presented by the received text? Do we not have rather the responsibility to ask first what the text intends to say, indeed, what kind of story it contains? It may be that the intention of the story is to give a naive description of historical events in the sequence of their occurrence. But it may also be that the story has a quite different intention. And it cannot be used as an historical source until that question is answered.

2. Beegle concludes that the story of Moses is really not about Moses but about God.[11] Moses appears in the narrative only in a supporting role. The history available for reconstruction is thus not the history of Moses but salvation history, the history of the Lord. It is quite clear that the tradition affirms God's inspiration for the leader who brought the people out of bondage. But does that fact lead to a denigration of the role Moses plays? Beegle does not in fact denigrate Moses. It is to Moses' merit that he plays second fiddle to the Lord. But how can this unique relationship between Moses and God be evaluated? How can the text attribute the first billing to God without reducing Moses to a mere instrument in God's hands, a tool that wields no more imagination in carrying out his deeds than does a hammer in the hands of the master carpenter? Do we not hear a tradition that asserts top billing to both God and his servant? So, in Exod. 14.31:

> The Lord saved Israel that day from the hand of the Egyptians; and Israel saw the Egyptians dead upon the seashore. And Israel saw the great work which the Lord did against the Egyptians, and the people feared the Lord; and they believed in the Lord and in his servant Moses.

And in the process do we not witness narratives that contain not only God's words and deeds, but Moses' words and deeds as well? It is only by recognizing this double character that reference to the Old Testament Torah as Mosaic, rather than simply Yahwistic, makes sense.

Elias Auerbach develops a similar approach to the Moses traditions. He observes:

> Our sources are exclusively biblical; nothing is known about Moses from any other source, such as Egyptian . . . Therefore, only the biblical narratives remain. They, however, cannot be used for historical research in their present state; indeed, they present peculiar difficulties.[12]

Thus, it is obvious that for Auerbach a literary critical evaluation of the traditions must precede a reconstruction of the history of Moses. Yet, the concern for Auerbach remains primarily construction of the history: 'Our first task in all the sources is to penetrate to the oldest accounts in the Moses legends'.[13] Auerbach knows the problems:

> We must not expect to find historical reports about Moses [even in the oldest accounts] since, strictly speaking, no such reports have been preserved. Scholars are in about the same position here as they would be concerning the Homeric poems, if nothing else were known about the most ancient history of the Greek tribes. Yet even then Homer would be a mine of historical information, not so much for the understanding of single events and of the people actually taking part in them, as for the geographical, political, social, and cultural background of that bygone period which, due to archaeological investigation, has come to life once more in a way which confirms Homer time and again.[14]

Auerbach offers, then, a sound methodology into the history of Moses. Historical reconstruction must depend on a careful evaluation of the literary shape in the sources. The prospects for developing any notion of the historical Moses, given the sources now available, must await a satisfactory evaluation of the traditions as literary art.

Yet, I would again recommend a little caution. Evaluation of the tradition as literary art may show that the style of the narrative calls for historical verisimilitude. That a story depicts the thirteenth century BC with historical and cultural precision does not prove that the *story* is accurate history. It proves only that historical and cultural background for the story is precise. That names and places in the story actually appeared in the thirteenth century BC does not prove that the persons in the story who carry those names actually did what the story attributes to them. For example, we know that the army of the United States burned Atlanta in 1864 in an infamous march to the sea during the period of the Civil War. And names like Rhett Butler and Scarlet O'Hara are not foreign to an American setting. But those data do not prove that the story in *Gone with the Wind* recounts factual events that occurred to a particular historical family of the old South. Even with historical verisimilitude, the novel remains a work of fiction. The background may be accurate. But a recovery of the historical Rhett Butler remains a remote possibility.

It seems wise, then, at least to hear voices that opt for some distance from easy historical pictures about Moses and his time. John Bright represents a kind of historical optimism about the quest for the historical Moses and guards against a reductionist methodology that would seek out only a small fragment of the Moses traditions as the historical kernel. Historical skepticism and reductionist methods cannot explain the great stature attributed to Moses at every corner of the tradition, particularly in the corners of Exodus through Deuteronomy. But one can hardly resolve a historical picture of Moses by overriding the reduction with an assumption about historicity. The antagonist for Bright was Martin Noth. He suggested that the Moses narratives embrace material from four distinct and originally independent themes of tradition: (1) the exodus out of Egypt, (2) the wilderness wanderings, (3) the gift of the law at Sinai, and (4) the conquest of Transjordan. But, Noth objected, since these four themes were originally independent of each other, Moses could not have played an equally original role in each one. He must have been attached primarily to only one of these themes and subsequently extended to the other three when the traditions were unified around an all-Israel perspective. Noth's suggestion is that Moses belonged at first only to the conquest theme, with the tradition about his death and burial in Transjordan the firmest point for defining the rootage for the stories.[15]

Gerhard von Rad followed Noth's suggestions about the themes in the Moses traditions, with some appropriate revisions.

> If it is true that the picture of the course of events given in the Hexateuch only arose from a confessional arrangement of different complexes of tradition, then the question of the historicity of Moses and his functions can only be put as follows: in which of these groups of tradition and in which of the separate traditions is the figure of Moses originally rooted?[16]

A certain historical skepticism thus emerges from von Rad's work and leads him to place greater importance on the character of portraiture in the various layers of the traditions than on a reconstruction of an historical configuration. It should be noted, however, that von Rad's skepticism was directed not only towards easy historical constructs, but also towards the constructions of tradition history.

> The question where it was that the figure of Moses was fundamentally at home and where not, and how it grew into traditions which originally had no knowledge of it, certainly throws a light on many a process that is interesting for theology as well. But the scientific basis of the matter is too slight to allow of a comprehensive picture. . . [17]

It seems necessary, nonetheless, for the historian to consider the character of the tradition before he uses it in a reconstruction of the historical Moses. I do not intend to imply by this observation that there are two 'historical' realities that compete for attention from the Old Testament scholar, the historical reality as the modern critical historian can reconstruct it, and the interpreted historical reality as it was presented by the Old Testament itself. Walther Eichrodt criticized the theological program of Gerhard von Rad in part by suggesting that von Rad separated too radically between real history as reconstructed by the disciplines of historical research and the tradition's history preserved in the Old Testament itself.[18] Franz Hesse makes much the same point: 'Für uns als christliche Theologen ist der wirkliche Ablauf der Geschichte Israels—die ja die Geschichte Gottes in besonderer Weise in sich trägt—viel erheblicher als die Vorstellungen, die Israel sich vom Ablauf seiner Geschichte machte'.[19] And finally, Walter C. Kaiser has criticized von Rad for making such a radical dichotomy in historical reality.

> Now there were two types of history: the one obtained from the reconstruction of the modern historico-critical method, the other from Israel's credal confessions supplied from the traditio-historical method. . . . In this dichotomy, the ghost of Immanuel Kant was still haunting academia. Von Rad . . . had managed to divide reality into two parts: there was the phenomenal world of the past (available to us from historico-critical research), and there was the noumenal world of faith. Israel's faith, like biblical theology, was to have as its object, not the real acts of God in real history, but that which the people of ancient times confessed to have happened in spite of modern critical doubts about its factual status.[20]

But the critics of von Rad's approach to Israel's history and Old Testament literature miss an important point. The methodology does not suggest that there are two realities available for investigation, the facts of history and the literary documents from ancient people of faith. It suggests that there are two ways for looking at one single reality: the methods of modern historical criticism, and the methods of ancient literary artisans who depicted their history as an expression of their faith in God, and whose insights can be recovered with the methods of literary criticism.

Moreover, all seem to agree that both methods have only the documents of the Old Testament to serve as source for the facts of history. The issue, then, is whether those documents of faith can yield the *bruta facta* of history. Certainly, they must be investigated for what they are, documents of faith, before *bruta facta* can be squeezed from them. And in this process, it will be necessary to recognize that the documents are not simplistic records of Israelite history, from which an accurate account of the life of Moses springs to life, ready for the television cameras. Rather, they are another way of looking at those *bruta facta* that composed Israel's past. To imply, as does Kaiser, that historico-critical research can abstract the true history void of interpretations, and that that true history must serve as the basis of faith is to ground faith on a utopian construct.

A far more judicious evaluation of the Moses tradition appears in the work of Roland de Vaux. As an historian, addressing the task of constructing a picture of the early history of Israel, de Vaux nevertheless evaluates the traditions for what they are: the stories of the folk. And he does so with sensitivity to their literary characteristics. Thus, for example, de Vaux recognizes in the traditions two ways for describing the exodus from Egypt. One suggests that when Moses petitions the Pharaoh for permission to go on a three-day journey into the wilderness for sacrifice, his negotiations fail. 'The matter is closed, the Israelites know that they cannot leave freely, and they can only flee. This is precisely what they do.'[21] The other describes the exodus more closely associated with the Passover. 'The Pharaoh drives the Israelites out.'[22] Then on the basis of the tradition history de Vaux offers his historical interpretation. 'The solution to this problem may perhaps be more easily found if we look in a different direction. Just as there were several entries into Egypt, so too is it possible that there were several exoduses, some groups being expelled, others fleeing from Egypt.'[23] The point here, however, is not to express approval of a particular conclusion but rather to highlight the method. Historical conclusions rest on a careful evaluation of the literature. James S. Ackerman thus captures the necessary element of a methodology:

> The Bible is certainly teeming with data very important to the historian, but concentrating exclusively on them will not bring the reader closer to an understanding of the text. The teacher of literature should not use the Bible to elucidate the 'history of Israel'. The history and culture of the ancient Near East are subsidiary concerns, important only as they provide the background out of which the Exodus 1-2 portrait will emerge.[24]

Sociological Studies

The second segment in my Moses bibliography includes items concerned to employ categories of a sociological analysis. It is necessary, however, to make an important distinction in the position of questions under review here. One school of Old Testament scholarship, to be reviewed in section C of this chapter, seeks to clarify the sociological context for Old Testament literature. What institutional forms within Israelite society account for the origin and preservation of particular types of literature? For example, a consensus now affirms that most of the Old Testament psalms did not originate as the product of poets who sat at their desks and composed religious verse. Rather, the poetry in the Psalter came into being as an expression of worship within the operation of the Israelite cult. That does not mean that there was no particular poet involved in the composition of particular lines. But it does mean that the motivation for the creation and preservation of the poetry in the Psalms came from the official institution for worship.[25] It is a relevant question to ask what social institution in Israel's past accounts for the origin and preservation of the Moses traditions. This question will be addressed in the body of the book.

There is, however, a second kind of question, related more closely to the historical research reviewed in section A than to the literary questions of section C. That question asks about the historical Moses: What sociological data clarify the questions about who Moses really was and what Moses really did? The quote from John Bright, at the head of section A, illustrates this perspective: 'Though we know nothing of his career save what the Bible tells us, the details of which we have no means of testing, there can be no doubt that he was, as the Bible portrays him, the great founder of Israel's faith'.[26] As founder of the faith, Moses would not only have made a contribution to the social structure of Israel's life, but he would have in fact shaped its structure for all time to come. 'Founder of the faith' would place him, as Bright observes, alongside Jesus and Mohammed. And the shape of the literature would reflect that status.

Klaus Koch observes in contrast that Noth's analysis of what the Bible tells us about Moses' career will not support the conclusion. If Moses belongs originally to only one of the major themes in the Pentateuch, he could hardly have exercised the dominating influence over all of Israel's religion that would be implied by the designation as *Religionsstifter*. 'Die Vorstellung von Mose dem Religionsstifter ist tot and bleibt tot.'[27] Koch's concern is then to explore other evidence for the rise of Israelite religion, noting little more about the importance of Moses in the process than his role in a special complex of traditions tied to the oasis in Kadesh.[28] His procedure places Israelite religion into the context of the society in Israel's environment. Her religion must have arisen in a fashion similar to the religion of her neighbors. But that process does not allow us simply to posit the existence of Moses as the founder of the faith.

Koch's description of the rise of Israelite religion apart from Moses depends on Noth's analysis of the themes in the Moses traditions. That analysis has not gone unchallenged. Yet, even should the analysis stand the test of critical evaluation and Koch's review of the history of Israelite religion apart from Moses as the founder of the faith be substantially correct, still the investigation of Moses traditions must address the present form of the narratives with Moses given a dominant role in all four of the relevant themes. Would that fact not suggest, quite apart from a proper resolution of Koch's question about the origin of Israelite religion and whatever unique quality may have been embedded there from the beginning, that somewhere in the history of the Moses traditions Moses gained all-inclusive stature denied him by Koch? And would that not mean that, even though the idea of a *Religionsstifter* might have been dead at the beginning of Israel's religion, it gained new life at some later point? So the question is put not so much as a part of historical investigation, but rather in terms of the literature. Does tradition not conceive Moses as the founder of the faith? Particularly in the post-exile period, for the priestly source of the Pentateuch or for Ezra, would this point not apply? How else would the reference to Moses in Ezra 3.2 carry weight? 'They built the altar of the God of Israel, to offer burnt offerings upon it, as it is written in the law of Moses, the man of God.'

J.R. Porter explores the Moses traditions in order to clarify a hypothesis that Moses functioned as a model for the monarchy.

> From early times, the clue to understanding the figure of Moses has been sought in viewing him as the typical representative of some religious and social category, for example, the classic king, high-priest, legislator, and the prophet of Philo. Of all the categories that have been proposed, the most inclusive and the one that best explains most features in the Pentateuchal picture of Moses would seem to be that of the Israelite king, more specifically the David monarch of the pre-exilic period.[29]

His argument is not that Moses was a king, although he comes very close to that. The term *melek* (king) never appears as an appellative for Moses. An exception to this observation may be found in Deut. 33.5, a text translated by the RSV as follows: Thus, the Lord became king in Jeshurun, when the heads of the people were gathered, all the tribes of Israel together'. But the Masoretic Text (the Hebrew text) does not have 'the Lord'. And the previous antecedent is Moses, the lawgiver. 'Thus, he [Moses?] became king in Jeshurun. . . ' Yet the text is ambiguous. Moses appears here as the lawgiver. And there is some obvious parallel between the lawgiver and the king, as the famous Hammurabi and his code would suggest.[30] But the subject of the description in vv. 2-4 is the Lord, not Moses. The text seems at best, then, to be inconclusive.

Porter develops various terms in the tradition as further evidence for his assertion. These terms suggest that the images used to describe Moses were images drawn from the monarchy and that therefore the Moses traditions show formative influence from the institution of the kingship. A case in point is the description of Moses as a 'meek' man, more so than any other person on the face of the earth, in Num. 12.3. The crucial term, *'ānāw*, describes a person who shows professional integrity in the execution of his official duties.[31] This term, according to Porter, and the related tern, *'ānî*, derive from the repertoire of virtues characteristic for the king (so, Zech. 9.9).[32] Yet, is the virtue exclusive enough to limit the Moses traditions, even this particular Moses text, to a setting in the institution of the monarchy? Would it even suggest influence from the royal institution on the traditions? Or must we consider a suggestion that the term, *'ānāw*, as well as *'ānî*, is a more general term, used for describing leaders of various offices? The use of the term in later stages of development to refer to a general group of 'meek' shows clearly that the term invites such connotations.[33] Is that not the case for *'ānāw* in Num. 12.3? Is the concern not to present Moses in ideal form as the model for a special leader, whatever the office?[34]

It must be clear, however, that Porter's argument rests on more than his exegesis of Num. 12.3. He collects several items from the Moses traditions which may be understood as royal in character. Among these is the important role for Moses as 'lawgiver'. This point will appear in my discussion in greater detail below. Suffice for the moment to observe that law-giving does not override the clear conception in the tradition that the law is older than the institution of the monarchy and that, indeed, the Davidic king stands in conflict with the law.[35] Moreover, a key part of Porter's argument asserts that the royal dimension of the Moses traditions had its inception in Jerusalem. Yet, remarkably, none of the sources for describing the royal tradition in Jerusalem refers to Moses (see, for example, the prophet Isaiah). Indeed, it is possible that an anti-Moses tradition held the seat of honor there.[36] In the light of Trent Butler's argument for such a conclusion, it would be difficult to defend Porter's view that the Moses traditions represent a pro-Moses, monarchy tradition from Jerusalem.[37] In view of these objections, then, would the suggestion that a common tradition lies behind both the Moses narratives and the royal element not carry greater weight? The precise character of the connection between the Moses traditions and the traditions about the monarchy would require careful attention.

Brevard S. Childs integrates his precise literary analysis with observations about the sociological context for the Mosaic office.[38] His discussion of the evidence opens with a depiction of Moses as covenant mediator as suggested by Deut. 5.5 (see also Exod. 20) and the conflicting picture that sees the covenant addressed immediately to the people in Deut. 5.4. The issue, in contrast to Noth's hypothesis that Moses must be understood traditio-historically as related to the conquest theme, suggests exploring the relationship between the office of Moses and the Sinai theme. 'What then can one say in respect to the Mosaic office, particularly in relation to his [Moses'] role as mediator of the law at Sinai?'[39] He concludes: 'A large consensus has emerged which agrees that more than simply a literary narrative is involved, but that the text reflects an ongoing religious institution of covenant renewal going back far into Israel's early pre-monarchial history'.[40] But even with this observation, a double factor in the tradition calls for some attention. One factor presents Moses as the mediator who stood in the gap between God and people following the terror that broke when the people heard the voice of God (so, Exod. 20.18-20). The other factor suggests that Moses' special role as mediator derives not from the terrified request of the people, but rather from God's design. (So, Exod. 19.19. Compare Exodus 34, where the commandments and the covenant come to Moses alone. The people simply hear of the new relationship or share in it through Moses.) These two offices do not derive from two different Pentateuchal sources, the one from E, the other from J, but rather from the combination of two distinct traditions about Moses, both lying behind the literary sources. And what image of Moses appears here? (1) Moses appears as covenant mediator in a covenant renewal festival. The festival was essentially cultic in character, suggesting that the Mosaic office should be seen as cultic. (2) Moses' office needs no act of legitimation before the people in the covenant renewal since the Sinai traditions assume the office from the beginning. Moses always mediated the will of God to the people. Moreover, this office stands in close relationship with the tent of meeting, the *'ōhel mô'ēd*. 'Moses functions as continual vehicle of the will of God in his office before the tent of meeting.'[41] And in the tent Moses exercises his office particularly as intercessor for the people. Both offices combine in Moses elements of both priestly and prophetic roles. Both cast Moses as the model for the authority of the office. In the course of time, the two traditions grew together, with the tent tradition and its view of Moses as the permanent mediator and intercessor receding behind the tradition that describes Moses as covenant mediator in a covenant renewal ceremony. The notion of a covenantal law given directly to the people seems to be a later reading of the tradition after the redaction of J and E placed the gift of the Decalogue before the validation of Moses' office.

Rudolph Smend approaches the Moses traditions with a methodological assumption like that of Dewey Beegle.

> In order to get to the beginning, and if possible to the historical nucleus around which the tradition has developed, it is important to exclude everything that is secondary, thus everything which can be explained obviously and naturally by more or less spontaneous acts of modifying..., 'etiological' or 'backward projecting' legend-development of a later time.[42]

The results of his study, however, are not simply historical but rather sociological. According to Smend, Moses belonged, not to the conquest of Transjordan, as Noth concluded, but rather to the exodus tradition as a leader in the institution of Yahweh war.[43] Part of the consequence in this exposition of Moses is recognition of the political as well as the religious dimension of the image. And it suggests a broad image, crossing various institutional settings. Perhaps the historical 'office' most nearly related to the image is the 'judge' who leads his people into holy war. And in this sense, Smend notes the intimate connection between Moses and the Ark of the Covenant. But still the Moses traditions describe a leader that integrates various offices, rather than isolating one particular office. Smend expresses this overarching character of the Moses image in this way: 'The sequence of narratives [including Exod. 5.3-19] can be understood as the history, or better, the series of stories of the charismatic hero Moses, whose person is quite inextricably inter-woven into Exodus traditions...'[44] His evidence for this position depends in part on the parallel he develops with the Jeroboam tradition in 1 Kings 12. But, he argues, 'the evidence that Moses is here being conceived of and represented as a charismatic leader could easily be augmented beyond what was brought forth in the Jeroboam account'.[45] That evidence he derives from an analogy with the later charismatic leaders. And characteristic for this position of leadership is a certain similarity to a king. One should ask nonetheless whether the similarity derives from royal images in the Moses tradition. Or does it reflect Mosaic images in the description of Jeroboam? Does the tradition not cast Jeroboam as a New Moses?

Ann Vater Solomon also emphasizes the importance of the charismatic in defining the role of Moses. For her, charismatic means a new form of leadership, a break from the previous institutions and offices, a style of leadership inspired to communicate a message to an audience that was unprepared for the event.[46] So, the charismatic in the office of Moses ties into the message Moses proclaimed to the people. The charismatic messenger here, however, does not appear as a king or a leader in Yahweh war. To the contrary, he looks very much like the prophet whose task is to deliver God's message to the audience designated by the divine commission. Maurice Luker makes the point explicitly. The image of Moses in the plagues is the image of the prophet.[47] James Muilenburg sees a similar connection, not only in the Moses traditions, but also in the layer of prophetic traditions: 'Moses is surely speaking here [Deut. 18.15-16] as mediator of the covenant, and, what is more, he is identifying the office of the mediator with that of the prophet'.[48] Lothar Perlitt also connects Moses with the prophetic tradition:

> Das Thema 'Mose als Prophet' ist in der ganzen Vielgestaltigkeit seiner Formen und Motive in der mittleren und späten Königszeit eine theologische Auslegung und Anwendung der schon von J kombinierten 'heilsgeschichtlichen' Hauptfunktionen des 'prophet-ischen' Offenbarungsempfängers, Mittlers und Volksführers Moses. Am Fürbitter und Wundertäter Mose in der Exodustradition ebenso wie as Mittler Mose in der Sinaitradition liesse sich dieser Zusammenhang 'prophetischer' Aspekte breit entfalten.[49]

The contribution to this discussion by Gerhard von Rad belongs more properly in the third section of this review. The broad literary base of his work provides nevertheless a platform for observations about the sociological context for the image of Moses, for example, in the major sources of the Pentateuch. In J, Moses appears as an 'inspired shepherd' whom God used for the purpose of delivering his will to his people. An important part of the office appears in Moses' role as intercessor. 'The prophetic style of what Moses says in J— "Go to Pharaoh and say: Thus hath Jahweh said" (Ex. vii, 16f. [viii, 1] viii, 16 [15] ix, 13)—is in harmony with this picture.'[50] Von Rad's description of Moses in J as inspired shepherd thus relates explicitly to a *prophetic* form. In E, the prophetic dress is more apparent. 'It is extremely probable that the whole source E comes from early prophetic circles. If so, it is not at all surprising that . . . this source viewed Moses as a prophet.'[51] For Deuteronomy, it is the same story: 'In it, too, Moses is נביא: indeed, he is the chief of the prophets (Deut. xviii 8) in that he is the archetype and norm of all prophets'.[52] There is, however, a distinction in Deuteronomy *vis à vis* J and E. Here the prophet takes on a noticeable role as mediator.

> Deuteronomy has no mention at all of any influence which Moses brought to bear on history by the instrumentality of miracles or the like. And further, it is only rarely in Deuteronomy that we find Moses acting as the leader who gives strategic orders (Deut. i 23, ii 20ff, iii 18), for his real office was to pass on to Israel, in the form of a proclaimed word, the word of Jahweh.[53]

In P, the conception of Moses breaks with the prophetic images.

> What Moses is for P can no longer be summed up under the generally accepted concepts of priest, worker of miracles, prophet, etc. Moses is something beyond all this—he is set apart for intercourse with Jahweh alone. . . . In proportion as he is taken over on to God's side, he is separated from men. They flee from him as he comes back, and he has first to cover the reflexion of God's glory on his face before he can speak to them (Ex xxxiv 29ff).[54]

The image of the Mosaic office is, unfortunately, not unequivocal, even for the individual sources. Despite the obvious contact between the Moses traditions and prophetism, there is also some effort to elevate Moses over the prophets. 'If there is a prophet among you, I the Lord make myself known to him in a vision, I speak with him in a dream. Not so with my servant Moses; he is entrusted with all my house. I speak with him mouth to mouth.' Von Rad speaks to this contrast: 'This restriction put upon immediate communion with

Jahweh could derive from the upholding of the prerogatives of certain priestly functions over against the prophets' reception of revelation'.[55] And with this observation comes a final reference to a sociological institution as a point of contact for the Mosaic 'office'. The tradition avers that Moses was born a Levite. Should the 'office' of Levitical priest be considered as the sociological setting for Moses or for the origin and preservation of the Moses tradition? Yet, before the question can be explored, some reference to the general problem of 'Levitical' heritage would be necessary. Is the birth tale designed to affirm Moses' genealogy within a Levitical family? Or does it reflect an intention to declare Moses' Levitical heritage as a means of entry into a particular 'office' or better, as a means for explaining the foundation of a particular 'office'. A.H.J. Gunneweg clarifies the Levitical terminology by reference to two points: (1) Moses was born into a Levitical family. The genealogical framework is certainly present in the tradition. (2) Levitical heritage comes to mean something about function in a particular office.

> Es kommt die Schwierigkeit hinzu, daß Worte wie 'Levit' oder 'Nabi' ähnlich wie überhaupt die als Termini technici fungierenden Vokabeln ... immer schon von der durch sie bezeichneten spezifischen Sache her in ihrer Bedeutung geprägt sind.... Unter diesem Vorbehalt wird man jedoch einer ursprünglichen Bedeutung 'Geweihter' 'Geliehener' den Vorzug geben können.[56]

Gunneweg does not, however, define the Mosaic office in terms of Levitical service. He suggests instead that Moses appears as covenant mediator.[57]

The tradition about Moses as Levite remains problematic, however. The problem can be illustrated by the role Moses played in the complex of traditions recounting Israel's life at Kadesh. That Moses was in some way attached to the oasis at Kadesh is not a new idea.[58] Geo Widengren concludes:

> This tradition is the oldest and the authentic tradition. It shows that there was in Kadesh a Yahweh-sanctuary where the Hebrew tribes celebrated their חג. Here Moses officiated as a priestly Levite. Here also he gave the תורה to the tribes of Israel, Ex. 18. I can see no reason to doubt the historicity of this tradition.[59]

But priestly groups in Israel and Judah were by no means unified in their dedication to the cult. There were struggles within priestly clans. And competing groups of priests apparently laid claim to Mosaic authority. Judg. 18-30 alludes to a Mosaic priesthood, quite distinct from Kadesh.[60] And the context for this verse suggests that the Mosaic line had some linkage to Levitical tradition. The point here is, thus, that although evidence for tying Moses to a priestly group is thin, there is nevertheless some evidence there. Yet, the evidence does not underwrite a clear picture. It is complex and ambiguous. And it points in more than one direction. It suggests at most that among various priestly groups more than one laid claim to Mosaic authority.

It is remarkably clear, therefore, that sociological questions have not produced a consistent and singular picture of Moses. To the contrary, the observation by Walther Eichrodt seems appropriate:

> It is characteristic of Moses that it should be impossible to classify him in any of the ordinary categories applicable to a leader of a nation; he is neither a king, nor a commander of an army, nor a tribal chieftain, nor a priest, nor an inspired seer and medicine man. To some extent he belongs to all these categories; but none of them adequately explains his position.[61]

The problem of the historical Moses thus remains as acute from a sociological perspective as it does in the analysis of the historian. Moreover, the effort to define the sociological context for the Moses traditions seems short-changed. It is, of course, too simple to transfer the argument for a sociological office for the historical Moses to observations about setting for the literature about Moses. To call him a king is not to conclude that the literature about him originated in the court. Nor does it suggest that the court preserved the tradition. Yet, insofar as I can understand the bibliography, no one before Childs pursues the question of setting for the literature. Is there anything in the literature that would clarify the sociological context and make sense of this wide range of possibilities about Mosaic office?

Literary Studies

To pursue the Moses traditions by means of a literary methodology does not mean to forsake interest in history or sociology altogether. To the contrary, key items in this section of the bibliography report an interest in literary studies in order to facilitate a more pressing interest in the historical shape of Moses or the character of the Mosaic office. Yet, the dominant question is not what really happened to Moses or what institutional office he held. It is rather a question directed to the literature itself. It focuses not on the importance of Moses as an historical figure or the sociological configuration that traces its lineage back to him, but on the verbal art that depicts him. Why did Israel remember Moses in just the peculiar way preserved by the Old Testament?

> This interest seeks to examine how and why successive stages of the tradition perceived its past, rather than to examine the actual contours of the past... It is based on a recognition that the literary question about the ideologies reflected in the various traditions is primary to a recovery of possible historiographical elements in the tradition...[62]

The term, 'literary analysis', does not, however, refer to a uniform methodological operation. It might involve investigation of authorship, along with historical and sociological circumstances that surround the author. It might explore oral stages preceding reduction of the tradition to writing. It might concentrate on the style and artistic merit in the writing. Does the text of the Moses traditions belong to any particular period or any particular hand? Questions about J, E, D, or P thus appear as relevant topics for examination. What process of development brought the traditions from the time of Moses to their formulation as written documents? Questions about the tradition's history also occupy an important position for the discussion. But in addition to these areas of interest, it will be necessary to explore the style and artistic merit in the shape of the text. Is the body of traditions about Moses composed of units that were originally independent stories? Can we recognize distinct, or even independent themes or organized grouping in the stories? Could we thus analyze the Moses traditions adequately by presenting a series of distinct essays, each investigating a story in the tradition or a theme that structures the presentation of stories? Or is there integrity in the traditions as a whole? And if so, does that integrity suggest an artistic shape of significance, a shape that might explain the diverse images of the Mosaic figure reconstructed by historical or sociological investigations? The guiding question here, therefore, is whether a single artistic configuration of the tradition carries the image of Moses. If so, what are the narrative patterns that produce the tradition? And where does the image of Moses fit into the patterns? Then we may ask: Does a single image of Moses effect the shape of the narrative? If so, what factors account for its singularity?[63]

A series of significant publications addresses these questions, with
the pace-setter the work of Hugo Gressmann.[64] He describes Moses
as the founder of the religion, a priest of the Yahweh cult who learned
his trade from Jethro, his father-in-law, during an extended
encampment at Kadesh. His work thus reveals a marked interest in
historical reconstruction. He wants to find a kernel of history that
will tell us something about who Moses really was. He carries out his
work nevertheless as a careful analysis of the literature and
corresponding conclusions about oral backgrounds. He asserts that
the genre of all the Moses narratives is 'Sage', a category of folk
tradition that resists precise historical definitions. 'Alle Erzählungen
dagegen über Mose und seine Zeit sind ihrer literarischen Art nach
als *Sagen* zu betrachten.'[65] Then he calls for identification of motifs
within each tale that carry the weight of the narration. Indeed, his
work with motifs enables him to make a certain distinction between
realism and fantasy, for in his program the typical motifs appear to
offer the context for fantasy, while the unique motifs represent the
real world adequately.[66] Yet, Gressmann does not assume simply
that representing the real world constitutes historical reconstruction.
The tale, with its balance of realism and fantasy, requires careful
evaluation as a piece of literature.

> Nun kann aber der Historiker die Sagen nicht so benutzen, wie sie
> in der Überlieferung vorliegen; wer speziell die Geschichte der
> mosaischen Zeit schreiben will, darf im allgemeinen nur die Ursage
> verwerten. . . . Darum kann der Historiker seine Arbeit erst
> beginnen, wenn die literargeschichtliche Forschung die jüngeren
> Schichten abgetragen und das Urgestein bloß gelegt hat.[67]

But again it is important to observe that Gressmann does not simply
rip through the later levels of the tradition in order to uncover that
Urgestein. His literary method enables him to evaluate the story for
itself.

Gressmann's literary analysis begins regularly with source
distinctions. He reflects no problems in dividing the text between the
priestly narrative and its earlier counterparts. The problem lies
rather in distinctions between J and E. Despite the problem, he avers
that J and E were originally distinct units, melded together into one
narrative by a later redactor. Therefore J and E should be considered
for their individuality in presenting Moses. The second step calls for
identification of the individual tales within the sources. Individual
tales are defined as narratives that have been rounded off, so that

they do not depend on other units for intrinsic introduction or conclusion. They focus on action, with only short speeches. The action develops in simple, vivid plots. Generally, the elements of the tale employ only two figures, with only two scenes to develop the stages of their relationship. The tales may have originated as cult narratives. But in their present form, they appear to be hero tales. Thus, Gressmann observes: 'In den Sagen, die vor Kades und in Kades spielen, tritt Mose so stark in den Vordergrund, daß man diese Erzählungen am besten unter die Heldensagen reiht'.[68]

The individual tales then emerge in collections around particular motifs. The largest collection (*Sagenkranz*) ranges from the birth of Moses to his death. But smaller, distinct collections also appear: (1) Israel's life at Kadesh, and (2) the relationships between Moses and Jethro. But an additional problem in the structure of the traditions emerges at this point. The larger whole seems to fall into two loosely related halves: (1) the tales that range from the birth of Moses to the arrival of Israel at Sinai, and (2) the tales about Israel's departure from Sinai and her movement to the promised land.[69] The problem lies in the observation that the Sinai complex disrupts the Kadesh collection. Gressmann suggests that the Sinai traditions represent the basic continuation of the exodus narrative, with the Kadesh stories secondarily inserted into the complex. The Kadesh collection would have held center stage in the earliest traditions, then lost ground to the Sinai narratives and entered the complex as a redactional addition.

A new direction for analysis of the Moses traditions emerged with the work of Martin Noth. He suggested that the literature in the Pentateuch can be divided into five themes, the Moses figure functioning as a bracket that welds four of them into a single narration. The bracket was, however, a secondary redactional device, not a part of the original form in each of the themes. Thus, Noth asked in which of the four possible themes Moses might have been at home.[70] The question is a matter of tradition history rather than of the literary shape in the narrative as it now stands. Yet, it has influenced sharply the judgment on the literature advanced by a generation of Old Testament scholars. Noth suggested that the Moses figure belongs originally to the theme of traditions about the conquest of Transjordan.[71] Childs, however, tied the figure to the Sinai theme.[72] Schnutenhaus suggested that the exodus theme provides the original home for the Moses of the Old Testament traditions.[73] Schmid pointed to the tradition of the event at the Sea,[74]

and thus, I might add, the wilderness theme enters the discussion.
But the fallacy in all of these observations about the history of the
tradition is that none provides a perspective for an examination of
the Moses traditions as a whole. If Noth's assumption that all four
themes were originally independent, and that therefore Moses could
have been at home in only one, should prove to be incorrect, then the
judgment that Moses was only a secondary bracket would rest on
sand.[75] The governing question, then, is not whether Moses appears
in only one theme; thus, which theme accounts for the beginning of
the tradition? It is rather whether the relationship among the themes
can be explained more adequately than would be the case on the
basis of Noth's hypothesis. Is Moses simply a bracket that binds the
themes together secondarily? Or can Moses be removed from the
various themes only by doing violence to the traditions?[76]

Gerhard von Rad uses his tools of form criticism and tradition
history not only to evaluate the Moses material for its contribution to
a history of Israel but even more directly to determine the value of
that tradition for an Old Testament theology. In his major work on
Old Testament theology he constructs a description of Moses images
in the major sources of the Pentateuch/Hexateuch. He does not
attempt to trace the history of the Moses traditions to their origins in
the life history of Moses. 'We can no longer look on it as possible to
write a history of the tradition attaching to Moses, and of where it
was at home.'[77] Part of the reason for this conclusion lies in Noth's
position about the role of the Moses tradition in the various themes
of the Pentateuch. 'Not the least of the difficulties in this connexion
consists in the fact that the figure of Moses is only a secondary
accretion in many of the traditions.'[78] But he does describe the Moses
portrait for each of the sources. In the Yahwist, the Moses figure
recedes behind the dominant role of Yahweh in the redemption of the
people. But that emphasis leaves the door open for a particular
construction. 'What then, in J's view, was Moses? He was no worker
of miracles, no founder of a religion, and no military leader. He was
an inspired shepherd whom Jahweh used to make his will known to
men.'[79] This designation of imagery for the Moses figure loses the
precision of a definition that would type Moses as a prophet, a priest,
or a king. There is no clear institutional office that calls for a
professional who might be called an 'inspired shepherd'. The image
suggests, rather, a folk category, a romantic figure whose characteristics evoke the processes of the storyteller rather than those of an
administrative or religious office.

Von Rad argues that in contrast to the folkloristic imagery for Moses in J,

> E has pushed Moses much more into the foreground as the instrument of God in effecting the deliverance. . . . It is extremely probable that this whole source E comes from early prophetic circles. If so, it is not at all surprising that on occasion the stories appear in the dress of prophetic concepts, and that this source viewed Moses as a prophet.[80]

And then von Rad's theological evaluation gains explicit expression. 'Since Moses on occasion also acts as priest (Ex xxiv 6), E's picture of him is perhaps not perfectly uniform. But still, its development on the whole represents a decided theological advance beyond J.'[81]

Deuteronomy maintains the prophetic imagery in its depiction of Moses.

> His real office was to pass on to Israel, in the form of a proclaimed word, the word of Jahweh which had been addressed to himself. In Deuteronomy Jahweh still speaks to Israel through the medium of Moses. . . But this concentration of all Israel's communion with God upon him now had a result which Deuteronomy clearly envisaged—Moses is a suffering mediator.[82]

Finally, von Rad describes the portrait of Moses in P as the product of tradition about God's revelation at Sinai. 'What Moses is for P can no longer be summed up under the generally accepted concepts of priest, worker of miracles, prophet, etc. Moses is something beyond all this—he is set apart for intercourse with Jahweh alone'.[83]

It is important to emphasize that von Rad perceives the Moses traditions to be about a man who for the traditions remains a man. He does not become a god. To be sure, he is the servant of God, the distinctive mediator of God's word to his people. But he remains a man. 'He was not a saint, an ascetic, one who stripped himself of all ordinary human feeling; equally, he was not a hero in the sense in which that word was ordinarily understood in ancient times. . . There was nothing divine about Moses. . . He was "the man Moses".'[84] This emphasis on the role of Moses in the tradition as man, not god, is certainly accurate and most appropriate. But the problem in the emphasis is that it leads to a denigration of the tradition's depiction of the man. Von Rad observes:

> But we have not yet come to the most important point of all. Not a single one of all these stories, in which Moses is the central figure,

was really about Moses. Great as was the veneration of the writers
for this man to whom God had been pleased to reveal Himself, in
all these stories it is not Moses himself, Moses the man, but God
who is the central figure. *God's* words and *God's* deeds, these are
the things that the writers intend to set forth.[85]

The stories about Moses are not really about the man, but rather
they focus on the God who stands behind the man. And in that
process, the assertions of the tradition about what this man was like
lose their force. But it is not necessary to reduce the role played by
the man Moses in these stories in order to emphasize the role of God
for the weight of the narration. Indeed, it is precisely in the dialectic
established by these two poles that the strongest dynamic in the
Moses stories appears. It is the task of this project to describe and
evaluate that dynamic.

Frank Schnutenhaus builds on the foundation laid by Gressmann,
Noth, and von Rad. And while he speaks to crucial issues of history
and sociology, his primary contribution to the discussion about
Moses rests on a careful literary analysis, in the manner of his
mentors. He does not tie down a formal, institutional office that will
account for the Moses traditions. Rather, he writes of configurations
that belong more naturally to literary portraits. 'Mose wird so als
Mensch gesehen und gleichzeitig als Sprecher Gottes; er wird nicht
mythologisiert.'[86] Moreover, this depiction of Moses in a very human
role is complemented by a pattern in the literature, fundamental for
the author's major thesis. Moses appears in a three-corner construct
as a messenger: God—messenger—people. Moses as messenger
cannot be understood apart from the God who sent him or the people
who heard him. The kernel of the Moses tradition is thus the
theological affirmation: 'Yahweh led Israel out of Egypt'. Moses did
the leading. He was the redeemer' (*Retter*). The credo confessions
presuppose that fact. But the articles confess that God acted in these
mighty deeds. They never mention Moses by name.

It is just at this point that one of the major issues in evaluating the
Moses traditions returns to the surface. What are the consequences
of the unique relationship between Moses and God, so central for the
presentation of Moses in the traditions? Must we assume from the
formulation of the credo articles that the Moses traditions are not
really about Moses after all, but rather about God? Schnutenhaus
makes his contribution to this issue particularly in his comments on
Exodus 14. In this pericope, he argues, God acts decisively to save
the people. Moses does nothing except in response to God's

commands. As a result, Schnutenhaus describes the Moses figure as a *Jahvemarionette*.[87] But does the tradition leave us, even in this particular instance, with only an image of Moses as instrument in the hands of the great puppeteer? And if it does, what can we say about the impact of the traditions on contemporary formulations of a theological anthropology, or, for that matter, on contemporary conceptions of ministerial leadership for the church or synagogue? Successes belong to God. Failures occur because the instrument resists God's direction.

Ann M. Vater (Solomon) also explores the Moses traditions in order to relate the literature in the Old Testament to her fundamental concerns for understanding messenger patterns in the ancient Near East as building tools for narratives. It is inappropriate, in her eyes, to limit definition of this image to one institutional role. 'The whole task of finding one role for the historical Moses is misconceived. Societies evolve from early complexity to later apparent simplicity of form.'[88] Vater's evaluation of the Moses traditions in the context of broader exploration into messenger patterns suggests that the presentation of Moses follows the lines of established form. 'The consistent image which emerges is that of the charismatic messenger in God's presence.'[89] The parade text for her analysis is the confrontation between Moses and the Pharaoh in the plagues account. Moses presents God's message to the enemy. Moreover, the problem arising from the comments of Schnutenhaus also arises here. 'God's speaking with Moses, which sometimes results in a brief notice about the delivery of the oracle . . . or no mention of delivery at all . . ., discloses the "charismatic messenger" whose own image melts into the words of God.'[90] But Vater does not leave her understanding of the messenger simply in the position of marionette.

> Thus, Moses is more than a prophet in this sense. Moses is also not the passive instrument used by God which Balaam represents. . . Moses has been let in on God's plan from the very beginning (Ex. 3.7-10). He has been sent to carry out this plan and whatever may be involved, speaking, acting, etc., he is sent to do. . . [91]

Robert M. Polzin sets his exploration of the Moses traditions in the Deuteronomic history into the context of a struggle with methodology: a synchronic evaluation of the text which can develop sensitivity to the character of the literature as literature stands in contrast to diachronic evaluation, genetic in approach, which seeks to cut through the text in a push to go back to the origin of the tradition.

His concern in developing such a probe, clearly weighted on the side of the synchronic but also fully informed by diachronic disciplines, is to hear how the words of Moses interpret the words of God throughout the Deuteronomic history. Indeed, part of the intention of the Deuteronomic History is to establish the authority of Moses to be the interpreter of God's word. But the intention is also to show that the Deuteronomic Historian stands in the same tradition as the interpreter of the Mosaic words. And he shares the authority of Moses to speak about the impact of God's words. This position, according to Polzin, is one that subtly diminishes the authority of Moses in favor of the successor, so much so that the Deuteronomic Historian now no longer sees the authority of Moses as unique. He shares that authority with his successors who interpret the post-Mosaic history with the same vitality reflected in the Mosaic interpretation of the post Exodus history.[92]

It is now possible to set my work into its proper context. I intend my method of procedure in the analysis of the Moses traditions to be literary rather than historical or sociological. If some insight into the sociological structure of early Israel can be won, either in terms of Moses' office or as the social setting for the literature, so much the better. But the concerns of this book are not for a biography of Moses or for an identification of an early office that traced its heritage to Moses. Rather, my goals are to determine how the traditions conceived Moses, how they put that image into literary form, and how that form communicated to Israel the importance of the man and his time. Moreover, I want to determine whether the literary construction of the traditions offers any way to account for the remarkably wide diversity of judgments about the image of Moses: prophet, priest, king, judge, covenant mediator, charismatic messenger, founder of the faith, leader of the people, inspired shepherd. And does it suggest anything about the literary locus for Moses: exodus theme, wilderness wandering, Sinai with its law and covenant, conquest at least in the Transjordan with the account of Moses' death and burial? Was the Moses tradition at home in only one of these themes? Or is the position of the tradition as the great bracket that binds them all together the original shape of the Moses story?

But again, caution must prevail. In what manner can the *original* shape of the Moses material come to light? The methods of form criticism and tradition history dominate the work of von Rad and Noth. With these methods, the path of development in the history of the traditions could, according to the theory, be established. But problems arise when one attempts to define the procedure for those methods. Polzin isolates three criteria for determining the temporal relationship among stages in the history of the tradition used by von Rad for his evaluation of the credo: (1) brevity, (2) simplicity in content, and (3) a setting in the life of the people that accounts for the character of the tradition.[93] Polzin then raises important objections about all three criteria. It is a weak step in constructing the history of a tradition to assume that the shortest or simplest example of the tradition is the oldest. It may still be the case in any particular example that the shortest or simplest piece among various witnesses to a tradition will be the oldest. But the fact of brevity or simplicity cannot be the decisive factor in such a conclusion. Moreover, the definition of setting can easily become hypothetical, difficult to control with precision. A subjective reconstruction of setting can easily replace a carefully controlled procedure.

The points are well taken. But again one must be careful. Even if all three points in the critique are granted as telling categories, the value of von Rad's method remains high for probing a text with its critical tradition. The ability of the form critic to establish a tradition history for the content of a pericope or a form history for its genre might be weakened by the critique. Yet, if some impression of the development in the tradition or the genre could be established, it would provide an invaluable control for defining the significance of the tradition or the genre at each critical stage. The tradition is obviously not of uniform character at all occasions of its appearance. To establish a control for placing the changes in some order of development obviously would help define the significance of the tradition's character along the way and, indeed, contribute to an evaluation of the changes.

But von Rad's method is not only diachronic. It also has critical value for defining the synchronic dimensions of a pericope, both for the analysis of structure and for the definition of genre. Moreover, it does not necessarily leave the pericope disintegrated. To describe the structure of the Pentateuch on the analogy of the credo, even if the credo should prove not to be ancient, even if the analogy does not prove a cultic origin for the Pentateuch, still would illumine the structure of the Pentateuch. And the value of the analysis is high for describing the nature of the unity in the whole, not simply for pulling the pieces apart and declaring them to be originally independent. The method does not require reconstruction of the original tradition in order to prove its value for interpreting the Moses images.

The primary goal for this book does not call for reconstruction of an original Moses tradition. My concern is to describe the various images used by various texts in the Old Testament for depicting the characteristics of this giant. The pursuit is thus properly synchronic. It asks about the shape of Moses imagery in the received text. But there is also a diachronic dimension for my work. If in the effort to describe how the tradition depicts Moses some competing images arise, it is an appropriate task to inquire about the relationship among those competing images. And that question can at least potentially open windows of diachronic relationships. An answer to the controlling question about the imagery for painting the portrait of Moses may be constructed simply as an observation about the dominant shape of the Moses story, not the original shape of the story. And yet, if the shape cannot be contested by evidence from early witnesses to the Moses tradition, one might ask why the dominant picture would not demand such an exalted status. It is nonetheless perhaps too much to claim that the clue for defining 'original' is uncontested dominance. The argument still depends on dating pieces of evidence. And that pursuit is currently under attack.

An assumption in the work that follows is that the Yahwist is older than Deuteronomy or the priestly source. And in those places where E appears, the source is an expansion of J, thus dependent on J.[94] Moreover, the priestly source represents the latest stage in the development of the literature, with Deuteronomy the middle term. But even these clues now stand under attack.[95] I am not concerned in the scope of this book with an absolute dating of the sources that would place the Yahwist in the court of David or Solomon. The issues are critical and demand attention. But my concern here is for relative relationships in the definition of the growth of the Pentateuch. The assumption of my work is that the classical definition of order in the relationships of the sources holds even in the face of challenges. But at key points the position will be argued rather than simply assumed.[96]

The Moses Narratives as Heroic Saga

In order to develop an analysis of the Moses traditions, I propose the following working hypothesis: *The Moses narratives can be understood, bracketed together, as heroic saga.*[97]

Several problems threaten the stability of this thesis:

1. Martin Noth observed, in response to a suggestion that Moses serves as a great bracket binding all the 'themes' together: 'But in view of the factors just presented, would not Moses perhaps undermine the whole thesis that there are different Pentateuchal themes?'[98] In order to meet this objection, Noth must either show that Moses was not originally a part of every theme and then discover which one represents the primary locus for the tradition (the patriarchs obviously falling out of consideration), or he must give up the thesis that the themes were originally independent. It should be noted just here that the logical consequence of the objection is not to undermine the thesis that there are different themes in the Pentateuch. It is to undermine the assumption that the different themes are independent of each other.[99] Noth chose to search for a single position in only one of the themes that would account for Moses' original home. It seems to me, however, that Moses cannot be eliminated so readily from the various themes of tradition, and, as a consequence, the assumption of independence collapses. Noth himself builds strong cases for concluding that Moses is closely bound with the exodus, or the wandering, or Sinai. And he then rejects the cases. But the reasons for rejecting them are not always strong.

One illustration will demonstrate the point. Noth dismisses Moses from the exodus theme in part because the birth and abandonment tale is 'one of the latest and most secondary passages of the Moses tradition'.[100] That it employs a narrative motif known all over the world is not evidence that it is literarily, or even traditio-historically secondary in the Moses tradition. That the motif does not mesh well with the oppression theme at the center of the exodus narrative may be.[101] And yet, the distinctive role of such Moses traditions as this one, the Midianite marriage, the battle with Amalek, or the humble image of Numbers 12 must not be overlooked. On the basis of this observation, I would reformulate the hypothesis: *The Moses narratives, structured as heroic saga, merge with narrative tradition about Yahweh's mighty acts, structured around confessional themes.* These two structural models stand as narrative opposites, at times complementary, at times contradictory. They find their largest expression in the structural opposition represented by the Pentateuch in contrast to the Hexateuch.

Some explanation of this point is in order. It is well known that the little historical credo suggests a structural unity for the themes about God's mighty acts. Moreover, that unity encompasses patriarchs and conquest as poles around the theme of promise and fulfilment. Those traditions now appear from Genesis through Joshua and suggest that the basic unit is Hexateuch. In what manner, then, is it possible to speak structurally of a Pentateuch? Is Pentateuch simply an accident in the process of canonization? Or is there a form-critical integrity that gives legitimacy to an analysis of the Pentateuch? In my opinion the Moses narratives constitute a body of tradition with valid form-critical character. That point suggests, however, that Exodus through Deuteronomy has integrity as a unit. What, then, can be said concerning the relationship between the Moses narratives and Genesis? One of the pressing problems, as yet unresolved in the scholarly discussion of the Pentateuch, concerns the relationship between the patriarchs and Moses or between the 'God of the Fathers' dimension of religion in the early tradition of Israel and the religious structure of Yahwism.[102] The point at issue here, however, is not the relationship between patriarchs and Moses but rather the structure of the Pentateuch/Hexateuch. The Moses traditions lend unity to the narratives from Exodus through Deuteronomy. The credo traditions draw distinctions between exodus, wilderness, and conquest, suggesting unity beyond the structure of the Moses saga. In what manner does that sign of unity contribute to the shape of Moses imagery?

2. Bernhard W. Anderson asserts: 'The exodus story is not a heroic epic told to celebrate the accomplishment of Moses as the liberator of his people'.[103] The issue here is not over the terms 'saga' or 'epic'. Rather, the problem turns on the designation of this story as 'heroic'. In order to speak to the issue, first, it is necessary to establish some definition of 'heroic' as an interpretative tool. In 1934, Lord Raglan, Fitzroy Richard Somerset, addressed the English Folklore Society with a study of folk heroes, designed to show a recurring pattern of structure for a heroic narrative. He drew on several works exploring heroic patterns, including the classical nineteenth-century study of the hero by Johann Georg von Hahn and Alfred Nutt. He proposed twenty-two elements in a heroic pattern: (1) The mother of the hero is a royal virgin. (2) The father is a king, and (3) often a near relative of the mother, but (4) the circumstances of the hero's conception are unusual, and (5) he is reputed to be the son of a God. (6) At birth an attempt is made, often by his father, to kill him, but (7) he is spirited away, and (8) reared by fosterparents in a far country. (9) We are told nothing of his childhood, but (10) on reaching manhood, he returns

or goes to his future kingdom. (11) After a victory over a king and/or a giant, a dragon, or wild beast, (12) he marries a princess, often the daughter of his predecessor, and (13) becomes king. (14) For a time he reigns uneventfully, and (15) prescribes laws, but (16) later he loses favor with the gods and/or his subjects, and (17) is driven from the throne and his city. (18) He meets with a mysterious death, (19) often at the top of a hill. (20) His children, if any, do not succeed him. (21) His body is not buried, but nevertheless (22) he has one or more holy sepulchers.[104]

The list should be used with caution. It has obvious contact with the Moses traditions, since one of the eighteen 'heroic' stories used to compile the list was the story of Moses. Lord Raglan apparently felt no necessity to prove that the Moses story was heroic before using it as material for the list or a definition of 'heroic' apart from the composite structure of the list. Yet, the list is useful precisely because it is a composite of eighteen distinct traditions and not dependent on the Moses story alone. Moreover, it suggests a distinction in the term 'hero' between the principal figure in a historical event, such as the 'hero' in the siege at Valley Forge, and the principal figure that gathers folkloristic traditions, such as the 'hero' of the *Nibelungenlied*.

A more recent study by a Dutch folklorist, Jan de Vries, offers a balance to the work of Lord Raglan. His list derives from medieval heroic tales and thus does not present an obvious dependency on the Moses tradition, although certainly he has been influenced by the study of Lord Raglan. The list includes the following: (1) The hero is begotten; (2) he is born; (3) his youth is threatened; (4) he is brought up; (5) he often acquires invulnerability; (6) he fights with the dragon or other monsters; (7) he wins a maiden, usually after overcoming great dangers; (8) he makes an expedition to the underworld; (9) he returns to the land from which he was once banished and conquers his enemies; (10) he dies.[105]

Again, the list should not be embraced simply as the necessary paradigm for any given heroic story. One or more elements may take on altered form or drop out altogether. The list is useful, rather, as an index for a recognizable structure that characterizes a particular type of story. It gives evidence of the structure, moreover, apart from the Biblical tradition, apart from Semitic literature and the period of literary history that produced the Moses traditions. It suggests not literary dependency or some kind of easy identification of types between the medieval hero and the Moses stories, but rather a typical story pattern that facilitates a definition of hero from evidence external to the Moses traditions. The hero would be a figure of folk tradition that meets certain kinds of needs for the folk, such as a representative for courage, leadership, and honor.

A consideration of the stereotyped structure faces several critical responses, however. Definition of 'heroic' cannot stand very long if it is simply the sum total of all the parts included by some prior definition of a heroic image. Is there not some qualifying definition that provides a point of control for the tradition included under this stamp? Yet, consideration of structure allows an initial and necessary assertion. 'Heroic' is a literary term, not an historical one or a sociological one. It is, moreover, a term at home in folklore, and while the heroic can certainly be created by an author, the category belongs not to the author who creates apart from the life blood of the folk, but rather to the folk and their storytellers who preserve their special traditions for the entertainment and edification of the people.

It would be helpful, then, to move beyond the structure typical for a heroic narrative to consider other elements in a definition. Is there a qualifying *intention* in the tradition that sets 'heroic' narrative apart from all general narration about some particular central figure? Joseph Campbell proposes one description: 'A hero ventures forth from the world of common day into a region of supernatural wonder: fabulous forces are encounted and a decisive victory is won. The hero comes back from this mysterious adventure with the power to bestow boons on his fellow man'.[106] The parallel with Moses is apparent. Thus, I would expand the working hypothesis with a qualifying definition for the intention of heroic tradition, particularly as it comes to expression in the Moses narratives: *This heroic tradition binds the hero with his people. Either by military might, or by skillful intercession, or by familiarity with surroundings and conditions, he defends and aids his own. He brings 'boons' to his people.*

But, someone might object, is it not possible to identify the *lone* hero who does what he does, not as leader and protector of his people, but rather as the paragon of the great individual champion? Samson might be an example.[107] Samson does not lead. He works as a lone giant and eventually dies that way. Moreover, despite his final success in conflict with the Philistines, his life appears marked with tragedy and even failure. He might be designated more appropriately as an anti-hero.[108] Yet, his lone deeds bring 'boons' to his people. He holds the Philistines at bay while he courts two of their women. And though the final moments of his life are tragic, the event marks a victory over Israel's enemy. The giant can be no hero, not even an effective anti-hero for folk tradition unless he is hero for the people. Even the Christian hermit cannot be a saint unless he is a saint for his people. His heroic quality makes sense only insofar as it serves the edification of the community.

One final problem in the composition of heroic tradition deserves some attention. There is some recurring tendency in heroic tradition to move the celebration of the deeds and virtues of the hero as a human being, committed to the health and peace of his own people, to a celebration of the hero as a god.[109] Hercules was a man. But at the moment of his entry to Olympus, he leaves his humanity behind and becomes one among the gods in the pantheon. Heroic tradition, then, balances the central figure between two natures. And the interplay of the human nature with the potential of its divine counterpart creates some of the tension in the dynamic of the tradition. Particularly in Hellenistic Judaism this dynamic effects the shape of the Moses traditions.

> For Philo . . . , Moses is the epitome of ideal humanity, reconciler and mediator between God and man, and revealer of the changeless law which existed with God before the creation of the world. Hellenistic Judaism views Moses in terms of its own ideals as a superhuman figure, a divine man (θεῖος ἀνήρ).[110]

This problem does not, however, effect the complexity of the Moses traditions in the Old Testament. The canonical texts reveal to the contrary a marked intention to withhold Moses from any form of apotheosis. In all aspects of the tradition, Moses remains a man, the man of God, the servant of God, but nevertheless a human being. It is in this context, then, that the complementary relationship between heroic man and the man of God who serves the mighty acts of God for the redemption of the people emerges with its strongest force. Moses is not simply an instrument in the hands of God. But he is also not the redeemer who initiates the salvation of the people. He fights for his people. But he does not make them into a people. They remain the people of God.

3. John Van Seters argues that the term 'saga' is inadequate for current Old Testament debate and should be dropped.[111] The primary reasons for his objections derive from a solid critique of the use various form critics have made of the term during the past decades.[112] It does not follow, however, that the term has no currency

for studies in Old Testament narrative. A more workable definition for saga suggests that as an analytic term for a narrative genre, it refers to a long prose, usually episodic narration built around a plot or a succession of plots.[113] Its intention is to capture the audience by the tensions in its story-line, thus, to entertain its audience with the skill of its storytelling. The consequence of this definition, among others, is that the genre belongs primarily to the repertoire of the oral story teller, although it would have been quite possible to transcribe the substance of the story-line at some point in its history. The episodic structure would enable the story teller to create his story with each performance by skillfully constructing the panels or episodes to fit his need. But the episodes would follow a typical, perhaps even a fixed pattern. It seems to me appropriate, therefore, to maintain the use of the term 'saga' in the working hypothesis, not as a wooden translation of the German word, *Sage*, but as a technical term for a very particular genre of narrative literature.[114]

To sum up, I would offer a final formulation of the working hypothesis: The Moses traditions, structured as heroic saga, emphasize a motif native to heroic tradition in one degree or another: *The hero identifies himself with his people. This structure merges with another, following the order of confessions about Yahweh's deeds for his people.* A major requirement for understanding the Moses tradition is, therefore, a definition of the relationship between these two structural patterns. Moses is the heroic man and the man of God.

Chapter 2

THE BIRTH TALE
AND THE MOSES-MIDIANITE TRADITION

In order to defend this working hypothesis, I propose to examine in detail the key elements of the tradition which carry the heroic saga structure.

1. *The Birth Tale: Exod. 2.1-10*

Heroic narrative typically enframes its story with some account of the hero's birth and death. That the J account of Moses' death is heroic has previously been suggested.[1] That his birth and adoption into the royal Egyptian court should be considered heroic is also not new, although it has not been explored in detail under a heroic rubric.[2] Heroic motifs include not only the threat to his life by the Egyptian pogrom, with the corresponding exposure that commits him to his fate, but also the irony that develops in the princess's decision to commit him to a Hebrew mother for his initial nurture. How could he do anything other than identify with his people?

Exposition of the birth tale begins with some consideration of structure and context. First, the structure of the pericope employs three major elements: (1) vv. 1-4, the birth and disposal of the child; (2) vv. 5-6, discovery by the Egyptian princess; and (3) vv. 7-10, adoption. It is important to note, with this pattern of structure in hand, that the tale does not focus on the birth of the child. To be sure, it reports that the child was born. But there is no miraculous quality in the birth report itself, no annunciation, no star to mark the place. To the contrary, there is only a sense of danger, identified in the observation of v. 2 that the mother hid the child for three months. The context stipulates the nature of the danger (see the comments below). For the tale itself, however, there is no such stipulation. Verse

2 reports only that the mother hid the child. Verses 3-4 carry this sense of danger to the point of tragedy. When the child could no longer be hidden, he must be committed to his fate. He must be exposed to the whims of the river, or better, as the reader knows, to the hands of God.[3]

The exposure motifs open the door to the second element in the unit. The child does not die by exposure. The royal princess discovers his ark in the river during an excursion with her attendants. Tension in the plot increases with the discovery. The princess recognizes immediately that the child belongs to the Hebrews, and the contrast between the royal Egyptians and the common Hebrews raises the level of anxiety marked by the opening element. Yet, at just this point of tension, the story teller foreshadows the outcome of the tale. 'She took pity on him...' The verb, *wattaḥmōl*, can mean simply 'to spare from death'. But it also connotes the intimate relationship between a parent and a child: 'I will take pity on them as a man takes pity on his son who serves him' (Mal. 3.17).

The tension breaks in the third element of this tale, just as the foreshadowing suggested. The child becomes a part of the Pharaoh's house by virtue of the princess's move to adopt him as her own son. It is significant that the structure particularly in the last element reveals stereotyped patterns formed by legal procedures for adoption as well as hiring a wet nurse.[4] The focus of the tale, then, does not highlight the birth of the child, although the report of birth is obviously a part of the unit. The focus is rather on the adoption of the child by the Pharaoh's daughter.

What, then, is the intention of such a pericope? It provides the occasion to introduce the Egyptian name of the child, a fact that lies hidden behind an explanation of the name as if it were derived from Hebrew.[5] But the intention of the pericope as a unit is not simply to give a name to the boy. The tale places Moses in an Egyptian culture. Moses would spend his childhood, at least from his weaning to his passage into manhood, in the Egyptian court. This observation does not support a conclusion that, as a matter of historical fact, Moses was really an Egyptian. It does set up an irony in that the figure that facilitates the victory of the Israelites and the exodus from Egypt comes from within the walls of the Pharaoh's own court. The irony is heightened by the description of the real mother of the child, hired by the Pharaoh's daughter as a wet nurse, responsible for the early years of Moses' nurture. The intention of the unit, however, does not appear to be an effort to make Moses an Egyptian. Rather, it establishes a significant contrast. All the physical signs point to Moses as an Egyptian (see v. 19), legally adopted into the social structures of the land of his birth. But by contrast, the adoption tale emphasizes Moses' true origin. And the early years of nurture place the decisive influence on his life among his own people, a fact of the tradition that was converted to Egyptian culture only by the legal procedure of adoption. In the tradition, Moses belongs to the Israelites.

The birth-adoption tale cannot stand apart from the story in 1.15-22 very successfully, at least not insofar as the structure of the received text is concerned. This story about the Pharaoh's pogrom against all Israelite baby boys provides the context for the birth tale. Why was the baby Moses hidden for three months following his birth? Why, then, was it necessary for the mother to commit him to an uncertain fate at the 'hands' of the river? Because the Pharaoh had condemned all males born to the Israelites to die, first at the hands of the midwives, then at the hands of all the Egyptians, the birth of Moses to his Levite parents occurred under the pale of tribal panic. A son born to an Israelite family should normally have been a reason for celebration. But in this case, it brought agony.

Verses 15-21 may constitute a story originally distinct in itself, not simply a context for the Moses birth tale. The Pharaoh condemned all male Israelite children to die at birth. And the midwives were to be the agents of the death. But the clever deceit of the two midwives, whose names are noted in the text, enables the children to live, the people to multiply, and the royal decree to fail. The midwives were themselves heroes for the people, a means for the continuing strength of the sons of Israel. And indeed, they received an appropriate reward for their plot. Because they 'feared' God, they won families for themselves (*wayya'aś lāhem bāttîm*). The facts that the midwives are named here, their plot described and carried to fruition, and their reward confirmed by God, while in 2.1-10 they receive no allusion at all would suggest an originally distinct life for the tale.[6] And significantly, at no point in the following Moses traditions or the entire exodus theme is the pogrom a part of the picture in the Egyptian oppression. If it should be appropriate to suggest that the midwives tale had its own distinct tradition history, then it would be clearer that 1.22 functions as a bridge between the midwives tale and the birth-adoption tale. It would be the product of a redaction that set the two traditions together. The intention of the redaction would have been to create the context for the birth of Moses explicitly in the oppressive policies of the Pharaoh. And it would heighten the irony of the narrative yet another step. The child adopted into the Pharaoh's house and subsequently the leader of the Israelites who engineered the defeat of the Egyptians should have died in the Pharaoh's pogrom. But instead, he escaped by the hand of the Pharaoh's own daughter.[7]

Moreover, the midwives' tale provides an additional bridge between the birth and adoption of Moses and the introduction of the oppression leitmotif in 1.1-14. In 1.1-14 the 'people' of Israel appear for the first time, the product of fruitful increase given them by God. But the increase leads directly to a policy from the Pharaoh to submit the slaves to oppressive hard labor (see 1.11 [J] and 1.13-14 [P]). The oppression leitmotif, however, does not mesh well with the pogrom scene or the birth-adoption tale.[8] Why would the Pharaoh kill off his labor force? Yet, it is not necessary to resolve this element of disunity by reconstructing the narrative in a more harmonious fashion. The disunity derives not from two different literary sources, but from the association of two distinct functional structures in the narrative: the Moses tale and the exposition for the exodus theme.

It would be relevant to ask here whether and in what manner the birth-adoption tale contributes to an interpretation of the Moses tradition as heroic. In order to address the question, I suggest *first* a comparison of the tale with the narrative about the birth of Sargon of Akkad:

> Sargon, the mighty king, king of Agade, am I.
> My mother was a changeling, my father I knew not.
> The brother[s] of my father loved the hills.
> My city is Azupiranu, which is situated on the banks of the Euphrates.
> My changeling mother conceived me, in secret she bore me.
> She set me in a basket of rushes, with bitumen she sealed my lid.
> She cast me into the river which rose not (over) me.
> The river bore me up and carried me to Akki, the drawer of water.
> Akki, the drawer of water, lifted me out as he dipped his e[w]er.
> Akki, the drawer of water, [took me] as his son (and) reared me.
> Akki, the drawer of water, appointed me as his gardener.
> While I was a gardener, Ishtar granted me (her) love,
> And for four and [. . .] years I exercised kingship. . .[9]

It has long been recognized that the accounts have some important parallels. The baby was exposed to his fate in a basket of rushes. His discovery introduces him into a family as an adopted son. And from that advantage he matures to become a leader of his people. In both cases, particularly if one considers Exod. 2.1-10 apart from the context, it is not clear why the baby was exposed. But in both cases, the exposure leads to adoption. Yet, despite the obvious similarities, the differences seem more significant. (1) Nothing is known of Sargon's father, and little is known of his mother. In contrast, Moses' parentage is clearly set forward.[10] Names for the parents are not given in this tale. But it is clear that Moses belonged to the Israelites, born to a family of Levites. Moreover, a sister watches over him and seizes the opportunity to bring the real mother to the princess as a wet nurse. The family of Moses is fully present. (2) If the intention of the Sargon tale is to introduce a blessing oracle which would determine the future by binding it to the past,[11] the Moses tale seems to move in a slightly different direction. It does introduce Moses into the royal Egyptian court. And it does establish Moses' past in a way that colors his future career. But the Moses birth tale seems even more intent on showing the connections between the baby and his own people. And in this direction, the heroic quality of the birth tale emerges. Threatened by the foreign king, as all male children among his people were, Moses survives by virtue of the protection given him in the Pharaoh's own house. But this past does not determine the future. That role belongs to the pericope in 3.1-4.23. (3) If Sargon can be described as hero, he is hero in this tale for the people who adopt him, the people he eventually rules as king. Moses is not hero for the Egyptians. In fact, the context shows Moses under threat from the host people. Rather, Moses is hero for the people of his birth. His elevation in the court of the Pharaoh plays no other role in this tale than as a contrast to the life that in fact is his. (4) Thus, the Sargon tale has no developed element for the adoption, no report of hiring a wet nurse. The interest of the narrative is not to account for the real origin of the child, from which he was taken by legal means. It is to show the important entry of the child into a royal position as the leader of his new people. Thus, the Moses birth-adoption tale qualifies as heroic in contrast to the Sargon piece because of its identification of the child with his own people.

I would argue *second* that the tale is heroic because of the mood of anxiety that threatens the birth of the child, a mood broken only by the careful planning of the child's family and, of course, the stroke of fortune which the audience can understand as the hand of God. The hero begins his life in the face of a contrast between Hebrews and Egyptians. And the contrast foreshadows the total scope of his career. A birth that foreshadows the conflict at the center of the hero's life work typifies the structure of heroic saga.

It is significant to note here that the priestly source has no claim to this tradition. In the first chapter of Exodus, P describes the plight of the people as a result of their fruitful increase. But the unit sets up the action of God, not the birth of Moses. The birth-adoption tale belongs rather to J, or with 1.15-21 to JE. To identify 2.1-10 as J and 1.15-21 as E might clarify the structure of the pericope. In that case E would provide significant context for the birth story, even though the present form of the text would preserve no trace of E's birth story narration itself. Yet, it seems probable to me that these two traditions circulated initially not as items in distinct literary sources, but rather as elements in the oral tradition that lies behind the written form of the tales. Their union reflects a combination of traditional elements that occurred before the material reached written form.[12]

If that conclusion is justified, then in what manner would the narrative motif, 'fear of God', enter the story? Does it not mark the work of the Elohist?[13] Would it then be a sign of the redactional revision of the Elohist, designed to bring the midwives tale into the scope of the narration about the exodus? The 'fear of God' belongs particularly to the midwives, not simply to the process of the story as a means for arriving at some other point. It accounts for the midwives' courage in combating the Pharaoh's instructions. Without it the plot that leads to victory over the Pharaoh's plan has no clear motivation. And the foundation for the reward given these women for bravery vanishes. So, v. 21: 'Because the midwives feared God, he gave them families (made houses for them)'. Would the 'fear of God' not constitute an intrinsic part of the story, not an item created *ad hoc* by the Elohist? At least it is not clear that the motif marks the story simply as a redactional element used only by the Elohist as a means for giving expression to the oppression leitmotif. And certainly it is not possible to conclude anything from this story about the Elohist's use of heroic tradition for the beginning of the Moses story.[14]

2. *Moses-Midianite Tradition*

a. *The Marriage Tale: Exod. 2.11-22*

This pericope comprises two subunits of structure, each built with essentially the same element: vv. 11-15a and vv. 15b-22. In the first element, the narrative depicts a point of tension. Moses, now a grown man, saw *his* people (*'eḥāyw*), working under the burden of Egyptian oppression (v. 11a). It is important to recognize that all Egyptian connections for Moses must be assumed for this verse. The explicit affirmation of the story here identifies Moses not with the Egyptians, but with the Hebrews. So, v. 11b: 'He saw an Egyptian beating a Hebrew, one of his people (*mē'eḥāyw*)'. The point of tension in the scene thus emerges with clarity. One of his people suffers under the oppressive hand of his opposition. Indeed, the verb 'beating' (*makkeh*) connotes not simply physical oppression, but killing. In this situation of oppression and in the light of the emphasis the text places on the identification between Moses and his people by calling the people his brothers twice, the tale has created the fundamental tension of the plot. What will Moses do?

The second part of this story features a resolution of the tension by describing Moses' intervention on behalf of the oppressed brother. Verse 12 represents the intervention with irony. Moses killed the Egyptian who had been killing the Hebrew brother. The verb used for the Egyptian's act of 'beating' now describes Moses' act of 'killing'. And the final result of the 'killing' stands out clearly in the reference to Moses' burial of his victim. This segment of the story demands careful attention. Moses' act of violence does not deserve denigration by interpreters as an act of 'murder'.[15] The text does suggest that Moses understands the risk of his act. Thus, it depicts him as initially cautious. 'He turned this way and that, and seeing no one he killed the Egyptian.' But his caution does not mean that he plans an act of 'murder' that would be a sin in the eyes of the Israelite God. Obviously, the oppressed Hebrew whom Moses defends would be a witness to the deed. And presumably he would have received the deed as an act of deliverance, not a crime of violence. The text represents the act, then, as a 'murder' only for the eyes of any Egyptian who might witness the event or hear about it from some primary source. For the Hebrew, for his own people, the act should be seen as heroic defense, a risk of his own life for the sake of protecting his brother.

But, we might object, Moses had not yet received God's commission to deliver his people. Would this act of violence not appear premature and thus inappropriate?[16] In no way! It is true that the call cannot justify the deed. But the call does not function to justify acts of violence anyway. If the deed were 'murder' in the eyes of the storyteller, it would still be murder even in the context of the call. Rather than justifying random acts of violence, the call commissions Moses for a very explicit responsibility. Here, that responsibility has not yet entered the picture. But this act foreshadows it.

The scene does not end with Moses' heroic intervention on behalf of his Hebrew brother. It develops a corollary element. Verse 13 places the hero among the Hebrews again, significantly in this case not explicitly called his brothers. When Moses sees two of them struggling (not the same verb as in the first element of the pericope) he intervenes against the one in the wrong. Moses attends not only to his own people against the Egyptians, but also to the cause of right, the opposite of the named opponent from among his own people. The guilty party responds, however, not with an apology and acquiescence to justice, but with an accusation of his own: 'Who made you a prince and a judge over us? Do you speak in order to kill me as you killed the Egyptian?' Moses might have explained that he killed the Egyptian in defense of his own people. But the tragedy of the scene is that the accusation comes from the Hebrews, not from the Egyptians, from the one oppressed by the enemy, for whom Moses risked the violent intervention. The accusation suggests rejection of the hero by the very one he claimed for his own. And even more, the public knowledge of the intervention from the previous day signals a violation of confidence from the man he rescued. The rejection comes not just from the people at large, but from the single person who benefitted from the intervention. Moreover, the public knowledge spells danger from Egypt. 'When Pharaoh heard this thing, he sought to kill Moses.'

The tragic scene of Moses' rejection sets a new scene in vv. 15b-22. In a fashion typical for the heroic pattern, Moses flees from his own people to a strange land (compare the *Nibelungenlied*). In Midian, a new incident of oppression occurs. At a well, a site for public meeting (see Gen. 24; 29), a site ripe for romance in the folk tradition of Israel, Moses stops to rest. Seven daughters of the Midianite priest arrive in order to draw water for their sheep. And this task they did. But then shepherds come and drive them away. In the same fashion of his first intervention for the sake of oppressed people, so Moses now arises to defend the oppressed. He drives the attacking shepherds away and waters the women's flock. And by virtue of the heroic intervention, Moses wins an invitation to the household of the priest and eventually the right to marry one of the daughters. The heroic tale of individual victory with the result of marriage into the clan's leading family thus characterizes this stage of the Moses tradition.

Yet, some caution must again control judgment. Martin Noth felt that the tale should not be considered a distinct tradition, but simply an introduction to the call narrative in Exodus 3-4.[17] If that judgment were correct, the marriage tale could not count as evidence of a heroic pattern apart from judgment about heroic or non-heroic elements in the call tradition. To call the marriage tale merely an introduction to the call tradition does not, however, appear to me to be sound. The marriage tradition cannot be simply subordinated to the call, even in the received text. Rather, it represents a distinct unit of Moses tradition in its own right.[18] And in its own field of meaning, it has distinctive heroic intention: (1) intervention for the sake of the oppressed, who happen to be the daughters of a Midianite priest, and (2) marriage to one of the women defended by his strength.

Still, one might object. The account is hardly a model for medieval romantic heroes. Moses saves the maiden in distress and thus wins her hand in marriage. But in fact, he saves all seven women. And no report of romance between Moses and his bride leads to an announcement of the wedding. Rather, the text gives only the barest of details, leaving the impression that the marriage was arranged by Moses and the father of the woman. Indeed, it would be possible to conclude that the intention of the tradition is to account for Moses' relationship with his father-in-law rather than the romantic relationship with his wife.[19] And this conclusion is supported by the tale in Exod. 18.1-8. Moses had sent his wife and her two sons away. And the father-in-law here brings them back. After the interval of absence, however, when Moses hears the news of their return, he runs to embrace and kiss, not the wife whom he missed as a romantic hero would, or even his sons, but the father-in-law. Verse 7b then paints a picture at odds with the image of a romantic hero. It is not his wife, newly restored to her husband, whom Moses takes into the tent for a time of intimate conversation. It is the father-in-law. The story may account for Moses' marriage to the priest's daughter. But it appears to be more of a Moses-Reuel tradition than a Moses-Zipporah one.[20] Indeed, if one asks whether the figure, Zipporah, was rooted traditio-historically in this pericope, the answer would necessarily be qualified.[21] Zipporah is, of course, named as the wife of Moses. And she bears him a son. But the name gives no distinctive quality to the development of the tale; even the birth report for Gershom constructs Moses as the active agent in giving the child a name. The search for a tradition that might feature Zipporah as a primary character would thus have to move beyond 2.11-22, in all probability to 4.24-26.

But if the marriage story cannot be described as a Moses-Zipporah tradition, in what sense is it genuinely heroic?[22] (1) It does feature Moses as a hero concerned for the oppressed, parallel to the hero who intervenes for his own brothers in vv. 11-12. Indeed, the two scenes stand much more tightly bound than the midwives and the birth of the baby. Thus, for this particular tradition, the heroic emerges from Moses' identification with his people; both his own brothers and the Midianite family become his own. (2) It fits into a general convention in Old Testament tradition that treats marriage as an event that establishes functional, familial relationships between the son-in-law and the father-in-law (so, compare Gen. 29-31). (3) While Moses remains with his father-in-law as a shepherd, he does so under the stamp of a foreigner, away from his own people. Thus, he names his son Gershom, and the tradition interprets the name by reference to the Hebrew word *gēr*, stranger or foreigner. Verse 22b makes the point: 'Because he said, "I am a *gēr* in a foreign land"'. And when he requests his father-in-law's permission to return to Egypt, he does so in order to make contact with his brothers in Egypt (*'aḥay 'ašer-bᵉmiṣrayim*). The heroic dimension which sets Moses in relationship to his own people thus looms through the marriage tale as the controlling orientation of the narrative. The tradition may intend to account for the relationship between Moses and Reuel, a relationship that returns to center stage in Exodus 18 (with the name of the father-in-law now Jethro). And it may offer a traditional element in a heroic pattern, accounting in a typical fashion for the marriage of the hero. But it does not lose contact with the focal emphasis in this heroic tradition for the relationship between Moses and his people.[23]

The entire pericope derives from the J source, with 2.23-25 a redactional piece designed to tie the marriage tale into the call narrative.[24] These verses would not be part of the major narrative tradition, but the work of the redactor who joined the Moses tales of Exodus 1-2 with the vocation tradition of Exodus 3. This piece may reflect influence from the cultic liturgy for lamentation.[25] But it is not now a cultic piece; its setting cannot be defined simply as cult. Rather, it is redactional in function. Its setting is the literary operation of the redactors. It is thus significant to observe that again the Yahwist features tradition about Moses that qualifies as heroic. The tradition behind the Yahwistic narrative centers in the marriage tale and thus preserves a typical heroic episode. The segment about Moses' intervention on behalf of his brothers does not appear to me to preserve older, originally distinct tradition. In contrast to the tale about the midwives, there are no names for the Hebrew brothers involved in the struggle. There is no final resolution of tension in Moses' intervention for those Hebrew brothers. Rather, the intervention scene seems to provide a bridge between the pericopes about Moses in Egypt and those about Moses in Midian. The whole unit, then, has the Yahwistic narrative about the marriage tale in view. And it confirms the conclusion from the birth-adoption tale that the Yahwistic story at this point is heroic in character. But it also suggests that the tradition incorporated by J was heroic. The cast of this Mosaic image was not simply created *ad hoc* by the Yahwist, but belonged to the tradition inherited by J from the lore of the people.

b. *A New Organization for Israel: Exod. 18.1-27*
This narrative unit comprises two principal sections, vv. 1-12 and 13-27. In vv. 1-2 Moses' family under the authority of Jethro, the father-in-law,[26] rejoins Moses in the wilderness. As suggested above, this tradition builds on a Moses-Jethro tradition rather than a Moses-Zipporah one. The focus of the narrative falls, moreover, not so much on the reunion itself, but rather on the report of Moses to his father-in-law and the corresponding response from the priest. The first element names the principal figures for the narrative and suggests the theme around which the narrative will develop. Jethro had heard of the events in Egypt established for Israel by God (v. 1). Verses 2-4 note as a parenthetical comment that Moses' wife and children were present. They do not, however, constitute a principal part of the narrative and drop from the scene. Verses 5-7 then establish the reunion between Moses and the father-in-law. And the key element for the section appears in v. 8. Moses recites the tradition for Jethro. It is not a tradition about Moses' deeds, but rather one of Yahweh's deeds: 'Moses recited to his father-in-law all the things the Lord had done to the Pharaoh and the Egyptians on behalf of Israel, all the hardship which had found them in the way, and how the Lord delivered them'. The unit here is thus not primarily heroic, but rather a part of the tradition about God's

mighty acts. But it also sets up the response of the Midianite to the
account of the mighty acts, reported in vv. 9-12. Jethro rejoiced over
the account. And the rejoicing leads to the confession of vv. 10-11
and the sacrifice described in v. 12. These elements have served
suggestions that Jethro must have been a priest of Yahweh and that
Moses introduced Yahwism into Israel's religious experience as a
result of influence from his father-in-law.[27]

The extent of Midianite influence on Mosaic Israel also constitutes
the subject of the second element in the pericope, vv. 13-27. Here the
father-in-law makes a recommendation concerning the organization
of the people. The background of the organization may be dominated
by the patterns of the military.[28] In this pericope, however, the
organization has to do with Mosaic leadership. Moses holds the right
to resolve civic disputes among the people. But the case load proves
to be so time-consuming that Moses could do nothing else (v. 14).
The father-in-law then poses a pattern of organization among the
people that would relieve the burden on Moses by investing
authority to assistants who could resolve minor cases. Significantly,
the text does not make a point of the authority of these assistants as
derivative from Moses (contrast Num. 11.17), Moses retains the
superior power. That power places Moses as the representative of the
people before God. And in return Moses must represent God to the
people, teaching them the proper way of life. The lower judges would
accomplish their part of the system as an extension of the Mosaic
position. But no explicit point confirms this relationship. Moreover,
the assistants must be men of integrity (8.21). But their qualification
for the office derives from the integrity, not by extension from Moses.
Thus, while Moses remains the leader of the people, and while he
receives the serious cases which the assistants cannot handle, the
intention of the unit is not to magnify Moses as leader, but rather to
describe the organization recommended by the Midianite father-in-
law. The organization does not derive from Moses' heroic leadership.
It does not derive from God's direction. It comes rather from the
Midianites.

This text, which has no apparent role for the heroic image of
Moses, has been commonly assigned to the Elohist. My impression is
that it would be methodologically unsound to conclude that E is non-
heroic in its depiction of Moses, while the heroic belongs to J. The
problem is rather one of tradition history. The tradition here belongs
more directly to a strand of Midianite tradition which happens to
include Moses. It may be intimately linked to Exodus 2. But the

heroic form of Moses in this link has faded. This non-heroic element is not peculiar to E but rather to the Midianite tradition.

c. *The Midianites and Baal Peor: Num. 25.1-18; 31.1-54*

The positive attitude toward the Midianites, assumed by the tradition in Exodus 2 and 18, stands in sharp contrast to the text in Num. 25.6-18 and its sequel in Numbers 31. The apostasy at Baal Peor occupies center stage for vv. 1-5 in ch. 25. By the seduction of Moabite women, the Israelites attached themselves to Baal of Peor. And as a consequence Moses pronounced execution for all those involved. The execution itself, however, does not appear as an explicit part of the narration. The tradition shifts in mid-stream at v. 6 to a particular incident involving one Israelite man and a Midianite woman. When these two persons were ritually executed by Phineas, the son of Aaron, the plague of God's anger stopped. Verse 9 may then assume some connection with the Baal-Peor incident, for here the narrator reports the death of 24,000 people because of the plague. Would this dimension not assume the guilt of the people as a whole for the violation? But it may be simply that the guilt of the individual jeopardizes the entire community (cf. Josh. 7.1). Verses 10-13 then use the tradition as grounds for a covenant with Phineas for a perpetual priesthood. And vv. 14-15 name the guilty couple executed by Phineas. The point of relevance for our consideration comes in vv. 16-18. Here the shift from the Moabites to the Midianites as the principals in the Baal Peor apostasy has been completed. And the impact of the shift is expressed in terms of a harsh, anti-Midianite saying: 'Harass the Midianites and smite them, for they harassed you with their plot which they planned against you in the matter of Peor'.

This anti-Midianite tradition also appears in Numbers 31. A speech from the Lord to Moses calls for war against the Midianites specifically to avenge the Israelites. The war brings victory, including the death of Balaam, the son of Peor, by the sword in the battle. The comment apparently assumes a connection between Balaam and the apostasy of Israel at Peor, a connection made explicit in v. 16. In these verses Moses remains the leader of the people and the spokesman for God. But the focus of the narrative is not on Moses. Rather, other elements of the community advance to center stage, such as Eleazar, the priest. Thus, the contribution of the narrative to a discussion of Moses traditions is not in terms of the Moses figure but rather in terms of the Midianites. Here the Midianites are the enemies of Israel because of their involvement with Israel in an act of worship of Baal.

Thus, the question returns sharply for evaluation. In Exodus 2 and 18, the Midianite father-in-law makes a significant and positive contribution to the life of Israel through his relationship with Moses. It is my contention that this tradition is positive, both in its depiction of Moses and in his relationships with the Midianites. There is no hint here of the tradition about the Midianite's violation with Israel at Baal Peor. And certainly there is not a hint of an anti-Moses tradition by virtue of his relationship with Jethro. Nor is there any suggestion that Jethro himself introduced Israel to an apostate cult. To be sure, both the Jethro tradition and the Baal Peor tradition connect the Midianites with Israel in some fashion through cultic activities. But there is no evidence to suggest that either the priest or the events in Exodus 2 and 18 should be seen as connecting Israel to an apostate cult. Moreover, no effort is made in Numbers 25 or 31 to connect the Midianites of the Baal Peor apostasy with Jethro. The connection is explicitly with Balaam. And that in itself is a significant traditio-historical problem.

Two forms of Midianite tradition seem obviously attested, one positive with supporting relationships for Israel, the other negative with Midian cast as a mortal enemy of Israel. But it is not a matter of relevance for the Moses tradition.[29] Moses speaks the words of Yahweh that establish a perpetual priesthood for Phineas or a perpetual enmity against Midian. But no negative configuration emerges for the Moses tradition itself. The two facets of Midianite tradition remain as separate as the Moses and Balaam facets in the book of Numbers.

Chapter 3

THE VOCATION TALES: EXODUS 3.1-4.31; 6.2-7.7

The accounts that set out Moses' call to a vocation hold a key for any definition of the tradition generally or for a description of the Moses figure in particular.

1. *Exod. 3.1–4.31*

This pericope requires no new structural analysis. The pattern features a combination of (1) a commission for the one called by a superior, (2) an objection to the commission by the one called, (3) the superior's reassurance for a successful execution of the commission, designed primarily to meet the objection, and (4) some indication of acceptance and even successful execution of the commission. These elements may appear in a variety of repetitions and even with other distinctive items, such as an opening theophany or a description of 'signs'. Yet, in all the variations and repetitions, the governing structural focus shines through. A figure receives a call, and despite his objections, he accepts it with his superior's reassurances and carries through on it to some kind of recognizable conclusion.[1] Parallels for the form appear in Gen. 24.1-67; Judg. 6.11-24; Isa. 6.1-13; Jer. 1.1-10, among others. And in each the same structural focus controls the presentation of the material.

The Moses pericope from the Yahwist begins with an account of theophany. Moses, the shepherd for his father-in-law in Midian, witnesses a phenomenon unique in the physical world: a bush burns without being consumed. Typical for the theophany are an account of unusual quality in nature or a natural event and some description of that quality in relationship to fire.[2] But the burning bush should not blind the eyes of the exegete to the dominant element in the structure. The fire serves only to attract the attention of the candidate, or perhaps better, the attention of the audience to the story. The divine speech is the more important part of the pericope.

In the speech, an initial vocative and response calls Moses to recognize the sanctity of the place (v. 5) and the relationship that sanctuary holds to the tradition about God (v. 6). God is present. And this God reveals himself as the God of the Fathers. The self-revelation formula in v. 6 uses the stereotype for the old traditions about the patriarchs. Doubtlessly it succeeds in establishing a connection between the Moses traditions and the patriarchal traditions. For the present form of the story, the Moses traditions are not independent from the patriarchs. The two stand together as a witness to the unity in the context of the Pentateuch. It is doubtlessly also true that the unity is secondary, a part of the redaction that fits the Moses story into the larger whole about the early life of Israel. But the initial narration nonetheless makes the Moses story a part of the larger whole.[3] It is difficult to conclude, however, that for the present form of the text a significant weight lies on the connection. There is an intention to connect exodus and patriarchs. But that is not the primary intention of the unit. The weight of the pericope rests rather on the commission speech in vv. 7-10.

But the commission element itself reflects a certain structural duplicity. And that quality demands immediate attention. Verses 7-8 present the Lord's intention to save his people. The plan introduced in v. 7 draws on the observation of affliction ($^{co}n\hat{\imath}$) imposed on the Hebrews by Egypt. But it also involves a response to the 'cry' of the people ($\d{s}a^{ca}q\bar{a}t\bar{a}m$). The Lord has heard the cry and now announces what he intends to do by way of a favorable response. A third element in the announcement connects the pain of the people ($mak\,'\bar{o}b\bar{a}yw$) to the Lord with the verb 'to know' ($y\bar{a}da\,'t\hat{\imath}$). The verb denotes intimacy, the intimacy of a marriage relationship with its sexual bonds (so, Gen. 4.1) or the intimacy of shared experience (so, Josh. 23.14). In the relationship God makes a personal commitment of his most basic nature. It is, therefore, a relationship that involves not only shared experience—God shares the pain of Israel's suffering—but a trust developed from the shared experience that affects all future events in the relationship. For God to 'know' the pain of Israel's suffering means for God to respond to it in his own essential way. The oppression becomes his own.

God's knowledge of Israel's oppression leads to a trust expressed in terms of the announcement. God *promises* to redeem his people from their suffering. The intimacy in God's relationship with his people, then, is expressed as a promise for the future, built on the trust in the relationship. And the validity of God's intimacy with his people depends on his ability to keep the promise. God trusts his people by sharing their pain. And in turn, the people trust God to keep his promise. Thus v. 7 carries the intimate commitment: 'Because I know their pain'. Verse 8 then announces the intention of God to act, his promise to redeem them from their plight. It will be a response undertaken personally by the Lord. 'I have come down to deliver them from the hand of the Egyptians and to bring them up from that land to a good and broad land, to a land flowing with milk and honey...' Verse 9, however, doubles back on the content of v. 7; indeed, it is set off from vv. 7-8 as a new start by two particles: 'Now, behold...' (w^e'*attāh hinnēh*). The duplicity in these verses stands out the more in the repetition of a key word: the 'cry' of the Israelites ($sa^{'a}qat$ $b^enê$-$yiśrā'ēl$). And v. 9b doubles v. 7a even though different vocabulary is used (*hallaḥaṣ*). But v. 10 does not describe a response to the pain in terms of what God intends to do for his people as an act of his redemption. Rather, it details the commission to Moses. 'Come, so that I may send you to Pharaoh. Bring out my people the Israelites from Egypt.'

How should this duplicity be interpreted? Martin Noth suggests, for example, that the first of these doublets belongs to J, while the second derives from E.

> According to J (vv. 7f., 16ff.) Yahweh's speech to Moses is simple and—in its original form—short. Yahweh has already begun to act. Not only has he heard the $ṣ^e$'*ākāh* of the Israelites, i.e., the cry for help of the helpless oppressed (v. 7); he has also already 'come down' (v. 8).... In E, where between v. 6 and v. 9 perhaps only the introduction to the divine speech of v. 9ff. is lacking, Moses receives the commission to 'bring forth' Israel since God has let the cry of the people of Israel come before him.[4]

Yet, it seems to me that the two elements do not constitute simple doublets of a single tradition and cannot be interpreted properly as parallels from two distinct literary sources. My principal reason for this conclusion lies in the observation that element *a* (vv. 7-8) presents God's intention to act for the sake of his people without reference to Moses. The verbs are first person active: '*I* have seen....*I* have heard....*I* have come down to deliver...and to bring up'. There is no second-person element at all. The principals are the Lord and his people. Element *b* (vv. 9-10), however, softens the first-person announcement by shifting the first statement to a participial clause: 'Now, behold, the cry of the Israelites is coming to me...' But of more importance, the intention is no longer to announce God's act for the salvation of the people, a direct intervention which he accomplishes for the sake of his people, but rather to announce his commission of Moses: 'I send you to Pharaoh...' And the goal of the commission now projects Moses' decisive contribution to the event: 'You bring my people the Israelites from Egypt'. The two elements, so it seems to me, have quite distinct functions, complementary to each other, but not identical. The relationship between the two can more appropriately be understood, therefore, in terms of the working hypothesis. Element *a* emphasizes God's mighty act to save his people, while element *b* is fundamental for the heroic tradition since it establishes Moses' vocational identity with the people. The people are still the people of God: 'my people' (*'ammî*). But Moses' vocation stands in intrinsic relationship to those people. He does not roam around as a lone giant, free to do whatever comes his way without consideration of the people. He must do whatever he does for the sake of the people. And what he must do is bring the Israelites out of Egypt. There is no way to understand a Mosaic office or even the Moses of literature apart from the people. But also, for this text, there is no way to understand the exodus apart from Moses.

This point is also apparent in vv. 11-12. Moses objects to the commission with a self-abasement.[5] And God's response promises divine presence. Indeed, the sign in v. 12 serves to validate Moses' office. 'I shall be with you [singular]. And this shall be a sign for you [singular] that I have sent you [singular]. When you [singular] bring the people out from Egypt...' It would appear here that God's presence in the exodus event is predicated on Moses' leadership, and that in itself might well stand as a dimension of the heroic. But the identity between heroic man and his people follows close on the heels of the image. 'You [plural] shall serve God on this mountain.' Moses and the people together will worship. Moses does not worship alone. He does not mediate the service to the people as something he experienced alone and now shares with them. He leads them. But he does not do so apart from them. In this case, the service involves both Moses and people. Moses is *primus inter pares*.

The sign, however, calls for more consideration. Moses does what he does in relationship to the people. But it is specifically Moses who represents God's presence for the people. The construction with singular suffixes in v. 12 emphasizes that point. Moreover, the verse sets up a means for validation of Moses' vocation. 'This shall be a sign *that I have sent you* [singular].' The *authority* of Moses to stand at the head of the people can now be identified as one of the principal topics in the pericope. And it is validated by the sign. Verse 12abα is, however, a problem, as Childs has shown.[6] What is the proper antecedent for the demonstrative pronoun 'this' (*zeh*)? Is it not the event suggested by v. 12b? The event apparently alluded to is the event to occur at Sinai when Moses and the people will gather there to receive the law. But how could an event yet to occur be taken as a sign for the authority of Moses' leadership? Particularly in light of the debate about the relationship between exodus and Sinai, the question is crucial. How can the Sinai event validate the authority of Moses in the exodus event? Childs develops a form-critical basis for the objection. 'Ordinarily, a sign takes the form of a concrete guarantee which follows the promise and yet precedes the fulfillment.'[7] And this observation he bases on a comparison of two patterns used with stereotypical consistency for describing signs. He suggests to the contrary that the pronoun *zeh* (this) does not anticipate a coming statement, thus v. 12b, but rather looks back in the pericope. The sign, so he argues, is the experience with the burning bush.

Yet, clarity in the perception of structure for the unit is crucial. The promise to be validated by the sign is the commission of Moses, not simply the exodus: 'I am sending you to the Pharaoh'. The issue at stake, to be confirmed by the sign, is the authority of Moses to carry out the commission. To be sure, the commission holds out a singular goal. 'Bring out my people the Israelites from Egypt.' Fulfillment of the commission, as it is guaranteed by the sign, would thus be escape for the Israelites from Egyptian oppression. The sign for guaranteeing this promise would need to occur before the report that the commission had been fulfilled, and the burning bush would be a candidate for the sign.

Yet, the burning bush theophany is removed from the demonstrative by several structural elements and cannot be obviously an antecedent for the pronoun. It would at least be an ambiguous construction. Moreover, the people for whom the sign serves as a guarantee for Moses' authority do not witness the burning bush. A sign at this crucial position in the Moses traditions that ignores the presence of the people would suffer from disjunction with the body of the Moses traditions. There is another alternative: The pronoun does indeed refer back to earlier parts of the pericope, rather than forward. But its reference is to the immediate context rather than a distant context. It is a part of the very speech that contains the demonstrative: 'I shall be with you, and this is a sign for you that I have sent you'. God's presence is fundamental for Moses' vocation. And the reality of it validates the vocation. Could it not be the sign that confirms his authority? Childs rejects this alternative because (1) the clause with its demonstrative pronoun connects to the preceding promise for presence with a *waw* conjunction, but to the following infinitive asyndetically, and (2) the sterotype 'I will be with you' does not function elsewhere as a sign. The first point would be a problem with any interpretation that looks backward for the antecedent rather than forward to the asyndeton. The second assumes a certain rigidity in the pattern. Would it be necessary to conclude that the stereotype cannot be the sign here because it does not appear so elsewhere?

The observation is important, however, and the construction of the verse is telling. Particularly, the parallel in Judges 5 provides helpful data. Again, the sign serves as a guarantee for the commission. The promise for presence is not the sign. It is a reassurance in the face of Gideon's objection. But the sign follows the promise and secures both the promise for presence and the promise-instruction in the body of the commission. Thus, the fulfillment of the promise is not the sign, as Childs suggests. In Exod. 3.12, a promise appears in the stereotype: 'I will be with you'. And that promise speaks to the crisis raised by Moses' objection. The fulfillment of the promise would thus be evidence for God's having been present.

But what, then, could be the sign? The text is ambiguous just here and does not spell out how God's presence might be made known. Could such a nebulous item function as a sign particularly when it never does so at other points in parallel texts? Moreover, it seems to imply a sign associated with successful completion. In that case, the sign would appear to me to be the event described in the clause of v. 12b. The construction in 1 Sam. 2.34 is exactly the same. The promise is that posterity for the house of Eli shall die. The fulfillment will be the death of the house. The sign occurs as a guarantee for the validity of the promise. Still, the objection remains. If the sign is worship on the mountain, in what manner can it relate to the promise for God's presence in the commission of Moses, to be fulfilled in the exodus? Child's objection to this alternative makes sense if we assume that the exodus is independent of Sinai. The exodus occurred, and then the event at the mountain occurred.

Indeed, they may have occurred for two completely different groups of people. And in that case, the event at the mountain could have nothing to do with a sign for the validation of Moses in the exodus.[8] But if this text should not assume such a distinction, if it should assume on the contrary that exodus and Sinai and even conquest all constitute the evidence of fulfillment in the promise, then the objection collapses. Coming out of Egypt is not the end of 'exodus' as God has promised it, and as a consequence the validation of Mosaic authority does not apply simply to an escape from Egyptian oppression. Rather, the authority of Moses continues (all the way to the land? so, v. 8), and its validation occurs *in the sight of the people*, not privately, when Moses and people together worship God at the mountain. The fact that the sign occurs after departure from Egypt— but before completion of the wilderness wandering—seems no more a handicap than does the death of the two sons of Eli as a sign that participates in the reality of the promise to eliminate all posterity from the family. And the fulfillment of the promise, a reality the sign already marks as a prolepsis, continues beyond the sign until its full scope reaches maturity. This conclusion does not undercut the thesis that exodus, wilderness wanderings, Sinai, and conquest are distinct themes. But it does weaken the argument that they were all independent. Especially, evidence for associating exodus and Sinai at a basic level seems to me to be present here.[9]

Verses 13-15 contain the classical center for discussion of this text, the revelation of the divine name in conjunction with the *idem per idem* formula. The objection Moses raises is that if the people should ask him the name of his superior, he would have nothing to tell them. God's response, v. 14, contains the formula: 'I am who I am'. It has long been correctly noticed that the formula contains a word play on the verb 'to be' (*hāyāh*). It is, moreover, a common explanation that the word play emphasizes God's promise to Moses for his presence.[10] I would support that interpretation with an observation that the word play represents a functional part in the structure of the pericope, rather than an external assertion. It is one in the series of reassurances addressed to Moses in the light of his objections to the commission. It seems unlikely to me that the play represents an abstraction of the verb in an effort to say that the Lord is the one who exists, or even the one who causes the creatures to exist.[11] Rather, I would suggest that the repetition of the form, *'ehyeh*, thus, *'ehyeh* *ᵃšer 'ehyeh*, plays on the same verbal form in v. 12, *'ehyeh 'immāk*. This point seems the more likely to me in view of the fact that the assistance formula, 'I will be with you', can be constructed in a proper way without the verb. So, for example, Jer. 1.8 reads *kî-'itt^ekā ^xnî*. Verse 13b then makes *'ehyeh* the divine name and thus parallel to the Tetragrammaton in v. 15. The Lord's name means his promise for presence. The name itself is the guarantee for the presence in the events of the exodus. The verbal construction for the formula appears also in Judg. 6.16. At that point, however, there is no apparent effort to play on the divine name. The construction is simply a way to express the promise. Yet, in the Exodus text, the formula does appear to play on the name and the verbal form from the root *hāyāh*. And if the play is in fact there, it would seem to me more likely to be an effort to explain the name by reference to the promise for presence.

Verse 15 completes the equation. In the place of *'ehyeh* from v. 14b, here the text employs the Tetragrammaton. It is the Lord who will accomplish the events of the exodus, Israel's redemption from oppression. But the parallel among the three distinct sentences, 14a, 14b, and 15a, shows clearly the intention of the text to establish an interpretation of the divine name. Yahweh is *'ehyeh*. And *'ehyeh* is the *idem per idem* formula. And the formula with its emphasis on *'ehyeh* is the divine promise for presence. Verse 15 also returns to the introduction of God from v. 6. This Lord is the same as the God of the fathers. And the continuation of the speech into vv. 16 and 17 picks up the motif from v. 8. God will deliver Israel and also give her the promised land. Thus, in this complex of traditions, the Pentateuchal themes, patriarchs, exodus, wilderness-Sinai, and the conquest belong together.[12] It is important to notice further that the references to the conquest appear only in those elements of structure that present the mighty acts of God, not in the ones dealing with the commission of Moses. It is as if the structure for the Moses traditions intentionally excludes that element from the parallel structure that deals with the conquest.

The remaining verses of this speech prefigure Exod. 4.29–6.1 and the plague cycle in 7.8–10.29. (1) Moses will command the obedience of the Israelites, and with the elders of the people he will go to the Pharaoh. At this stage in the presentation of the tradition, negotiations with the Pharaoh will take place under the leadership of Moses. But the event will involve the unique union of Moses with his people, represented by the elders. (2) Moses and the elders will appeal to the Pharaoh on the basis of a request to go into the wilderness three days journey for sacrifice. At no point in the tradition is the plan for a journey into the wilderness actually communicated to the Israelites as the Lord's instructions for worship. Rather, the motif represents a plot for deception. The implication in the request to the Pharaoh is that the Israelites would return after the sacrifice. It does not imply that the Pharaoh would release the slaves from their bondage. The narrative does suggest, however, that the request is a ruse. If the Pharaoh should let the slaves go for three days, expecting them to return in another three days, he would face a surprise, for they would obviously keep on going. And so, the text prefigures the Pharaoh's response. The ruse will fail. And with the failure will come the signs and wonders. (3) Verses 21-23 then anticipate the despoiling, a motif that functions as a topos for the exodus event itself (see the comments below). The motif contributes to the pattern of the heroic Moses by suggesting a tradition about the exodus as a secret escape under the leadership of Moses. The despoiling text in Exod. 11.3 rounds out the image: 'The Lord gave the people favor in the eyes of the Egyptians. Moreover, the man Moses was exceedingly great in the land of Egypt, in the eyes of the servants of Pharaoh, and in the eyes of the people'. Moses' stature was recognized by both Egyptians and Israelites. And that stature made the exodus possible.[13]

Chapter 4 continues the pattern of objection and reassurance.

(1) The Israelites will not listen to, i.e. obey, the voice of Moses (v. 1). This point Moses advances in direct contraditiction to the Lord's promise in 3.18. Obedience to Moses becomes in itself a key leitmotif for the Moses traditions. And it relates to the heroic pattern specifically by raising a question concerning the people's relationship with Moses. Moses is hero for the people. But can the people embrace him as their hero, or must they reject him? 3.18 carries a projection of obedient, supportive, embracing relationship. The people will see Moses as their own. But 4.1 proves to be a more accurate barometer for the coming storms, at least insofar as the preserved text is concerned. Moses fears that the people will not hear him. And that means that they will not obey. They will rebel. Thus, a leitmotif for the Moses tradition highlights various poles for considering the nature of obedience. What does it mean for Israel to obey Moses? As a religious question, what constitutes obedience to Moses? And how does that obedience relate to Israel's faithful obedience to the Lord?

(2) The Israelites will not believe in him (*lō' ya^ʾₐmînû lî*). The term is parallel to the reference to obedience. To believe in Moses is not simply to affirm that in the opinion of the people Moses did in fact

meet with God and promise deliverance from the oppression of Egypt. It is to act on the affirmation. It is to obey. The parallel between belief and obedience can be supported by reference to the same term in Gen. 15.6.[14] Abraham believed in the Lord. And his belief undergirds a designation of his virtue as righteousness. Righteousness cannot mean an internal virtue. It connotes rather the kind of relationship that ties two parties together. In this case, it is Abraham's obedience within the covenant and not simply his affirmation of trust in the promise that underwrites the designation of his relationship with God as righteousness. Again, the point is clear in Ps. 119.66, even more so in Deut. 9.23. The distinctive formulation here, however, is the suggestion that belief and obedience belong (or do not belong) to Moses. So, in 2 Chron. 20.20, the king appeals to Jerusalem to believe in God and in his prophets. Belief defines a relationship with God. But it also defines a relationship with the prophets. And belief means more than affirming that the prophets are indeed prophets of God. It means obedience. In Exod. 14.31 the same formulation appears. The people believe in God and in his servant Moses. And belief means commitment to follow God and his servant in the wilderness. It seems to be clear, then, that belief in God and in Moses functions as a counterpart to the Lord's intimate knowledge of the people's pain. It is the people's intimate commitment to the Lord and to his servant.[15]

(3) Thus, a key item in the Moses traditions is a theologoumenon about obedience. The signs and wonders now serve that theologoumenon. On one side of the relationship, they establish Moses' authority. He has the right to command obedience. On the other side, they promote obedience. Thus, the term, 'believe', recurs at key intervals: 4.5, 8, 9. And belief now appears clearly as a term for obedience. The signs will establish Moses before the elders as one who has the authority to command action. At the same time, they establish the authority of God.

It is important at this point to consider the role of the rod (*hammaṭṭeh*). In this chapter the rod is closely attached to *Moses* as his instrument for accomplishing the signs. It is not difficult to see the rod as the typical magician's wand, the key to power for performing signs and wonders. Certainly, the initial sign would support this view. Moses throws the rod on the ground, and it turns into a serpent. And when he does the trick before the Pharaoh, the magicians of the court do the same trick with their rods. But the rod is more than a magician's wand. A parallel would appear in the scepter of the king (so, Ps. 110.2). As a symbol for the power of the throne, the ability of the monarch to accomplish his goals, it represents performance to the public. But the symbolic and functional value of the rod in the Moses tradition is not limited to depiction of power. It stands for the authority Moses carries for commanding obedience.

It should be noted here that in the tradition, the rod does not always belong to Moses. It is on occasion Aaron's rod (see Exod. 7.12; 8.1; *et al.*). These texts apparently refer to the same rod rather than two different ones employed by the two different figures. Thus, in 8.1, the rod of Aaron is the instrument for creating the plague of frogs, just as in 9.23 the rod of Moses is the instrument for bringing thunder, hail, and fire from heaven. It is necessary to ask, therefore, whether the rod belongs primarily to Moses or to Aaron. Horst Seebass suggests that the original home for the symbol was in the Aaron traditions and that Moses subsequently took over the position of authority Aaron occupied, including the symbols and motifs that serve the tradition.[16] As support for this position, we could cite Numbers 17 with its description of preeminence for the rod of Aaron. Yet, precisely in Numbers 17 the character of the Aaron tradition as a secondary intrusion into the Moses narrative is clear. (1) The issue here is not the power or authority of Aaron to demand obedience from his followers, although that function might lie in the background. It is rather the relative position of the Aaronic priesthood within the organization of the people of Israel. (2) The rod at this point stands for the position of sacral preeminence for the group, not so much the authority of the leader. The relationship of the leader to the people in the execution of the exodus does not enter the narrative as a central feature. The dominant form of the tradition in the received texts suggests to the contrary that the rod belongs to Moses and symbolizes the authority he wields *before the people*. It does not limit the authority it attests to a sacral sphere. Rather, it demonstrates evidence for obedience to its wielder in all areas. I would tend to think, therefore, that the symbol was from the beginning a part of the Moses traditions and became attached to Aaron as Aaron was introduced into the narrative. The process, moreover, would reflect that period in the history of the tradition when the Aaronic priests struggled within the structures of the cult to establish authority and dominance for execution of priestly rights.[17] The question of the original form of the rod as Aaron's rod would hang together, therefore, with the question about the original form and function of the Aaron tradition.[18]

An additional complication also demands some attention. Part of the pattern of evidence for the question is the description of the rod as the rod of God. Exod. 4.20 and 17.9 illustrate the combination. And in both cases, the collocation serves to emphasize the peculiar relationship between God and Moses. The rod symbolizes Moses' power to act on behalf of his people. The action is not limited to sacral acts. To the contrary, political events dominate. But the rod carries the name of God and points to the source of authority and power for the act as God. Moses acts with the rod, therefore, by virtue of the authority of God that is expressed in the symbol of the rod. Moreover, the term, *maṭṭeh*, appears in parallel with the hands of Moses. So, in 9.22, the Lord instructs Moses to stretch forth his hand. But the notice of execution for the instruction describes the event as stretching forth the rod (see also 10.12, 13). And in 10.21-22 the same kind of event occurs, but in this case the hand of Moses has completely replaced the rod. Thus, it would appear to me that the instrument is not simply the magician's rod, but rather the symbol of Moses' personal authority. In this one symbol, the heroic man who acts for the benefit of his people and the man who functions as the representative of God merge. Reference to the rod as the rod of God does not suggest that traditio-historically the rod belongs originally to either of the two figures who led Israel. It points rather to the theological dimension in the tradition.

In contrast to this representation of the authority of Moses, 4.10-17 presents the next round of objections and reassurance. Moses complains that he is not a man of words, that in fact he has a 'heavy' mouth and a 'heavy' tongue. But this objection does not mean necessarily that the man Moses suffered from a physical handicap. It does not mean that for the literature, a stammering tongue was Moses' heroic flaw.[19] To the contrary, the description must be evaluated in the light of the stereotyped pattern. The stereotype demands the objection in order to set up a reassurance related to the mouth of the subject. Thus, Isaiah objects that he is a man of unclean lips. And the reassurance has one of the seraphim touch his mouth with a burning coal (Isa. 6.5-7). The second servant poem avers that the Lord who called the servant from the womb made his mouth like a sharp sword (Isa. 49.2). Jeremiah complains that he cannot speak because he is only a youth. And the Lord reassures him by 'touching his mouth' (Jer. 1.9). And for Ezekiel, the Word of God becomes

sweet as honey in his mouth (Ezek. 3.3). Moses' objection that he has
a heavy mouth and no words should not be taken as a sign of literal
physical handicap, or even as an element in a non-heroic or anti-
heroic picture in the literature, but rather as a marker that sets up
the reassurance. Thus, in 4.12: 'Now go, and I shall be (*'ehyeh*) with
your mouth and I will teach you what you shall say'. Moreover, it is
particularly in this context that we can see the promise for presence
as a uniquely personal promise to Moses. But the personal character
of this promise lies not so much in the promise for presence with a
part of Moses' body. It is more deeply rooted in his *vocation*, in what
Moses must *do*. God's presence underwrites Moses' mission and
authority. And it is out of that presence that his heroic relationship
with his people is possible.

The objection in v. 13 relates to the complaint about a heavy
mouth and a heavy tongue: 'I pray, O Lord, send by the hand of the
one you will send' (RSV: 'send some other person'). The objection
provokes God's anger. And with the anger God introduces Aaron as
a means for meeting Moses' objection. Aaron can speak well (*dabbēr
yᵉdabbēr hû'*). But again, the stereotype should be recognized. Moses
objects, a typical element in the vocation scene. The objection does
not suggest that a handicap belabored the work of Moses. Nor does it
suggest a literary construct designed to highlight Moses' heroic flaw.
Rather, it is a literary construct that introduces Aaronic tradition
into the Moses story. That tradition appears to me to be clearly a
secondary insertion into the Moses complex. And the process,
especially in v. 16, clearly subordinates Aaron to Moses. 'He shall
speak to the people for you. He shall be a mouth for you. And you
shall be God for him'. One must be cautious here. The tradition does
not elevate Moses to the status of God, a feature that does appear
commonly in the patterns of heroic tradition,[20] but never emerges in
the Old Testament tradition about Moses. The statement does not
suggest that the hero Moses becomes God. Rather, it establishes an
analogy. To the extent that Aaron *functions* as a mouth for Moses, to
that extent Moses *functions* as god for Aaron. Moses does not become
god for all of his people. He does not even become god for Aaron
except in terms of functional relationships. When Aaron, who is not
literally Moses' mouth, functions as a mouth for Moses, saying the
words Moses gives him to say in the way that a person gives his own
mouth words to say, then Moses functions as a god for Aaron, and
only for Aaron, giving him words to speak. This relationship is
confirmed by the parallel in Exod. 7.1. In that text, Moses stands as

god to the Pharaoh. And Aaron will be the prophet. 'God to the Pharaoh' suggests an image that demands obedience. But the crucial part of the picture for the discussion of the Exodus 3–4 text is the relationship between Moses and Aaron. Aaron, Moses' prophet, will speak the words Moses gives him to say. And that relationship confirms the pattern in Exodus 4.

Verses 18-20 break the dialogic structure of the commission with its responses of objection and reassurance for a narrative report of the conclusion. Moses returns to his father-in-law in order to ask permission to return to Egypt. Jethro grants his leave and Moses packs his family for the trip. The functional role these verses play for the unit does not focus, however, on the relationship between Moses and Jethro, as it does in ch. 2. It is rather to report the execution of the commission to *Moses*. Moses heard the Lord, sending him back to Egypt. Now he goes. Thus, v. 20: 'So Moses took his wife and her sons, and he made them ride on the ass. And he returned to the land of Egypt. And Moses took the rod of God in his hand'. Verses 21-23 also belong to the pericope. But they are not a primary part of the structure. Rather, they represent an addition to the conclusion that associates the plagues to be established by Moses (thus, the reference to the rod in v. 20) to the Passover. But the relationship appears to me to be clearly secondary. These verses represent an extension of the basic exodus tradition in order to make room for the Passover tradition (see the comments on the Passover below). Two important motifs for the plagues also appear here: (1) the Pharaoh with the hardened heart, and (2) an appeal to the Pharaoh to release the Israelites for service to the Lord. But in both cases, the motifs derive from the plague tradition. They do not constitute primary elements for the vocation tale or for the Passover tradition.

Verses 24-26 have nothing to do with the vocation tradition. Indeed, it is not clear to me that this little unit can in any manner be assigned a primary role in the Moses traditions at all. The principal figure is Zipporah. The context identifies the passive figure as Moses. Verse 20 notes that Moses takes his family with him on the journey back to Egypt. Yet the unit in vv. 24-26 makes no reference to Moses by name. The RSV inserts Moses into v. 25 in order to clarify the antecedent for the unnamed passive male in the narrative. But the MT has no name, no allusion that would identify this figure. And in fact the male is relatively unimportant. The primary principal is Zipporah. Indeed, the unit may represent the original locus for Zipporah in the traditions of the Pentateuch. Moreover, the circumcision of Zipporah's son supports a performative ritual apparently directed, not to Moses as the RSV would suggest, but to the Lord. The tradition history for the unit appears in detail in Childs's commentary.[21] For the purposes of this discussion, it is sufficient to note that no contribution from it adds a critical element to the Moses traditions.

Verses 27-31 now compose the second half of a frame around the bridegroom unit and appear to be another expansion of the vocation account. They report a detail in the process of execution of the commission instructions. Verses 27-30 belong clearly to the Aaronic addition, noted already in vv. 13-16. Aaron makes contact with Moses and receives his share of the commission that sends the two of them to the Pharaoh.

Specifically, Aaron now carries the responsibility for doing the signs before the elders of Israel. This point, not suggested by vv. 13-16 and in fact contradicted by v. 17, places the authority that belongs to Moses, symbolized by the signs, into the hands of Aaron. But significantly, in v. 17 the rod does not pass over to Aaron. Would this point not provide substantial evidence for the primary attachment of the rod to the Moses tradition? In contrast v. 31 appears rather ambiguous. The people believed. But the text does not specify the nature of the belief. One might anticipate that they believed in Aaron, since he did the signs. And the belief would signify their obedience. But the signs belong to the Moses traditions. Aaron performs them as Moses gives him instructions. So, perhaps the people believed in Moses. The corollary to the notice about belief reports: 'They heard that the Lord visited the Israelites and that he saw their affliction. So, they bowed and worshipped'. The point would seem to suggest that the people believed the Lord, thus, obeyed the Lord. Something of the image is created by Exod. 14.31: 'Israel saw the great deed which the Lord did against the Egyptians. And the people feared the Lord. And they believed in the Lord and in his servant Moses'. The ambiguity in 4.31 is not relieved by this parallel. But perhaps it suggests that the belief of the people, directed to Moses, embraced the Lord at the same time. To believe in Moses is to believe in the Lord. And to obey Moses is to obey the Lord.

The unit can now be defined as a tale about vocation, a narrative that describes the beginning of a career and leads the audience through stages of tension, created particularly by objections to the commission, to the point of acceptance and execution of the vocation task. As vocation tale, it can thus play a significant role in the larger

Moses saga. Vocation tale sets up the narrative pattern for the larger saga. How will Moses execute the instructions in the divine commission? What lengths will be necessary to fulfill the whole scope of the call? The vocation tale plays a key role for the entire exodus theme: Everything that follows is in some sense execution of the divine commission. For the final form of the text, the pericope does not end until Exod. 12.36.

The vocation tradition thus makes an important contribution to the pattern of the Moses traditions as heroic saga. It describes Moses' vocation in relationship to the people. Moses becomes the one who will lead the people. But the point is not so much to describe him in terms of the shepherd. It is to establish his authority as leader of the people. His authority raises the question of obedience to Moses, both from the people and from the Pharaoh. In what manner will the people or the Pharaoh recognize the unique position Moses holds? Moreover, it is important to ask how this pattern of authority for Moses effects the narrative image. Who, according to the literature focused on the topic of Mosaic authority, was Moses? It is clear that the authority is not simply resident in the person of Moses. Moses derives his unique position from God. There is, then, a sense in which Moses functions as a mediator for the authority of God. This point can be seen in the fact that while the rod belongs in a special way to Moses, it is still on occasion called the rod of God. Yet, Moses is not simply an instrument for mediating God's authority to the people. The focal concern of ch. 4, indeed, the intention of the signs in ch. 4, is to enable the people, or at least the elders, to believe in Moses. Moses, according to the tradition, was the heroic leader of the people, the one to whom the people committed their loyalty.

But can this image of Moses be defined with more precision? Hugo Gressmann suggests that the pericope builds on an early level of tradition derived from a *hieros logos* for a sanctuary.[22] The burning bush tradition accounts for the original discovery of a holy place. And the account involved a Midianite hero whose name is no longer preserved.[23] The setting would thus be cultic. But this stage would not reflect influence from the Moses traditions or anything about the image of the Moses figure that carries the narrative. The local tradition, should the hypothesis be correct, would have been appropriated as exposition for the Moses tale. And certainly any guesses about the character of the hypothetical Midianite hero would offer no controls for evaluation of the guiding questions about Moses.

Brevard Childs rounds out the tradition history of this pericope by pressing for a definition of the setting for the Mosaic stage in the tradition. 'In my opinion, the evidence points more convincingly towards seeing the setting of Exodus 3 in the prophetic office.'[24] Yet one must remain cautious just here. There is clearly some kind of relationship between this tale and the form of various prophetic vocation units. But one cannot argue from that connection to a setting for Exodus 3 in the prophetic office. And particularly, one cannot argue from that connection to a conclusion that the image for the figure of Moses in Exodus 3 is prophetic. Childs speaks to the problem: 'This is not to suggest that the form of prophetism which developed in the monarchial period was simply read back into the Mosaic period. Rather . . . the tradition linked Moses' call as Yahweh's messenger with the later phenomena of classic prophetism'.[25]

But if the tradition about Moses' call as Yahweh's messenger stands a step removed from classical prophetism, linked by tradition to the later phenomena of prophetism, what enables us to conclude that the setting for Exodus 3-4 is the later linking? Even if we agree that at some stage in the history of the Moses tradition the prophetic office exerted some influence on the Moses tale, what underwrites the conclusion that Exodus 3 derives from that setting? But the question goes even farther: If one should concede that at some point in the history of the tradition the setting for Exodus 3 must have been the prophetic office, what consequence would the conclusion have for defining the character of the Mosaic image in the pericope? It would not follow that the story therefore presents Moses as a prophet. A later setting for the story might influence the shape of the figure. But it would not necessarily control the image. Some shape of its original image would still compete for a hearing. Childs develops the point by connecting 'the deep disruptive seizure' in the Moses story with the experience of the prophet,

> for whom neither previous faith nor personal endowment played a role in preparing him for his vocation. However, it is also clear that the later prophetic office influenced the tradition of Moses' call. Particularly in the expanding form of the present text, the series of questions raised by Moses in objection to being sent echo [sic] the inner and outer struggles of the prophets of Israel.[26]

But prophets were not the only figures who raised some kind of objection or expressed some form of doubt or hesitation about being sent on a mission. In Gen. 24.5, the servant of Abraham responds to his master's commission to go to Mesopotamia in order to find a wife for Isaac by objecting: 'Perhaps the woman will not be willing to come with me to this land...' And Abraham responds by reassuring him that in that event he would be free of the oath binding the commission. Beyond the pattern, with its feature of a series of objections, no other item in the pericope necessitates a conclusion that the setting is prophetic or that the image of Moses casts him as a prophet. The office of the prophet limits the range of the narrative to a narrow and restrictive definition. Would we not profit, therefore, by suggesting a setting for the pattern in various kinds of such call units that would lie behind the prophetic office and the Moses tale? Childs leaves such an alternative open by recognizing a tradition about Moses' call linked with the later phenomena of classical prophetism and the character of the pre-prophetic tradition he describes as 'Yahweh's messenger'. Could we not suggest an original setting for the typical patterns as commissioning a messenger?

Norman Habel argues in this direction, with evidence garnered from the description of a messenger commission in Genesis 24.[27] Ann Vater developed a similar position by suggesting that the image of Moses that carries the narrative is shaped by the patterns of the charismatic messenger. The charismatic dimension of this represents Moses in a dynamic position as a messenger figure, one who has the vitality to break with the past in order to initiate new processes, new forms.[28] Moreover, the new forms facilitate the authority of the messenger's mission. The charismatic dimension enhances the ability of the messenger to inspire his audience to loyalty and obedience.

Childs objects to a definition of the setting in terms of charismatic messenger. 'It is becoming increasingly difficult to subsume the prophetic office under the simple title of messenger. Too many other factors are involved. Habel's attempt to find the provenance of the call in the specific practice of commissioning messengers is artificial.'[29] Yet, the simple title of messenger may facilitate the description of Moses more adequately than more complex offices such as 'prophet'. The point would not be to suggest that an institutional 'office' of prophet gives us the text or shapes the image of Moses. The common bond would be in the functional dimension of the messenger. But the point is also not to suggest an institutional 'office' of Yahweh's messenger or even a secular office of messenger as the formative home for the pattern of the call narratives. The office may have exerted its influence. But the point is to suggest a stereotypical pattern for describing a commission to a vocation served the call to a messenger or the call to a prophet or the call to a judge. The pattern would not be tied to a particular office but would represent a fixed oral or written form for depicting a call to any recognizable task. The image of Moses, then, would not be a prophet, or even a messenger, if by the term one means an institutionalized office. It would be a messenger in the sense of a simple title but yet a descriptive one, depicting a figure sent by God but with the charismatic freedom to meet the needs of the people, indeed, to enact the redemption of the people. The setting would then be the literary activity that produced the story about the messenger, this hero of the people who combines all the merits of Israel's ideals. The image would be shaped by ideals in folk tradition rather than an institutionalized office.

The heroic tradition in this pericope appears again in J. Martin Noth analyzes the two chapters as primarily J, suggesting that E also appears in 3.4b, 9-14 (15); 4.17, 18-20.[30] It is necessary, however, not to offer a resolution of traditio-historical problems by parcelling out the problematic elements to different sources. It may be that the problems indicate a conflation of written sources. But the methodological question should not be confused. Thus, for example, to attribute 3.4b to the Elohist on the basis of the name change, the Tetragrammaton in v. 4a and *ᵉlōhîm* in v. 4b, would reflect procedure typical for source analysis. But the question hangs together with the designation of v. 6 as E. Again, the name for God is *ᵉlōhîm*. But here the disunity reflects a traditio-historical problem. The Moses traditions have been combined with patriarchal traditions about the God of the fathers. And I cannot assume simply that all of the 'God of the fathers' tradition belongs to E. If that should be the case, then the point would require explicit demonstration by showing that the God of the fathers element is a special Elohistic subject, reflecting a special Elohistic bias. The combination of these names may therefore reflect a process of tradition history. But if the tradition about the God of the fathers enters the Yahwistic narrative as a result of combining major themes before literary fixation, can v. 4b be denied the J source simply on the basis of the name change? Moreover, the parallel between vv. 7-8 and 9-10 also reflects a traditio-historical problem, the combination of tradition about the heroic Moses with tradition about the mighty acts of God. The apparent doublet cannot, therefore, serve as evidence for two literary sources.

Verses 11-14 constitute the classical text for the Elohist in the

Moses narrative. And in this text is the word play on the name of God, a play that emphasizes the promise for God's presence with Moses. If this text is properly E, it would suggest that at least a part of the heroic traditions appears in E and is thus perhaps a part of G, the basic tradition that lies behind both J and E. Yet, the critic cannot simply slice these verses away from the Yahwistic narrative without suggesting something similar from J for the parallel, for these verses carry a key element in the structure of the whole. If they are E, they must be taken not as evidence for an independent Elohistic narrative, but as an expansion of the Yahwistic structure. E would thus not represent an independent witness to the heroic tradition about Moses, but rather a witness that depends on the basic Yahwistic narrative. And the evidence for reconstructing a basic level G source would disappear. In ch. 4 the same kind of caution would be required. Noth suggests that v. 17 belongs to E.[31] The reason is that the rod, the only constitutive motif in the verse, corresponds to the rod of God in v. 20. But again, the problem is not a source-critical one, but a traditio-historical one. A traditional designation of the rod is *maṭṭeh hā'ᵉlōhîm.* In Exod. 17.9 the point is clear. But such a technical combination, so it seems to me, would belong more nearly to the tradition about the rod than to the peculiar vocabulary of one source for referring to the rod. It would at best be weak evidence for designating vv. 17 and 20 as E. I am inclined to conclude, then, that while the Elohist is doutblessly present in this pericope, it cannot be defined as an independent source and thus as an independent witness to the heroic tradition. It is more likely that E is an expansion of J and thus draws its perspective about Moses, the recipient of the promise for God's presence, from J. The intention of the E expansions would thus be to comment on the character of the tradition in J by giving a significant interpretation of the name of God.

2. *Exod. 6.2–7.7*

This pericope constitutes a doublet of Exod. 3.1–4.31. It is not simply a repetition of the structure and content of the JE counterpart. It has its own peculiarities. But the functional pattern of structure is the same. And the variations in content can be explained as the result of the peculiar interest of the source.[32]

The character of the tradition as a tale in the Moses narrative suffers a compromising alteration in the first element of structure, however. There is no clearly defined exposition for the narrative, no theophany. Rather, it begins virtually *in medias res* with a speech. The speech contains elements of the parallel J tradition, nonetheless, and suggests by its contents certain dependency on the structure of its counterpart. Thus, God addresses Moses with a self-revelation. And the self-revelation integrates the tradition of the unit with the patriarchs and the conquest. 'I am the Lord. I appeared to Abraham, to Isaac, and to Jacob as El Shaddai. But by my name, the Lord, I did not make myself known to them. And also I established my covenant with them to give them the land of Canaan, the land of their sojournings where they sojourned.' The process of tradition history, noted in the parallel, still shows itself here. But the rougher edges have been smoothed off. The shift from one tradition to the other is not so abrupt but rather fits more naturally into the flow of the unit.

Verse 5 contains the commission, remarkably parallel to 3.7-8 and 9-10. The key vocabulary is now different. The Lord hears the complaint of the people. But the term is no longer *ṣaʿaq* but now *naʾᵃqat bᵉnê yiśrāʾēl*. But it has the same tradition clearly in view. 'I heard the groaning of the Israelites whom the Egyptians oppressed' (*maʿᵃbidîm*). A new element here is the reference to the covenant between the patriarchs and God (v. 4) or now between the people and God (v. 7). The relationship between people and God thus does not in any way depend on Moses. The announcement of the exodus in vv. 6-7 attributes the entire scope of the coming exodus event to God. There is nothing here to correspond to the commission of Moses in 3.10. Moses is simply to speak the words of the announcement. If the image here is again the messenger, it is no longer the charismatic messenger who speaks in the spirit of inspiration, but now simply a messenger who functions as an instrument to be moved as God so desires. The primary affirmation is rather that God now intends to fulfill his promise.[33] And the promise for both redemption from oppressive slavery and a gift of the land speaks appropriately to the audience of the priestly source.

Verse 9 might correspond to the objection of 3.13. In this case, however, it is not a part of the dialogue controlled by a pattern of commission, objection, and reassurance. Rather, it reports that Moses followed the instructions but met with resistance from the people (contrast 4.31). Indeed, the explicit assertion that the people refused to listen to Moses, i.e. refused to obey Moses, stands in contrast to the belief of the people noted in 4.31. Moses does not demand the same kind of believing commitment here that he holds in the parallel. Verse 10 does not address the problem of v. 9. Rather, it moves the focus of the commission from the report to the people to a confrontation with the Pharaoh. Verse 12 now follows the structural pattern of objection to the commission with Moses' self-abasement. Doubtlessly, this element in the tradition reflects the excuse of 4.10. But the formulation here spiritualizes the objection. 'Behold the Israelites have not listened to me. How shall the Pharaoh listen to me, for I am a man of uncircumcised lips' (cf. also 6.30). Something similar appears in Lev. 26.4; Deut. 10.16; Jer. 9.24-25; 4.4; 6.10; Ezek. 44.7, 9. In each case the term seems to suggest a part of the body that does not work in the proper way. But it does not connote physical failure, as if for example, the uncircumcised heart does not pump blood adequately. It suggests willingness or unwillingness to obey. Thus, in Jer. 6.19, the text argues: 'Behold, their ears are uncircumcised. They are not able to pay attention'. Uncircumcised lips are, therefore, not simply lips that are heavy, as in ch. 3, but lips that cannot obey the commission.

Verse 13 does not represent a reassurance as response to the objection. There is no promise for presence here. Rather, the verse simply reports that the Lord established the commission despite the objection. And the commission belongs to both Moses and Aaron alike. Verses 14-25 contain a genealogy for Aaron and thus a special emphasis on Aaron as an intrinsic figure in the unit. Verses 26-30 then summarize the tradition to this point and thus close the frame that binds the genealogy into the unit. 7.1-5 repeat the commission speech, now directed to Moses but designed explicitly to include Aaron. Significantly, the pattern that subordinates Aaron to Moses in the J text disappears here. Aaron is still prophet for Moses. But now Moses is God not for Aaron, but for the Pharaoh. Moreover, the commission itself has Moses and Aaron strictly as messengers who simply announce what God is going to do. There is no reference to Moses as the one who would execute the exodus. The unit ends in vv. 6-7 with a notice that Moses and Aaron executed the commission as it came to them and a note about their ages at the time.

There are obvious differences between this unit and the vocation tale in chs. 3-4. The event occurs in Egypt, not Sinai. It involves both Moses and Aaron. Indeed, one of the major intentions of the unit seems to be to include Aaron. The commission takes the pair beyond the elders of Israel to the Pharaoh. There are no signs to be used with the Israelites. But the most important change is the shift from heroic images to obvious non-heroic ones. Moses and Aaron here recede behind the dominating form of God. And they function simply as instruments in the hands of God. The unit belongs, according to a scholarly consensus, to the priestly source. But the impact of that observation is not simply that P employs non-heroic tradition, while J or JE uses heroic images. Rather, the point of the observation is that P apparently intentionally rejects the heroic dimension. It seems likely that P knew the J tradition. The self-revelation of God, the witness to Israel's moaning because of the Egyptian oppression, indeed, the announcement of God's intention to bring Israel out all point to such a conclusion. The shift to non-heroic images would emphasize the fact of tradition, already present in J, that depicts God's mighty acts. But the point of importance would be that the shift represents a distinctive element for priestly theology. For P, so we may now anticipate, all these stories about Moses or Moses and Aaron are not really stories about the human leadership of Israel in the exodus. They are stories about God. The image of Moses that carries the tradition, now shared with the image of Aaron, is one that represents these figures, not as creative leaders, but simply as messengers, instruments in the hands of God. Not even the charismatic dimension remains. They do not inspire loyalty among the people to follow their leadership. They inspire loyalty to God.

Some more systematic attention to the impact of Aaron on the Moses traditions would be in order just at this point. In the priestly narrative Aaron appears rather forcefully as the founder of the priestly group, the brother of Moses and spokesman to the Pharaoh. Noth observes: 'As the brother and the closest associate of Moses, Aaron was especially well suited for the important office of priest. Moses himself held a position that was too all-embracing for him to undertake one single office, even if it were the office of the high-priesthood, which was central for P'.[34] Thus, even for P, Aaron would not represent a figure whose leadership would have detracted from Moses. For the older tradition, the Aaron figure is more problematic. Noth finds the evidence ambiguous for determining the origin of the tradition. Many appearances of Aaron are simply secondary. But even in the ones that are not, the image of Aaron remains ambiguous.

> Just as there is no true substantive agreement among these passages. . . , so there is no discernible way to move from them to the view of Aaron in one instance as the instigator of the cult of the

'golden calf', in another as the brother of Moses and as the 'Levite',
or still again as Moses' rival for the claim to have a prophetic
relationship to God... Thus, we can only conclude that for a
considerable period... Aaron was a living figure of tradition
concerning whom new and different things continued to be related
without any direct reliance upon older narratives.[35]

In a study focused on the traditions about Aaron, Heinrich
Valentin agrees substantially with Noth's judgment about the figure.
(1) In the pre-priestly tradition Aaron is not the eponym of a priestly
group, not the founder of a priesthood from Bethel. (2) The traditio-
historical origin for Aaron tradition is not in Exodus 32. (3) The
oldest literary witness to Aaron is in Exod. 17.10, 12; in contrast to
Noth, Valentin concludes that no evidence for an older connected
tradition, perhaps one that failed to survive except in fragments,
exists. (4) Aaron became a priestly figure, e.g. in Exodus 32 and even
in Exodus 17, because the narrative development set him into such a
context. The role of Aaron in the older tradition seems most clearly
understood in its narrative function rather than in a historical,
sociological setting.[36] And in its narrative role, the Aaron image
supports Moses, or at least it does not detract from the heroic
dimension of Moses. The Aaron tradition does not appear in itself to
be heroic. Rather, it has been subordinated in its supporting role to
the heroic character of the Moses tradition. The depiction of Aaron
as brother of the hero is a device of the subordination. The same kind
of conclusion would also be in order for the designation of Miriam as
the sister of Moses.[37]

Chapter 4

MOSES' DEALINGS WITH THE PHARAOH:
EXODUS 5.1-12.36

The narrative tradition in these chapters constitutes the execution of the commission assigned to Moses in the vocation tale. In the present form of the text, therefore, it is not possible to see this material as distinct and independent from the context. Whether two or more originally independent traditions lie embedded in these narratives will appear more clearly as the result of the analysis of the texts.[1]

1. *Exod. 5.1-6.1*
Structure in this pericope builds around three major subsections: 5.1-4; 5.5-19; and 5.20-6.1. The first and last of these depict the role of Moses and Aaron in the process of negotiations with the Pharaoh. The second describes events in the negotiations that occurred without Moses or his prophet. Is there any manner of construction that would suggest that the structure in these verses reveals some kind of unity?[2] And what image of Moses emerges from the scene? Is it compromised by the close association of Moses with Aaron?

(1) 5.1-4 appears in the pattern of a dialogue between the Pharaoh and his opposition, Moses and Aaron. The opening speech presents the first confrontation of the Pharaoh with the demand for the exodus. It is prefaced by the messenger formula: 'Thus says the Lord, the God of Israel'. The authority for the demand thus does not reside in Moses himself or in his prophet. He mediates divine will and divine authority. In this speech, Moses is simply a messenger. Moreover, the demand itself is not constructed in a fashion that might be suitable for courtly appearance. It is an imperative, not a jussive or cohortative, a direct address, not a third person appeal. There are no particles that might soften the tone of the demand. It does not say: 'Let my Lord the king send, I pray, my people away'. It

is blunt: 'Send my people away, that they may celebrate a festival to me in the wilderness'. But this blunt demand does not contribute to the image of Moses in the pericope. Moses clearly functions simply as messenger. It contributes rather to the image of the Lord. Moses speaks with the authority of God.

Accordingly, the Pharaoh responds with a rejection of the demand. The first part of the speech in v. 2a is formally an insult. And it functions to negate the content of the *ꜥašer* clause in the second part of the speech.[3] 'Who is the Lord that I should obey his voice to send the Israelites away?' The rejection is then made explicit in v. 2b. The text builds here on a contrast to the statement of the Lord's intimate relationship with Israel in 3.7. There the Lord knows Israel's suffering. Here the Pharaoh does not know the Lord. And as the verb 'know' connotes intimacy between God and Israel in 3.7, so here the negative connotes a rejection of such intimacy. Rejection of intimacy means denial of validity for the authority in the demand. 'I do not know the Lord. And moreover, I will not send Israel away!'

The speech in v. 3 is a remarkable contrast to the initial speech Moses sets before the Pharaoh. It, too, is not constructed in third-person courtly style. But in every other way, it forsakes the blunt form of the speech in v. 1. It is not a message from the Lord. There is no messenger formula. Rather, it is cast as first person plural, the speech of Moses and Aaron and the people. It begins with an assertion of the condition for the following request. The appeal will rest on a justification constituted by a past event, 'The God of the Hebrews' had met with the Israelites, or perhaps just with Moses and Aaron, and because of that fact, Moses and Aaron must present their request. The appeal itself now appears not as an unsupported imperative, but as a cohortative with a supporting particle of entreaty. 'Let us go, I pray, three days journey into the wilderness, so that we may sacrifice to the Lord our God.' Then the appeal is framed with another supporting clause to provide justification for the request, a *pen* clause that shows a pressing motivation: 'Lest he fall on us with pestilence or sword'. The results of the appeal, however, look very much like the results of the initial demand. Verse 4 addresses Moses and Aaron directly. And the form of the address is not the insulting rejection of v. 2, but rather an accusation, a question that functions to set Moses and Aaron on the defense. 'Why, Moses and Aaron, do you take the people away from their work. Go to your burdens.'[4] Thus, the request is denied. But the point to be observed here is that the negotiations change mood abruptly. The reason for the change might be attributed to the difference between direct negotiations between the Lord and the Pharaoh (conducted, of course, by the Lord's messenger) and the indirect negotiations that employ the initiative of Moses and Aaron. But the point is nonetheless clear. Moses and Aaron appeal. They do not demand. And it is clear that the appeal does not accomplish the goal. The negotiations fail.

What image of Moses supports this scene? In what manner does this story relate to the heroic form of the tradition in the vocation tale? It would seem on the surface that this pericope forsakes the heroic image of the tradition. God is strong and demanding. Moses softens the character of the demand. Yet, Moses does not cower before the Pharaoh. The cohortative verb and the entreaty particle, *nā'*, do not require such an anti-heroic interpretation (compare Gen. 22.2; Isa. 7.3 for the particle *nā'*; for cohortative with *nā'* simply as a form of polite speech, see 1 Kgs 1.12). A more prominent characteristic of the appeal is the identification between Moses and the people. Thus, the plural form of the verb implies a subject that cannot be understood simply as Moses and Aaron. It embraces Moses, Aaron, and all the people. They must all go into the wilderness in order to sacrifice, just as the subsequent account of Moses' dealings with the Pharaoh shows clearly. But still two significant problems demand attention: (1) The negotiations with the Pharaoh fail; the ruse with the justification in the Lord's instructions to sacrifice or face punishment is simply dropped. Does this fact not raise immediately the question about how and when the commission to Moses might be expected, or even whether it can be executed? And if so, what happens to the image of Moses in the unit? Does the failure of the negotiations compromise his heroic stature? (2) Moses' image carries the weight of the narrative. But it is tied closely to the image of Aaron. Are conclusions about the image of Moses applicable also to Aaron? Or does Aaron water down the heroic dimensions of Moses and his relationship with his people? These problems return in the larger cycle of scenes about Moses' dealings with the Pharaoh. Yet, the traditio-historical issue in the negotiations tradition may reside precisely in this text. Does the primary form of the tradition not show itself most clearly here?

This possibility comes more sharply to light when the second element of the pericope comes into consideration. Verses 5-19 contain only a veiled reference to Moses or Aaron. Verse 5 repeats the speech formula for a new speech from the Pharaoh. And the speech is apparently addressed to Moses and Aaron: 'Now the people of the land are many, but you make them rest from their burdens'. It is significant to note an obvious change between the two Pharaoh speeches. In v. 4 the king of Egypt sends Moses and Aaron back to the people by reference to '*your* burden' (*l*ᵉ*siblōtêkem*). But in v. 5 the same word appears with a third person suffix: '*their* burdens' (*missiblōtām*). In the first case Moses and Aaron share the burden of the people. In the second, they stand removed. Does the shift suggest something about heroic, non-heroic patterns?

The removal then sets a new tone for the narration of the element. Moses and Aaron recede completely into the background. The Pharaoh imposes new burdens on the people. They must now find their own straw to make their quota of bricks. So the negotiations are renewed, but in this case under the leadership of the foremen of the people rather than Moses and Aaron. The goal for the process, however, has changed. It is now not the intention of the negotiation process to gain freedom to sacrifice but simply to restore the old order. It is sufficient to note that for the rest of the element, the negotiations conducted by the foremen fall under the same blight as the negotiations made by Moses and Aaron. They fail. And as a result, the burden on the people remains severe.

The third element in the unit returns Moses and Aaron to the scene. The foremen meet the two leaders who were waiting for them to leave the Pharaoh. Moses and Aaron thus seem on the fringe of the negotiation scene. But the exchange between the foremen and the leaders marks some continued involvement for the pair in the problem. The substance of the meeting is expressed by an accusation: 'May the Lord look on you and judge, because you have made our odor stink in the eyes of the Pharaoh and in the eyes of his servants, by giving a sword into his hand to kill us'. The reply to the accusation comes now only from Moses. But it is not a reply to the accusers. It is rather a lament to God. The lament focuses on the personal issue: 'Why have you done evil to this people? Why did you send me? From the time I came to the Pharaoh to speak in your name, he has done evil to this people. And you have not delivered your people at all'. The conclusion in 6.1 seems to override the negotiation structure. It suggests that the results of the efforts will come not as the product of negotiation, but rather as the product of divine intervention. The image, so it seems to me, has the Passover tradition in view and stands therefore as a parallel to the same movement in 4.21-23. This point is suggested by the strong vocabulary of 6.1. 'The Lord said to

Moses, "Now you shall see what I shall do to the Pharaoh, for with a strong hand he shall send them away and with a strong hand he shall drive them from this land".' The strong vocabulary includes the verbs 'to send' (*šālaḥ*) and 'to drive out' (*gāraš*). The Passover scene in 12.29-33 fits such a pattern. In 12.33, the text uses a similar picture: 'The Egyptians pressed the people to hurry, in order to send them out from the land. . . ' The verb here is *šālaḥ* (*lᵉšallᵉḥām*). And in Exod. 12.39: 'They baked dough which they brought from Egypt, unleavened cakes, because it was not leavened because they were driven from Egypt. . . ' The verb here is *gāraš* (*gōrᵉšû*).

Again, therefore, the question arises: Does this unit not represent an anti-heroic image of Moses? Moses and Aaron await the results of the negotiations when the foremen of the people leave their efforts with the Pharaoh. Does this picture not undercut the image of Moses as leader of the people (and of Aaron as his assistant)? Martin Noth argues this case:

> In this section Moses recedes completely into the background and the Israelite overseers negotiate alone with the Pharaoh while Moses, as it surprisingly turns out in v. 20, waits outside! . . . Manifestly, in Exod. 5.3-19 we come upon the fossil remains of a stage in the history of tradition when the figure of Moses had not yet been incorporated into the theme 'guidance out of Egypt' and when the elders of the Israelites still acted as spokesmen to the Egyptians.[5]

His point of view would suggest, moreover, that not only was Moses not a part of the exodus theme at this stage and thus not the heroic leader of the people, but also that this stage of the tradition originally prefaced the plague cycle. Indeed, one might explore whether this 'fossil' preserves the traditio-historical roots of the exodus-plague tradition. If that should be the case, then in the primary form of the tradition, the plagues would not be the execution of the vocation tale but tradition of independent importance. A critical evaluation of this hypothesis must wait examination of the cycle of narratives about Moses' dealings with the Pharaoh in Exodus 7-12, and indeed, the completion of the discussion about this pericope.

Yet, we must remain cautious in concluding simply with Noth that this fossil removes Moses from the picture in the exodus traditions. The text as it now stands does not represent the foremen as negotiating for the release of the Israelites for a festival celebration in the wilderness. They negotiate for reduction of the work burden, which has increased in the wake of Moses' (and Aaron's) failure. We might hypothesize that the original form of the tradition actually set the foremen as the primary negotiators for the exodus. That is apparently the position Noth would take. But there is no evidence to support that hypothesis. The foremen appear only as negotiators for reduction of the work load. What, then, are the alternatives? Rudolf Smend makes the following observation in a convincing fashion:

> The state of affairs in Exodus 5 [as Noth described it] seems to me to be indisputable, but not the explanation. The fact that Moses does not appear in this passage does not have to mean that originally he did not at all belong to the leading forth from Egypt. On the contrary, to begin with, one can regard it as quite appropriate that in those situations in which it is a question of the aggravation of compulsory labor and the measure to be affected by it, the (Egyptian) 'taskmasters' (נגשים) and the (Israelite) 'overseers' (שטרים) are for the Pharaoh the partners that exist in order to receive his instructions or else to complain to him, even if the initiative for the entire incident came from the other party. As a result it is significant when Moses in this phase remains in the background. By all means, then, even the disappearance of Moses (and of Aaron) at the beginning of our passage and still more the manner of reappearance in verse 20 do seem to be strange and strongly favor Noth's supposition of a special position of our passage, even if not an implicitly literary one. Verses 1, 2 (4), and 20ff. apparently do not originally belong together with it. Does it consequently exclude the role of Moses? I do not believe so, and for the explanation of the peculiar situation in Chapter 5, I would like to refer to a phenomenon which occurs in a completely different connection, namely in 1 Kings 12. The situation has features similar to that in Exodus 5. The people of Israel beg the king (or rather the one who is to become king) Rehoboam for an easing of the burdens which lie upon them. The king reacts negatively, whereupon the people rebel against him. Instead of Rehoboam, they make Jeroboam their king. According to the original text, which is still preserved in the Septuagint, he had not participated in the negotiations with Rehoboam. Rather, he had stayed in Egypt, whence he had once fled from Solomon, and returned upon the news of his death... Israel learns of that after the failure of the negotiations with Rehoboam, sends for him, has him called into the meeting, and makes him king (verse 20). According to the precepts of the narrative art, this course of events is the proper one. A figure destined to help in such an emergency... tends to put in an appearance only when it is necessary. Before that he exists only in

secret, known to the listener or reader as already appointed... A
deliverer seldom comes too early... I suspect the same process in
Exodus 5, even if it is no longer perceptible there on the basis of
textual criticism... Moses, in fact, does not belong in the
negotiations there, not because he does not have anything to do
originally with the leading forth from Egypt, but because his public
appearance already presupposes the ineffectual development of the
negotiations... The sequence of narratives can be understood as
the history, or better, the series of stories of the charismatic hero
Moses, whose person is quite inextricably interwoven into the
Exodus tradition, whereon... his absence in Exodus 5.3-19 cannot
be confusing.[6]

I would conclude, then, that while this unit may not contribute new
material to the image of Moses as a hero, it does not detract from the
thesis. Indeed, if Smend's observation has merit, it supports the
thesis in a very particular way. Moreover, it would appear to me that
failure in the negotiations process would not detract from the heroic
image. Rather, it introduces a particular kind of challenge to the
hero. If the Pharaoh refuses to let the people leave as a result of the
formal negotiations, how will the hero accomplish his goals? This
problem cannot be answered on the basis of this chapter. Insofar as
this unit is concerned, the commission remains unfulfilled, and the
unit points beyond itself to a conclusion in coming narration.

But if that opinion is correct, can we find in chapter 5 the fossil of
ancient tradition that gives us a handle on the original shape of the
negotiations narrative and Moses' role in it? Smend argues effectively
that this pericope does not constitute convincing evidence for
excluding Moses from the exodus theme. If it does contain a fossil of
ancient tradition, Moses would be a part of it. The subject of the
negotiations seems to me to argue for the same point. The foremen
negotiate only a reduction in the work requirements, not the release
of the people. Moses is intimately connected to all negotiations for
release. And if we hypothesize about an original form of the tradition
that had the foremen seeking the release of the people, we must deal
with the weakness of the hypothesis, for no evidence in the text
supports the picture. It would seem to me, therefore, to be clear that
this fossil preserves the role of Moses in the negotiations process. At
this early level, Moses is the charismatic hero of the Israelites whose
work makes possible God's redemption of the people from their
bondage. Would this image be compromised by Aaron? That does not
appear to me to be the case. The text always relates Aaron to Moses.

But here Aaron never does anything of significance. He does not do Moses' work for him. And he does not block that work. He is at best a peripheral supporting character, if not obviously secondary.

What, then, can be said about unity in the pericope? I do not see any fundamental inconsistency between the role of Moses as negotiator for the release of the people and the role of the foremen as negotiators for reduction of the work load. Moses negotiates and fails. Then the foremen try to reduce the negative results of the failure. The final scene fits the picture also, for here Moses waits to see whether the increased work load can be reduced. This pattern of unity would not support Smend's hypothesis, however; for in it, Moses would simply not have made his public appearance. The primary tradition would involve negotiation for release without Moses. Some such original form of the negotiations tradition might perhaps lie behind the text. My reconstruction of the narrative would not, however, contradict Smend's observations. It would suggest simply that while Moses had made a public appearance, negotiated for the release of the people, and failed, his stature as heroic leader only emerged the more completely as he attempted to deal with the failure. That attempt would fit into the pattern suggested by Smend. But the full scope of the tradition about the attempt would come to light only with the continuation of the negotiations narrative. The unity of the pericope thus appears to me to be in proper order. It may reveal signs of early tradition. But it is not disjointed.

Should the narrative be divided into different sources? Reference to the antagonist as the Pharaoh in almost all cases, but once as the king of Egypt (v. 4) might suggest such a conclusion. Moreover, the double speech by the Pharaoh in vv. 4 and 5 would also point in that direction. It is possible, however, that the concern of the speech in v. 5 is to introduce the motif about the large number of Israelites and thus the parallel element in these traditions about God's blessing (so, Exodus 1). Heroic man tradition in v. 4 combines with the tradition about the blessing of God in v. 5, with v. 5 anticipating God's action in the exodus. The complexity of the scene would thus reflect the tradition's history rather than a combination of literary sources. I would be inclined to agree with Noth, then, that the unit as a whole is J.[7] Heroic man dominates the view of the Yahwist's narratives about Moses. But with it is the important role of God's intervention. And the combination of the two characterizes the special presentation of J. Heroic man is at the same time the man of God.

2. *Exod. 7.8–12.36*

The received text of Exodus seems to suggest that the execution of the commission of Moses unfolds through a series of signs and wonders that culminates in the Passover, with the Pharaoh expelling the Israelites in a desperate response to the death of the firstborn. The structure of the series would appear to support this assumption. A succession of episodes pits Moses and Aaron against the Pharaoh in dogged negotiations for the release of the people. Regularly, each scene begins with a speech from the Lord, addressed to Moses or Moses and Aaron together. Regularly, the speech specifies instructions for establishing a sign. Commonly, but not on every occasion, the instructions send Moses or Moses and Aaron to the Pharaoh in order to negotiate for permission to leave the land with the people. Motifs from Exodus 5 recur at just this interval. Thus, Moses appeals for permission to take the people into the wilderness to 'serve' the Lord (7.15, 25 [RSV 8.1]; 8.15; 9.1, 13; 10.30). But regularly, the Pharaoh hardens his heart or the Lord hardens his heart for him. To be sure, a series of concessions appears. But the hard-hearted Pharaoh so limits his concessions that Moses will not accept the condition. But the reason for the Pharaoh's obstinacy is not simply the hard heart; it is his impression that Moses plans to deceive him. So, in 10.10, he rejects the concession Moses wants: 'See, you have some evil purpose in mind'. Thus, regularly, each scene suggests that the negotiations or the demonstrations of power fail. The series thus moves from one sign to the next. And the Passover sign stands at the conclusion.

Narration of the Passover sign occurs in the same sequence and clearly appears as the continuation of the series. It is the sign that finally exerts enough pressure against the Pharaoh to secure release of the people. So, in 12.31-32: 'He summoned Moses and Aaron by night. And he said, "Rise, go out from the midst of my people, both you and the Israelites. Go and serve the Lord as you said. And take your flock and your herd just as you said. Go and bless me also"'. Moreover, the construction of the scene shows clearly that the Passover episode is one more in the series: The Lord instructs Moses (not Aaron) to anticipate one more plague, despite the explicit break in the negotiations represented by 10.28. And while no commission sends Moses to the Pharaoh to warn him of the plague and negotiate for the release of the people, the scene apparently assumes such a warning. Thus, the speech in v. 4 announces the plague to the Pharaoh in advance of the event itself. Verse 8b shows clearly that the announcement occurred before the Pharaoh and that the event led again to frustration. So, in the present form of the text, the climax of the negotiations, with increasing physical and political/religious pressure developed to support the appeal, appears in Exodus 12. In vv. 29-32 the Pharaoh accedes to the appeal of the Israelites. And v. 32 marks the climax: 'Take both your flocks and your herds just as you said, and go. And bless me also'. Then vv. 33-36 narrrate the execution of those instructions.

It is important to note that in this configuration, the exodus occurs not as a consequence of the negotiations of Moses, but rather as a consequence of the proper celebration of the Passover ritual. Verse 28 makes this point explicit: 'The Israelites went and did just as the Lord commanded Moses and Aaron; thus they did'. This formulaic report of execution for instructions established by some previous speech sets up the event that marks the climax to the series. And the parallel to it in vv. 50-51 shows the connection clearly: 'All the Israelites did just as the Lord commanded Moses and Aaron; thus they did. And on that very day, the Lord brought the Israelites out from the land of Egypt according to their hosts'. Thus, if we ask this text how the exodus occurred, the answer must be that it happened when Israel kept the ritual in a proper manner. It was a cultic event. And though Moses and Aaron played a role in it, it was not their deed. The Passover tradition, then, does not appear to me to be a part of the heroic saga material that belongs to the Moses narratives. It affirms rather that God acted to save his people when they kept faith in the ritual.

It seems to be clear, then, that there is some kind of relationship between the series of plagues and the Passover episode. Martin Noth describes that relationship in terms of the primary position of the Passover in the history of the tradition:

> Substantively, the plague story is intimately connected with the narrative of the celebration of the Passover at the time of the exodus from Egypt. In fact, it results precisely in a validation of the passover rite since the last plague, in which the divine pressure brought to bear upon the Pharaoh and the Egyptians reaches its greatest intensity, occasions the very first performance of the annually recurring Passover... Therefore, there is scarcely any other possibility than that the development of the narrative of the Egyptian plagues had its beginning in the Passover.[8]

If Noth's conclusion is correct, then we might very well assume also that the plague series has nothing to add to the picture of Moses as heroic man. The Passover tradition does not appear to represent Moses as heroic. And if the plagues developed out of the Passover, they would theoretically share the same kind of non-heroic picture for the leadership of Moses.

There is, however, another facet of the tradition. Exod. 11.10 suggests that the signs were the work of Moses and Aaron. And Deut. 34.10-12 glorifies Moses precisely for the signs in the series:

> And no prophet like Moses has arisen in Israel since then, whom the Lord knew face to face, for all the signs and wonders which the Lord sent him to do in the land of Egypt before the Pharaoh and all his servants and all his land, and for all the strong power and for all the great and terrible deeds which Moses did before the eyes of all Israel.

Is there not, then, a duplicity in the content and structure of the tradition? Noth had himself observed that the Passover was an independent narrative unit and that the plagues represent the subject of a narrative complete in itself. The issue, then, is a problem in the tradition's history rather than simply an adequate perception of the structure in the pericope. Does the plague sequence function simply to support the final, most disastrous plague? Or is there some other element of tradition that might have constituted the original center of the plague narrative?

The issue comes into sharper focus as a result of descriptions of the symmetry in the narrative unit. Moshe Greenberg identifies three sets of three plague episodes, each with balanced and parallel structural elements.

> Plagues one, four, and seven all begin with a variation of the following charge: 'Go to pharaoh in the morning as he is coming out to the water, and station yourself before him at the edge of the Nile'. Plagues two, five, and eight all begin 'The Lord said to Moses, Go to Pharaoh and say to him: Thus said the Lord, let my people go that they may worship me'. Plagues three, six, and nine all begin with a command to the Hebrew leaders to do something that will set the plague in motion—there is never a warning. That is to say, the plagues are arranged in three sets of three by formal criteria alone.[9]

But the important point to note in this description of the plague units is that the Passover plague also does not fit into the symmetry. The series begins with the commission to change the water to blood, and it ends with the darkness so thick that it could be felt. The Passover stands apart from this group. If, then, the Passover does not constitute the climax of the series insofar as this structure is concerned, what does it do? And what does the problem suggest about the original independence of the plagues? Moreover, what would have constituted the climax for the structure of the plagues? These questions are the more pressing in light of the fact that Greenberg's analysis depends on the received text, a combination of the literary sources that produced the final version of the narrative. In the present form of the text, how are we to understand the proper climax to the plague sequence? But equally important, how does the tradition's history cast the climax of the story?

Dennis J. McCarthy analyzes the structure of the narrative in a different way, yet with remarkably similar results.[10] In his construction, the pattern of the story appears as a chiasm. The first scene corresponds in structure to the tenth scene, the second to the ninth, the third to the eighth, the forth to the seventh, and the fifth to the sixth. This description of the plague series assumes that the first episode is not the water to blood scene, but rather the rod to serpent one. But some would suggest eliminating the serpent episode from the sequence. An initial point might be that the identification of the event as a plague is weak, for the event is little more than a magician's trick and hardly deserves a place beside the grievous challenges posed by the remaining signs. Indeed, Childs observes: 'The miracle which he performs was in no sense a plague and even in its structure lay outside the sequence of the ten ensuing disasters'.[11] Yet, a key motif for the plague sequence begins here: Moses and Aaron confront the Egyptian magicians who challenge their authority to make demands on the Pharaoh. Moreover, the concluding formula, so regularly a part of one plague structure, appears for the first time in the sequence here. And the internal structure of the episode certainly follows the pattern of the following scenes. I cannot therefore see the cogency of the argument that the scene lies outside the sequence of the other episodes particularly in its structure. All of the appropriate elements of structure are there. And the magician's motif requires that this scene be taken together with the following ones.

The following diagram illustrates the pattern, with the words in italics corresponding to an element in the parallel member.

I. Rod to snake 7.8-13
  A. Lord to M and A
    1. Instructions to A
    2. *No warning*
  B. Execution of sign

  C. Magicians, wise men,
    sorcerers

  D. *Hardened heart (ḥzq)*, NL,
    AYS

II. Water to Blood, 7.14-25
  A. Lord to M (go to Ph)
    1. *Hard heart (kbd)*
    2. Instructions, including a
      warning
  B. Lord to M, A to do sign

  C. Execution of the sign
  D. Magicians

  E. *Hardened heart (ḥzq)*, NL,
    AYS
  F. Conclusion

III. Frogs, 7.26–8.11 (RSV 8.1-15)
  A. Lord to M
    1. *Go to Ph*
    2. *Instructions to warn*
      (negotiations)
  B. Lord to M
    Commission to A to execute
    sign
  C. Execution of sign

  D. Magicians
  E. Negotiations
  F. Hardened Heart (kbd) NL,
    AYS

X. Darkness 10.21-29
  A. Lord to M
    1. Instructions to M
    2. *No warning*
  B. Execution of sign
    1. In Egypt
    2. Not in Goshen
  C. Negotiations
    1. Ph concessions
    2. M conditions
  D. *Hardened heart (ḥzq)*, NLPG

IX. Locusts, 10.1-20
  A. Lord to M
    1. *Hard heart (kbd)*
    2. Catechism

  B. MA to Pharaoh, a *warning*
  C. Pleas of servants
  D. Negotiations
    1. Ph concessions
    2. M conditions
    3. Ph rejections
  E. Execution of the sign

  F. Concession and stopping
    the sign
  G. *Hardened heart (ḥzq)*,
    NLPG

VIII. Hail 9.11-35
  A. Lord to M
    1. *Go to Ph*
    2. *Instructions to warn*
  B. Lord to M
    Commission to execute sign

  C. Execution of sign
    1. Against Egypt
    2. Not against Israel

  D. Negotiations
  E. Hardened Heart (ḥzq)
    NLPG, AYS

IV. Gnats 8.2-15 (RSV 8.16-19)
    A. Lord to M
       Instructions to A to execute
       sign, no warning
    B. Execution of sign
    C. *Magicians fail*
    D. *Hardened heart (ḥzq)* NL,
       AYS
V. Flies 8.16-28 (RSV 8.20-32)
    A. Lord to M
       1. *Instructions to go*
       2. *Warning*
       3. *Separation*, Israel from
          Egypt
       4. KF
    B. Execution of sign
    C. Negotiations
    D. *Hardened heart (kbd)*
    DLPG

VII. Boils 9.8-10
    A. Lord to MA
       Instructions to execute
       sign, no warning
    B. Execution of sign
    C. *Magicians expelled*
    D. *Hardened heart (ḥzq)* NL,
       AYS
VI. Murrain on the cattle 9.1-7
    A. Lord to M
       1. *Instructions to go*
       2. *Warning*
       3. *Separation*, Israel from
          Egypt

    B. Execution of sign

    C. *Hardened heart (kbd) DLPG*

These corresponding elements suggest, then, that a chiastic structure governs the pattern of the narrative. Particularly strong in this structure are the relative positions of the key words for the Pharaoh's hardened heart, the one exception to an exact parallel being in the concluding formulas for elements III and VIII. Indeed, the pattern includes shifts in episodic structure from instructions to return to the Pharaoh to warn him of an impending plague, should he continue to hold the Israelites, to instructions that effect a plague without warning. And the hardened heart motif provides the transition from step to step. Each occasion ends in failure. The Pharaoh is convinced, as he was in Exodus 5, that the appeal is a trick. And he holds firm to his intention not to let the people go. Moreover, the series ends with a clear break. The chiastic structure excludes the Passover. The negotiations end. And the concluding interview, 10.28-29, makes it possible to continue the series. Moses cannot see the face of the Pharaoh again. And he agrees to the ban. Whatever happens in this series will happen without the head to head negotiations that have functioned without success to this point. Thus, the question returns: Where is the climax of the series? In the light of the apparent exclusion of the Passover from the structure of the series, can some other point of conclusion be identified? Is there another tradition about exodus?

It should be clear that the correspondence between elements in the chiastic structure is not a wooden repetition from one parallel element to the other. There is movement in the narrative. (1) In the beginning the Egyptian magicians duplicate the signs effected by Moses and Aaron. There is, however, a foreboding anticipation from the very first sign: The serpent rod of Moses and Aaron swallows the serpents of the Egyptians. Moreover, in the plague of the gnats, the Egyptians try to accomplish the same thing Moses and Aaron have done, just as they have in the preceding episodes. But they cannot (8.14; RSV 8.18). And as a result, they confess: 'This is the finger of God!' And finally, in the plague of boils, the Egyptians suffered the attack in their own bodies and could not stand before Moses. They were defeated. And the victor is explicitly Moses. 'The magicians were not able to stand *before Moses* because of the boils.' (2) Moses and Aaron begin together. Moses tells Aaron whatever he should say. But Aaron slips into the background. For example, 10.3 reports that Moses and Aaron went together to confront the Pharaoh. But v. 6 notes that departure from the Pharaoh involved only one person. And v. 7 contains a plea from the Pharaoh's servants to allow the exodus because 'this one' (*zeh*) was a snare (*môqēṣ*) to them. The one is not named. One might argue that this scene preserves a memory of Aaron as the one who effected the plagues. But the point is not crucial. It is sufficient to note that for this scene, one figure keys the action, not two. Moreover, in the development of the scene, Aaron drops completely away. From 10.9 to the Passover scene Aaron plays no further role. The acting leader is Moses alone. (3) Moses or Moses with Aaron negotiate for the release of the people in the face of each plague. The negotiation meets rejection initially. And closely associated with the rejection is the motif of the Pharaoh's hardened heart. The negotiations do, however, win some concessions. At first the concessions are severely limited. The Pharaoh agrees to let the people go to sacrifice as they have asked (8.4). But when the plague ends, the Pharaoh revokes the concession (8.11). Or he agrees to let the people sacrifice, but only within the borders of Egypt (8.21). Or he agrees to let the people go into the wilderness, but not very far away (8.24). Or he agrees to let the men go where they will (9.11). Or he agrees to let the families go, but not the herds (10.24). The movement clearly anticipates some breaking point. (4) It would be possible to argue that the intensity of the plagues increases with each new encounter. Thus, the trick with the rod is rather innocuous. But when water turns to blood, pressure begins to build. Frogs, gnats, and flies discomfort the people. But death of the cattle introduces a more severe threat. Boils then attack the physical health of the population. Hail and rain, then the locusts interrupt the fertility of the land, a matter of concern for the economic health of the Egyptians. And the darkness shifts the scene of activity to a realm controlled by the gods. Thus, all the more is it necessary to ask where the conclusion to the series might be.

In the structure of the plague story, as well as in the history of the tradition, the most outstanding characteristic of the narration is the depiction of the negotiations ending in failure. The hardened heart motif clearly emphasizes the failure. And the opening round of negotiations set forth in Exodus 5 shows the result of the negotiation with painful clarity. Indeed, ch. 5 may well offer the most basic level of the tradition's history.[12] And if so, then the negotiations tradition would from the beginning represent the results of Moses' efforts in dealing with the Pharaoh as failure. This point gains weight in light of the concluding scene in 10.28-29. These verses stand apart from the stereotyped structure of the series. And they express the final break in a negotiations pattern. If Moses presents himself before the Pharaoh again in order to pursue the negotiations, he will die. And Moses accepts the closure. Moreover, the renewal in ch. 11 seems somewhat artificial in the face of the closure. Thus, the Lord instructs Moses concerning one more plague. The formulation is peculiar in the series: 'Yet one more plague. . . ' (*'ôd nega' 'eḥād*). The brittle relationship seems to me to confirm the conclusion that the series moved originally to some other kind of climax than a renewal of the negotiations.

I would suggest that the series originally depicted the exodus event as an alternative to a negotiated release of the people. When the negotiations failed, according to the tradition, Moses urged his people to leave Egypt anyway, in haste, without the Pharaoh's permission or even his knowledge. This original conclusion to the series would then have been overshadowed by the Passover story.

But is there positive evidence for such an original conclusion? The answer can be established first by the history of the Israelite cult. It seems to be clear that in the course of history, the Passover celebration assimilated to its structures the traditions and means for celebration from an originally quite distinct festival, the Festival of Unleavened Bread.[13] And, indeed, the Passover itself overshadowed the festival of Unleavened Bread, leaving it simply as a skeleton around the rituals for the Passover meal. Moreover, the unleavened bread symbol fits more cogently into the story of departure from Egypt in haste than an account of extensive preparation for the Passover event. Departure in haste would constitute the event of the exodus for the traditions of the Unleavened Bread Festival, just as departure by proper execution of the ritual constitutes the exodus event for the Passover.

But is there anything more to fill in the edges of the tradition about a departure in haste? And what role would Moses have played in the picture? The textual evidence for the tradition, preserved in fragmented pieces by the exodus narratives, depicts the departure as an escape without the knowledge of the Egyptians or the Pharaoh, but with spoil taken by deception from unsuspecting slave owners.[14] It is crucial, in order to understand this tradition, not to interpret the event as a moment of unguarded good will from the Egyptians, as though the Egyptians were giving gifts to their departing friends.[15] Nor does the text represent this event as a proper, legal payment to slaves dismissed from their slavery in good standing.[16] Rather, the image of the tradition is of a slave people who trick their masters and by virtue of their wit win the spoils of war which their cunning victory deserves.

But why, one might ask, would the Egyptians be so gullible as to give away the spoil without suspecting the true intentions of the Israelites, especially in view of the Pharaoh's constant vigil against the plans of Moses to deceive him? The text does not give us an historical answer to the question. We cannot expect an answer that would resolve the incredulity of the modern historian. Rather, the text supplies a theological answer. In 11.3, an explicit response appears: 'The Lord gave the people favor in the eyes of the Egyptians'. But at the same time, the text combines its theological answer with a heroic one: 'Also, the man Moses was very great in the land of Egypt, in the eyes of the servants of Pharaoh, as well as the eyes of the (Israelite) people'. The despoiling occurred, then, because God intervened and made it possible, but also because Moses had a reputation in the land that made it possible. The two poles go hand in hand.

Thus, 12.34-36 responds to the question about the exodus. When did the exodus occur?

> The people took their dough before it was leavened, their kneeding bowls bound in their mantels on their shoulders, for the Israelites had done according to the word of Moses. They had asked from Egyptians the vessels of silver and vessels of gold and clothing. So

the Lord gave the people favor in the eyes of the Egyptians, and
they asked them, and they despoiled the Egyptians.

The exodus occurred when, by the intervention of God and the
reputation of Moses, the people obeyed Moses and despoiled the
Egyptians.

This second tradition about the exodus would, so it seems to me,
fit into the plague narration as the proper climax of the sequence
more effectively than would the tradition about the event at the
Sea.[17] The issues in the Sea tradition are, from the beginning of its
history to its latest Pentateuchal form, different from those controlling
the shape of the plague stories. The despoiling would also rest very
close to the oral stage of tradition history, with its fossil form
projecting an image of negotiations that fail and a leader who finally
seizes the opportunity to take his people away despite the failure of
formal appeals. The heroic man enables his people to meet *the*
political and religious crisis of their lives. Moreover, this tradition
would more readily fit with the skein of narrative depicting Moses as
the heroic man whose work complements the mighty acts of God.
Not only does the tradition recognize as complement to the signs and
wonders effected by God a tendency to attribute the same signs and
wonders to Moses, but it also affirms that the exodus event itself, that
final sign that redeemed the people of God, occurred in part because
of the stature of 'this man' whom the servants of the Pharaoh
feared.

This perspective provides a valuable position for evaluating a
problem in the narrative development of the plague events. In
Exodus 7, v. 17 introduces a speech of Yahweh, addressed apparently
to the Pharaoh, and prefaced by a messenger formula. Moreover, the
speech opens with a typical formula about 'knowledge' of the Lord,
constructed in first person. 'By this you shall know that *I* am the
Lord.' The speech itself, cast in the first person as a statement about
Yahweh's intention to act, described an event that assumes Moses'
action. 'Behold, I will strike the water which is in the Nile with the
rod which is in my hand. And it shall be turned to blood.' Then v. 25
concludes the scene with a repetition of Yahweh's action: 'Seven days
passed after the Lord struck the Nile'. Does this panel in the plague
series not assume that God acted directly in effecting the plagues?
Does it not eliminate the role of Moses as an intrinsic part of the
plague tradition?

But the issue is not whether Moses effected the plagues without reference to Yahweh or whether Yahweh himself did the job without Moses. The issue is to understand the intricate relationship between Moses as the leader of the people and representative of God to the Pharaoh and Yahweh as commissioner of Moses to the Pharaoh. When Moses speaks to the Pharaoh, he does so in the name of the Lord. This point is made clear by the messenger formula. The speech of Yahweh, addressed by Moses to the Pharaoh, then assumes that when Moses acts, his action is the action of God, just as when he speaks his words, they are understood as the words of God. In the same manner Hosea announces an act of reconciliation with the woman he loves, but recognizes that the act is like God's act, indeed, introduces God's act with the people he loves (Hos. 3.1). But the actions merge more sharply in Hosea 2 where the description of the divorce is apparently something that applies to Hosea and Gomer but moves almost imperceptibly to something that applies to Yahweh and Israel. Hosea's divorce initiates Yahweh's divorce.[18]

Would this representation of Yahweh's action through Moses suggest that prophetic influence shaped the image of Moses in these traditions? It is necessary to recommend caution about the consequences of this observation. It is clear that some kind of relationship between this image and prophetic figures exists. However, it does not follow, at least from this text, that prophetic images shaped the literary representation of Moses, much less that Moses is represented as a prophet. It is at least as likely that the shape of the image here is formed by tradition patterns of the messenger, by general patterns of any person sent by a superior, as it is that Moses appears here as the model of the classical prophet, shaped by classical prophetism as a model for subsequent generations. It seems to me to be clear that in the plague the image of Moses is general and heroic, a literary creation, rather than specific and institutional, a product of the historical or sociological configurations of a particular office. The image of God effecting the plague with the rod in his hand, then, is an image that participates in the two-fold character of the tradition. God acts. But those acts must be executed by the work of Moses.

Finally, some comment about the rod is in order here. The rod obviously belongs to Moses. It is in some manner a sign of his authority before the Pharaoh and before his own people. But here, with Moses acting for God, it apparently becomes a rod for God's action. The authority of Moses merges with the authority of God. And in the same manner, the rod of Moses merges with the rod of

God (see Exod. 17.9). It is a part of the same duality, the heroic man coupled with the acts of God, noted in the principal thesis for this entire investigation.[19]

The structure of the plague sequence and, incidentally, the tradition's history emerge more clearly when the characteristics of the literary sources enter the discussion. The youngest of the sources, P, appears in 7.8-13, 19, 20aα, 21b-22; 8.1-3, 11aβb-15 (RSV 8.5-7, 15aβb-19); 9.8-12, 22, 23aα, 35; 10.12-13aα, 20-22.[20] The following outline illustrates the pattern:

    I. Rod to Serpent
       A. Lord to M and A
          1. Commission to A
          2. Rod to serpent
       B. Execution of the sign (N.B. *Aaron's rod*)
       C. Magicians
       D. Hardened heart (*ḥzq*), NL, AYS

   II. Blood to water
       A. Lord to M
          1. Commission to A
          2. Rod over the water
       B. Execution of the sign
       C. Magicians
       D. Hardened heart (*ḥzq*), NL, AYS

  III. Frogs
       A. Lord to M
          1. Commission to A
          2. Rod over the water
       B. Execution of the sign
       C. Magicians
       D. Hardened heart (*ḥzq*), NL, AYS

  IV. Gnats
       A. Lord to M
          1. Commission to A
          2. Rod over the dust
       B. Execution of the sign
       C. Magicians fail
       D. Hardened heart (*ḥzq*) NL, AYS

   V. Boils
       A. Lord to M and A
       B. Execution of signs
       C. Magicians expelled
       D. Hardened heart (*ḥzq*) NL, AYS

VI. Hail
  A. Lord to M
    1. No reference to A
    2. Moses' hand
  B. Execution of sign—rod
  C. Hardened heart (*ḥzq*) NLPG

VII. Locusts
  A. Lord to M
    1. No reference to A
    2. Moses' hand
  B. Execution of sign—rod
  C. Hardened heart (*ḥzq*) NLPG

VIII. Darkness
  A. Lord to M
    1. No reference to A
    2. Moses' hand
  B. Execution of sign—hand
  C. Hardened heart (*ḥzq*) NLPG

No chiasm marks this arrangement. Rather, these verses reveal a regular pattern of scenes, each repeating the basic structure of the preceding one. The point is particularly clear in the first five episodes. The Lord speaks to Moses and Aaron (I, V) or instructs Moses to commission Aaron (II, III, IV) for the execution of the sign. The first four feature Aaron using the rod to establish the event. No warning precedes the act. Aaron simply performs the required ritual with the rod, and the sign occurs. The only movement in this rather static sequence is effected by the role of the Egyptian magicians. In the first scene, the Egyptians duplicate the trick of Moses and Aaron. But a sense of the outcome nevertheless grips the confrontation when the serpent of Moses and Aaron swallows the serpents of the Egyptians. Scenes II and III report simply that the Egyptians duplicated the sign of the Israelite leaders. Scene IV reports that the Egyptians were not able to repeat the sign as had been the case, but rather they confessed in their failure that the event occurred by the finger of God. And scene V notes that the sign from Moses and Aaron affected the bodies of the Egyptian magicians so severely that they could not appear in Moses' presence. The defeat and expulsion of the Egyptians mark a sharp contrast to the steady failure of the negotiations with the Pharaoh. The final element in the structure reports that the Pharaoh's heart was hardened. With a *waw* consecutive Qal imperfect, or on two occasions (9.12; 10.20), a *waw* consecutive Pi'el imperfect of the verb *ḥzq* with the Lord as the subject, the conclusion repeats the refrain. The Pharaoh's heart was hardened, or the Lord hardened the heart of the Pharaoh. And regularly, the refrain concludes that the Pharaoh would not listen, just as the Lord said.

It is possible, moreover, that P originally reported three more signs: the hail, locusts, and the darkness. Evidence for this hypothesis resides in the conclusion to each of the three relevant scenes. In a context that may belong primarily to J, these conclusions employ the distinctive verb from the P source for reporting the hardened heart motif. Once the verb is Qal, twice Pi'el. The remaining part of the concluding formula shifts from the notion that the Pharaoh did not listen as the Lord had said to a note that he did not let the people go (compare the J scenes for the flies and the cattle murrain). The static pattern appears in all three scenes with no reference to Aaron or to the magicians and no marker for movement in tension. Thus, in the P sequence, the one element of drama focuses on the defeat of the Egyptian magicians. And the victory belongs explicitly to Moses. In 9.11, the point is clear: 'The magicians were not able to stand before Moses because of the boils'. It would appear, then, that something of the heroic victory of Moses in a face to face encounter with the Egyptians belongs to P. This tradition is perhaps weakened by 8.15, for in that moment the Egyptians confess that the struggle belongs to God. Yet, still, an important heroic motif surfaces here in the priestly narrative. It may reflect simply the influence of early tradition on P, or even immediate influence from J. But it does suggest that the heroic element is not simply limited to J. It is a part of the tradition which both J and P inherit. But significantly, P does not do much with the tradition. It stands like a signal from the past, no longer instrumental in the construction of the narrative, perhaps not even clearly understood in its complementary relationship with 8.15.

But in addition to the element of movement in the conflict with the Egyptians, the text also reveals the problem of identifying the final climax of the sequence. The structure of the preserved scenes moves in a linear fashion to embrace some final occasion of confrontation. For P this final scene must be the Passover. The Passover in P, however, does not appear as a new occasion for negotiations with the Pharaoh. 11.9-10 marks a conclusion to the negotiations, just as 10.28-29 does for J. Moreover, it suggests that for P the negotiations end in failure. Verses 9-10 constitute a general conclusion to the sequence. And they feature the key priestly verb for the hardened heart motif, a *waw* consecutive Pi'el imperfect from *ḥzq*: 'The Lord said to Moses, "The Pharaoh will not listen to you, in order that my signs might be multiplied in the land of Egypt". So Moses and Aaron did all these signs before the Pharaoh, and the Lord hardened (*wayᵉḥazzēq*) the heart of the Pharaoh and he did not send the Israelites away from his land'. Thus, for P the Passover is not simply a new plague. The Passover event itself appears in Exodus 12 and establishes the exodus from Egypt totally in terms of a cultic event. To keep the ritual is to leave Egypt. The ritual preserves Israel from the death of the first born. There is a plague dimension: All the Egyptian first born, even the first born of the Pharaoh, die. But the exodus does not occur because the sign has convinced the Pharaoh that Israel should go (contrast J, 12.31-32). It occurs because the ritual has been fulfilled, and thus, God makes the departure possible. The plagues end in failure. But the ritual, given by God, enables that failure to be converted into liberation from the Egyptian bondage. And that for P is the climax to the plagues. The concluding statements in 12.28 and again in vv. 50-51 confirm this point: 'The Israelites went and did just as the Lord had commanded Moses and Aaron; thus, they did it'. 'All of the Israelites did just as the Lord had commanded Moses and Aaron. So they did it. And on that very day, the Lord brought the Israelites out from the land of Egypt according to their hosts.' Moreover, at this crucial point, Moses and Aaron play only an instrumental role. They facilitate proper performance in the ritual. But they do little more.

In contrast to the structure of P, J reveals the pattern of the chiasm preserved by the final form of the text (see overleaf).

In order to see the chiasm in J, we must assume that J, like P, began with an account of the rod to serpent sign. But the assumption can be supported by the J reference to the rod in 7.15: 'Take in your hand the rod which turned into a serpent'. Then, like P, J presents eight scenes in the negotiations sequence. The pattern itself begins regularly with the Lord's instructions to Moses (Aaron never enters the picture) to perform the sign, commonly in the presence of the Pharaoh. And the sign promotes negotiations for the release of the Israelites. It is here that the series of concessions begins. But finally, all progress in the negotiations collapses, and the negotiations end in failure. The chiasm is supported, moreover, by the motif of separation between Egypt and Israel and by concluding formulae. Finally, we might assume that scenes I, II, VII, and VIII originally

I. Rod to Serpent

VIII. Darkness
   A. Lord to M
      1. Instructions
      2. No warning
   B. Execution of the sign
      1. In Egypt
      2. Not in Goshen
   C. Negotiations
      1. Ph concessions
      2. M conditions

(*ḥzq?*)

   D. Conclusion (*ḥzq?*)

II. Water to Blood
   A. Lord to M
      1. *Hardened heart (kbd)*
      2. *Instructions, go to Ph*
      3. *Warning*

VII. Locusts
   A. Lord to M
      Instructions, go to Ph
      2. *Hardened heart (kbd)*

   B. MA to Ph: *Warning*
   C. Pleas of servants
   D. Negotiations
      1. Ph concessions
      2. M conditions
      3. Ph rejections

   B. Execution of sign

   E. Execution of sign
   F. Plea for intercession

   C. Conclusion (*ḥzq?*)

   G. Conclusion (*ḥzq?*)

III. Frogs
   A. Lord to M
      1. *Instructions, go to Ph*
      2. *Warning*

VI. Hail
   A. Lord to M
      1. *Instructions, go to Ph*
      2. *Warning*
   B. Lord to M: commission to execute the sign

   B. Plea for intercession

   C. Execution of sign
   D. Negotiations

   C. Conclusion (*kbd*) NL/AYS

   E. Conclusion (*kbd*) NL/AYS

IV. Flies
   A. Lord to M
      1. *Instructions, go to Ph*
      2. *Warning*
      3. *Separation, Israel from Egypt*
   B. Execution of the sign
   C. Negotiations
   D. Hardened heart (*kbd*) NLPG

V. Murrain on the cattle
   A. Lord to M
      1. *Instructions, go to Ph*
      2. Warning
      3. *Separation, Israel from Egypt*
   B. Execution of the sign

   C. Hardened heart (*kbd*) NLPG

carried an ending that reported the hardening of the Pharaoh's heart. Could it be that J employs here the verb *ḥzq* as P normally does and that the text gives us, in fact, nothing of the endings in P for these scenes? If so, the ending would contrast sharply with the other J allusions to the same motif. Those texts employ a *waw* consecutive Hiph'il imperfect of the verb *kbd*. And, moreover, scenes II and VII employ the same verb in the opening speech of the Lord to Moses as an allusion to the previous experience. Indeed, this position shows most convincingly the pattern of the chiasm for J.

In addition to this pattern of structure in the chiasm, the sequence also shows movement toward a goal. Thus, the signs are used more directly as occasions for negotiations. And accordingly, Moses warns the Pharaoh of the coming sign, at least on occasion. But the signs can also function as evidence to promote a new intimacy for the Israelites with the Lord. Thus, the knowledge formula, for example, in 10.2 shows that the event will produce knowledge of the Lord for Moses and Aaron and, through them, for subsequent generations. The knowledge will not belong to the Egyptians. It will be the experience of the Israelites. And this growing act of redemption will establish a relationship that will promote Israel's fullest life.

With Martin Noth, I would conclude from this pattern of structure that the plague narrative has no sign of E. Brevard Childs argues to the contrary that E appears in 7.15b, 17b, 20b, 23; 9.22-23a, 24a, 25a, 35a; 10.12-13a, 15a, 15b, 20, 21-23, 27; 11.1-3.[21] There is, however, some problem in the conclusion, 'The E source is preserved in a rather fragmentary form'.[22] But the problem is more extensive than simply the fragmentary character of the suggested verses. Childs counters the problem offered by the fragmentary state of the text by observing: 'In spite of this, there does appear to be a discernible pattern which would speak against its being considered as a series of glosses rather than a continuous strand'.[23] But a part of the evidence for identifying the E fragments in the first place is the pattern. 'The decisive argument seems to be that the material which has been isolated apart from J and P does reflect a definite form-critical pattern.'[24] But the issue is precisely whether material can be successfully isolated from J and P. Or do the fragments under consideration constitute simply glosses on the other sources? That question must be resolved before one considers the form-critical integrity of the fragments. Otherwise, a circular argument emerges. In order to avoid a circular argument, this isolation and identification of the fragments must be completed without reference to the pattern.

But then the question must be: What criteria enable the E fragments to be identified?

Georg Fohrer is a key critic for consideration of this question. He argues for three distinct formal patterns within the narration of the plague sequence, each the product of one of the principal sources.[25] All three employ a structure comprising three basic elements: (1) Preparations for the sign. (2) Execution of the sign. (3) Results. The distinctions among the sources emerge in the development of each element.

Thus, in the first pattern, (a) preparation involves a command to Moses to deliver a message to the Pharaoh. The message will contain (i) a demand to release the Israelites, (ii) an announcement of the plague, in case the Pharaoh refuses the demand, and (iii) a special motif about exemption from the plague for the Israelites. The second element will be (b) a report that the instructions given to Moses have been executed. Execution of the sign involves simply a report that the plague occurred by the hand of the Lord and some narration of the details. And then (c) the results of the plague are set out.

The second pattern develops the three principal elements in the following way: (a) Preparation embraces (i) a command to Moses to stretch out his hand or his rod over a particular area or to a particular area, and thereby to institute the plague, and then (ii) the details of the plague. (b) Execution of the sign will involve (i) a notation that Moses followed the instructions, and (ii) details of the event. (c) Then the results follow.

The third pattern has a slight modification in the first element. (a) Preparation involves (i) a command to Moses, to be delivered to Aaron, who should stretch out his hand with the rod over the affected area, and (ii) the details of the event. (b) The second element reports (i) execution of the command by Moses or by Aaron, (ii) the details of the event, and (iii) the special motif of the magicians.

The first of these patterns belongs to J, the second to E, and the third to P. Moreover, J presents the plagues as punishment according to Fohrer, with a marked pedagogical goal. The Pharaoh might respond to the pressure of the punishment and change his policy. E and P, on the other hand, have nothing of the pedagogical character. For them, the event is strictly a demonstration of miraculous power and authority. As such, the plague is limited in time, quite apart from the Pharaoh's reaction.

Fohrer observes, however, that the sequence and the different traditions in the sequence derive from the redaction of the sources by a later hand.[26] In his opinion, distinction between the sources in fact rests on style, peculiarity of treatment, and formal structure of each scene. For example, in the water to blood plague, he sees three sections: '1. Das Nilwasser durch Fischsterben verpestet (J), 2. das Nilwasser durch Verwandlung in Blut (E) und 3. alles Wasser in Ägypten durch Verwandlung in Blut (P) unbrauchbar gemacht wird'.[27] But the distinctions here seem painfully thin to me. Is the change of all water anything more than a narrative technique of intensification for the change of the Nile water? Do we have anything more than a double form of the tradition? The key words for the hardened heart, *ḥzq* and *kbd*, would seem to me to point in the same direction. Moreover, the three-fold pattern of the plague scenes described above would constitute the most important criterion for identifying E. But even there the distinctions seem to me to be thin and incapable of supporting the hypothesis. Thus, the command to Moses to stretch out his hand with the rod seems remarkably similar to the command to instruct Aaron to do the same thing. Is Aaron the critical criterion? Or does the presence of Aaron in this sequence, as well as in J, reflect a particular traditio-historical problem? Would the three-fold structure of this material be so obvious if Fohrer were not already working from the perspective of three independent sources? Thus, for example, in his treatment of the water to blood scene, he breaks the unit in v. 15 between elements a and b, attributing v. 15b to E.[28] But it is precisely this break that enables him to identify what E is. If he had no necessity to find J and E here, no hypothesis that J involves an address to the Pharaoh while E involves the act of stretching out the rod over the river, it would not be so necessary to break the unit. I cannot see that v. 15b or even v. 17b is anything more than the natural completion of the opposite part of the verse. The point in common between v. 15b and v. 17b is the rod. But why can the rod not appear alongside the hand in J or P? Thus, these distinctions seem to me incapable of supporting the weight of a hypothesis that argues for three distinct sources. The structure as described by Fohrer facilitates a distinction between two sources, not three. The structural patterns he identifies for E merge so closely with P (or, on occasion, with J) that they resist justification of an argument for three independent sources.

It seems to me, therefore, that Noth's thesis remains the best explanation of the phenomena. The plague narratives reveal two basic, distinct sources, with E a dependent collection of glosses. In order to be consistent, we would need to consider the same question with regard to the distinction between J and P. But here vocabulary (*ḥzq* vis à vis *kbd*) coupled with structural duplicity (7.14-18//7.19) provides some solid critical control. Indeed, the chiastic structure of J sets one pattern with integrity over the regular structure of P. Thus, it seems to me to be in order to distinguish between J or JE and P. But to draw a sharp distinction between J and E does not appear to be justified.

The J narrative of the plagues develops a sequence that excludes the Passover from the intrinsic pattern of its structure. And with the pattern, the question is posed concerning the proper climax of the tension. In what manner did the exodus occur for J? The Passover scene does appear here as a renewed occasion for negotiations with the Pharaoh. And the event presents the Egyptians at the point of collapse. The death of the firstborn has brought them to their knees. The Israelites must now leave; the Egyptians drive them out. But it is precisely here that the distinction between the plague cycle and Passover emerges most sharply. The plagues appear in a cycle of narration that completes its pattern without the Passover event. It is rounded off by the structure as well as the note in 10.28-29. The Passover episode is thus the more artificially constructed as a new plague. And the construction casts the Passover as an appendix. Insofar as J is concerned, the Passover tradition is now the conclusion to the plagues. But the Passover narrative also reveals the evidence for the distinct tradition about the exodus, casting the event as an escape in haste with the spoils taken from the Egyptians. This part of the tradition, as noted above, houses the presentation of Moses as hero.

I conclude, then, that the plague tradition experienced extensive changes in the course of its history. Initially a presentation of Moses' negotiations with the Pharaoh, ending with failure and anticipation for the necessity to escape in haste without the permission of the Pharaoh, it became an account of the efforts of Moses and Aaron to secure release for the people by pressure negotiations, ending with the most severe of all pressures, the death of the Egyptian firstborn. And with this event, the goal for the negotiations is reached.[29] The Pharaoh drives Israel out. In summary, two forms of the exodus tradition appear. The Passover version of the story places primary focus on God's intervention. Moses and Aaron simply facilitate the event. But the escape in haste combines divine intervention with the heroic stature of Moses. Moses calls his people to leave under his leadership, without the permission or even the knowledge of the Pharaoh.

Chapter 5

GOD'S AID TO ISRAEL IN THE WILDERNESS

A series of tales in Exodus and Numbers recounts God's aid to Israel in the face of particular crises experienced by the people in the wilderness. Beginning with Exodus 14, these tales describe problems such as attacks by various enemies (Exod. 14; 17; Num. 21), thirst (Exod. 15; 17; Num. 20), and starvation (Exod. 16; Num. 11). In addition, the spy story (Num. 13–14) sets out an account of Israel's initial foray into Canaan. In each of these tales the murmuring of the people against Moses or Moses and Aaron together dominates the received text.[1] This motif recounts Israel's rebellion, an act that challenges Moses' position as leader of the people in the exodus from Egypt. The pattern of the murmuring stories includes: (1) some account of the crisis confronting the Israelites; (2) the response of the people to it as a challenge to the validity of Mosaic leadership; (3) an explicit goal announced by the people to return to Egypt or an implicit wish expressed as an accusation against Moses or Moses and Aaron for their role in facilitating the exodus, thus an element that would reverse the exodus. (4) Some tales include the response of Moses or Moses and Aaron and, on occasion, the response of God, either by defending the issue challenged or by punishing the people as rebels.

Typical vocabulary for this stage includes the verb, 'to murmur' or, better, 'to rebel', 'to complain' (*lûn*), and a series of synonyms. The murmuring tradition, so it seems to me, is a relatively late narrative revision of an older tradition, converting an originally positive account of Israel's life under Mosaic leadership to a negative account of rebellion. The reason for the conversion is still a subject for debate. It is probable, nevertheless, that a polemical redaction from the interests of the Jerusalem court and the Davidic king shifts the tradition to its negative form in order to show that Israel, the ancestors of the northern kingdom, forfeited the privileges of divine election, leaving the door open to a new act of election for David and Zion.

The traditio-historical rootage for this murmuring redaction is the account of the rebellion by Dathan and Abiram.[2] This account does not center on an event of natural crisis or even an attack by an external enemy. Rather, it shows resistance to Moses within the ranks of the people themselves. Thus, Dathan and Abiram refuse to continue their participation in the exodus with an accusation against Moses' leadership. In Num. 16.13, the text quotes the accusation: 'Is it too little that you brought us up from a land flowing with milk and honey to kill us in the wilderness? Will you also make yourself prince over us?' Thus, the tradition shows a direct challenge to Moses' leadership. And the challenge leads to rejection of the rebels. Moreover, the rebellion is the substance of this story, not a secondary reinterpretation of an earlier, positive story. Rebellion against Mosaic leadership raises immediately the question of validity for the Mosaic figure.

This interpretation would suggest that the traditions about Moses as leader of the people who followed him in obedience would have been at home in the northern tribes, a hypothesis strengthened by the singular reference to Moses as the prophet who led the exodus in Hos. 12.13. Moreover, the tradition equates the leadership of Moses with the leadership of God. To rebel against Moses is to rebel against God. If the rebellion tradition reflects a southern, anti-Israel perspective with a rejection of the privileges of election associated with the exodus, it is not at the same time a rejection of Moses. Moses remains the leader appointed by God to care for his people in the wilderness setting. And that appointment is confirmed in the face of the rebellion. Thus, in the Dathan-Abiram story, punishment for the rebels will at the same time establish Moses' authority to lead the people: 'In this you shall know that the Lord sent me to do all these deeds, that it is not from my own heart. If like the death of all persons these rebels die, and the fate of all persons is imposed on them, the Lord has not sent me. . . ' When the earth swallows the rebels, clearly a death that fits Moses' conditions, Moses' position before the people is validated.

The strongest vestige of the heroic tradition now preserved by the murmuring stage of the narratives is the facet that depicts Moses as the intercessor.[3] Despite the rebellion of Israel against Moses, the hero nevertheless defends his people against the plan of the Lord to execute them.[4] And in the process he risks his own position before God and, indeed, his own life. In Num. 14.11-25, the Lord announces his intention to destroy the people. Moses responds with an appeal to the Lord's reputation with the nations who know of the promise to give Israel the land, to his character as a God of great loyalty (*k^egōdel hasdekā*), and to his oath in the exodus event itself. On the basis of the intercession, the Lord changes his plan. The rebels will not die immediately. But they lose their right to inherit the land. Divine punishment remains a part of the pattern. But the degree of punishment drops.

It would be in order to consider here the scene of rebellion and its consequences in Exodus 32-34. This act of rebellion cannot be simply equated with the murmuring scenes. The murmuring motif regularly involves the leadership of Moses. But it centers in the exodus tradition with a reversal of the escape from Egypt as well as the theological significance that goes with it. In contrast, for Exodus 32 the issue is explicitly the absence of Mosaic leadership. Since Moses is no longer physically present, the people look for a replacement. The concern is not to replace God. Moses was the leader of the exodus. And the gods to be created by Aaron and his people would replace him in order to carry on the exodus. 'Up, make us gods who will go before us, for this Moses, the man who brought us up from the land of Egypt—we do not know what happened to him.' The rebellion leads God to announce to Moses that his intention to slay the entire group and start over with Moses and his descendants will solve the problem. The response in 32.11-13 is again intercession. Moses appeals again to the reputation of the Lord in the eyes of the Egyptians, as well as the Lord's promise to the patriarchs. Another scene of intercession appears in vv. 31-32. And in this case, Moses who is innocent of the people's apostasy, identifies himself completely with his apostate people. 'Now, if you will forgive their sin. . . But if not, wipe me out from your book which you have written.' Moreover, Moses' intercession for the people begins with some distinction between the two. In 32.33-34, Moses remains aloof from the people's sin. But the results of the sin spell the Lord's absence from the people. And that prospect affects Moses. Thus, in 33.16: 'In what shall it be known then that I have found favor in your sight, *I and your people*? Is it not when you go with *us* that we are set apart, *I and your people*, from all the people who are on the face of the land?'

The intercession assumes a remarkable intimacy between Moses
and God. Moses risks his position as leader and his life itself in order
to negotiate for his people. And that kind of risk calls for trust and
open frankness between Moses and God. Moreover, the text makes
that level explicit by describing the intercession process as a face to
face encounter between Moses and God. The Tent of Meeting
provided the place for the event. Moses would go in there regularly,
and the Lord would meet him there. And there the intimacy occured.
'The Lord would speak to Moses face to face (*pānîm 'el-pānîm*) just
as a man speaks to his friend (*rē'ēhû*)'. To confront God as a man
confronts his friend is to enjoy a unique position. And indeed, this
position founds the intercession process. In v. 12, Moses avers:

> See, you say to me, 'Take this people up', but you have not made
> known to me the one you will send with me. You have said, 'I know
> you by name, and also you have found favor in my eyes'. So now if
> I have found favor in your eyes, make known to me your ways, so
> that I shall be known to you in order that I may find favor in your
> eyes.

Thus, Moses as the intercessor stands for his people before God, and
even offers to share the fate of his people. And the power of his
intercession, rooted in the past traditions of God's acts, but also in
the stature he himself holds with God, succeeds in winning the
concession from God for his continued presence in the exodus. In
33.14, the Lord promises: 'My presence shall go, and I shall give you
rest'. And again in v. 17: 'This word also which you speak I shall do,
because you have found favor in my eyes, and I know you by
name'.

In contrast to the murmuring stage in the history of the wilderness
traditions, an earlier, pre-murmuring stage still leaves its mark in the
received text. This stage of the tradition recounts the same groupings
of narratives according to distinctive elements of content: crisis
posed by enemies, thirst, and hunger. But in this case, the
relationship between people and Moses, and thus between people
and God, is positive.[5] In Ps. 105.40-41, this tradition appears
forcefully: 'He asked and he brought forth quail. With bread from
heaven he satisfied them. He opened a rock, and water flowed. It
moved in the desert like a river'. The third person masculine singular
verb in v. 40, *šā'al*, may have the people in view as the subject. But
the construction is ambiguous, as the variants in the manuscripts and
the Septuagint seem to suggest. Could we not think, therefore, that

the tradition preserved here corresponds to the tradition of the Pentateuch in Numbers 11 and its priestly parallel, Exodus 16? Perhaps the singular masculine subject is Moses. In any case, the presentation preserves an image of the traditions free of the negative perspective in the murmuring. The pattern of the tradition would embrace (1) a description of some kind of crisis, whether an attack by enemies of the wilderness, a threat of death by thirst or hunger, or even a challenge of leadership, (2) a complaint by the people to Moses, not taken in itself as an act of faithless rebellion, but as an act within the rights of the people, (3) an intercession by Moses to the Lord, in effect, a mediation of the people's complaint, and (4) some resolution of the crisis. Typical vocabulary for this stage of the tradition includes the verb 'to cry out' (*ṣā'aq* or *zā'aq*). Again, it is important to note that the act of 'crying out' is not in itself negative. A person of faith has the privilege to complain before God, and thus also before Moses, without being labelled by that fact as a rebel or even as a complainer. And the same verb then describes Moses' plea to God for aid.

Thus, in Exodus 14, the people find themselves blocked from further progress by the waters of the Sea and pressed from behind by the pursuing Egyptians. In the priestly account of the event, continuity within the exodus story emerges from repetition of the hardened heart motif. The Pharaoh changes his mind about sending the Israelites away, deciding rather to pursue them into the wilderness. This account of murmuring or aid is thus not independent of the exodus tradition, a fact suggested also by the key role of the Pharaoh. It is not appropriate to assume, then, that Moses must have been originally in the one account or the other, but not in both. The exodus and the Sea event, along with the other traditions about the wilderness, belong together in a single complex of tradition. And thus they offer equal rootage for the Mosaic figure.

Yet, even for P the scene is not a simple repetition of the signs leading to the Passover.[6] The event at the Sea is not simply a renewed plague. The Israelites do not fall under more severe oppression or languish under a royal decision to hold them in their slavery. Rather, the fruits of the Pharaoh's hardened heart come in a command to the army to pursue the Israelites, now free from the Egyptian's oppression. Moreover, Moses' heroic response to the confrontation does not appear as renewed negotiations, efforts to convince the Pharaoh to allow Israel the privilege of worship in the wilderness. Rather, he must respond by defending his people in the face of danger in the wilderness. Thus, a new phase in the tradition begins. Moses has already led the people to freedom from Egyptian slavery. Now he must defend that freedom in the face of crisis. This same tradition is even more clearly the case for the Yahwist. Egypt and slavery lie in the past. It is not a forgotten past, irrelevant to the present crisis. But the present crisis is a new challenge to the freedom of the people. Now, in the face of that crisis, the people cry out. In v. 10, J reports: 'The Pharaoh drew near. And the Israelites lifted up their eyes and behold the Egyptians were marching after them. They were exceedingly afraid. And the Israelites cried out (*wayyiṣ'ᵃqû*) to the Lord'. There is nothing negative in the cry, no sign of faithless apostasy. The people face a crisis. And as a faithful worshipper cries out in his complaint before God (so, Pss. 77.2; 107.6, 28; cf. also Exod. 3.9), so the faithful Israelites cry for help from God. This cry for help stands in sharp contrast to the murmuring question to Moses in v. 11. And it contrasts also with the choice of service to the Egyptians in v. 12. Rebellion is not the same thing as the question of faith, even the accusation from faith in the complaint. And accordingly, God responds to the cry by giving Moses instructions for resolving the crisis. Indeed, the opening line in v. 15 assumes that the cry to God was mediated by Moses. His intercession in the face of the crisis makes the cry of the people audible to God. It should be clear here that the tradition does not make the aid to the people in the wilderness simply the work of Moses. Moses cannot save his people from the death threatening them in the shape of Egyptian armies. The tale is thus not simply a heroic account of the exploits of Moses. Indeed, the earliest version of this event, the so-called Song of Miriam in 15.21, recounts the occasion of salvation for Israel in the wilderness without reference to any contribution from Moses. It is clear that some tradition in the Old Testament knows of God's mighty acts accomplished for the benefit of Israel without giving any role to Moses. The one side of the tradition completely dominates the other. But what does this fact mean for an evaluation of the Moses traditions? In the mythopoeic form of v. 21, God acts directly. And the couplet makes no assumptions about Moses at all. This tradition must be balanced against the narrative account of the same event. God acts to save his people. And that action is a central body of Old Testament tradition in itself. But the narrative joins that tradition with a Moses image. Moses does not save the people in this facet of the tradition. It is still God's act. But in the same vein, God does not save his people from that death in the wilderness by direct intervention apart from Moses. Moses acts. He follows God's instructions. He makes God's redemption possible. But still the point remains. Moses acts. And the account is not simply a thinly veiled presentation of God's intervention; it is not accurate to say that this narrative does not really depict Moses, but rather only God. To the contrary, Moses emerges as the servant of God who effects God's act. And as a consequence, the conclusion in v. 31 does not highlight the act of God alone. The two stand together. 'Israel saw the great deed which the Lord did against the Egyptians. And the people feared the Lord. And they believed in the Lord and in Moses his servant.' Belief in Moses, like belief in the Lord, is not simply propositional assent. It is commitment to obey, to follow leadership. And it signs the relationship of the people to Moses and the Lord, just as Moses' heroic stature signs his relationship of loyalty and defense for his people.

But would this combination of Moses' heroic deeds and God's acts for his people suggest that the Moses traditions enter the field at a secondary level, that the earliest traditions knew only an account of Yahweh's deeds? This conclusion would not follow necessarily, any more than the argument about the plagues necessarily leads to a conclusion that the original form of the tradition cast Yahweh as the lone wielder of the rod of God. The two facets of the tradition stand more closely together, complementary and not contradictory.

A parallel makes this point more visible. In Num. 11.1-3, the people complain about bad things in the hearing of the Lord (*kᵉmit'ōnᵉnîm raʿ bᵉ'oznê ᵃdōnāy*). This complaint is not equivalent to the murmuring acts, although it sets up a negative point. Because of the complaining, 'the fire of the Lord burned among them and consumed the ends of the camp'. This much of the pericope seems so constructed to account for the name of the place. Thus, the word play between 'burning', *bāᵃrâ*, and the name, *tabʿērâ*, founds the etiology. The point of relevance for the Mosaic tradition lies in v. 2. The people cry out, *wayyiṣʿaq*, to Moses, and Moses then intercedes, *wayyitpallēl*, to the Lord. And because of Moses' defense, the crisis ceased. Thus, the heroic dimension of the Moses tradition becomes the content of the local etiology.

Still another parallel expands the perception of this pattern. In Num. 21.4-9, the storyteller recounts a crisis faced by the people in the wilderness in the form of fiery serpents attacking the people. Yet, here the pattern shifts. The crisis does not provoke the murmuring; rather, the murmuring provokes God to send the crisis as punishment.

The content of the murmuring is general: no food, no water, and hostile reaction to the manna. Murmuring seems therefore to be a more general term, embracing all the problems, rather than a reinterpretation of a tradition that focused on God's aid to the people in various wilderness crises. Yet, the aid stage also appears. The people appeal to Moses for aid, although the typical verb does not appear here. Moses then intercedes for the people. And God provides the aid. In this case, the aid itself seems an expansion of a tale that supports an etiology for the Nehustan, the bronze serpent of the later temple cult (see 2 Kgs 18.4).[7]

The point can be supported by one further step. The description of the event at the Sea reveals images drawn from holy war tradition. This language includes the panic-stricken cry of the Egyptians in 14.25: 'Let me flee from Israel, for the Lord fights for them against the Egyptians'. Holy war imagery clearly affirms that military conflict occurs in response to the Lord. Yet it also includes Moses' speech to the Israelites in v. 13. 'Fear not! stand firm! See the salvation of the Lord which he shall accomplish for you today.' The victory still belongs to the Lord. But the leader has responsibility for his people and thus encourages them: 'Fear not! Stand firm!' And indeed, it is his act with *his* rod or *his* hand that effects the delivery (see v. 16). And his rod or his hand demonstrates his authority in the act. The power of God does not save the people apart from the work of the military hero. Indeed, the military hero, by the power of God, wins the victory in head to head confrontation. That is the character of Mosaic leadership in this narrative.

It is appropriate now to ask what kind of image for Moses appears in the various sources. The Elohist appears here only in fragments. It may be that v. 5a belongs to E because of its special term for the opposition. J normally calls the antagonist the Pharaoh. But the text here uses 'the King of Egypt'. Yet, a simple variation of terms does not apppear to me to be convincing evidence in itself for a distinct source. Why would an ancient writer not vary his vocabulary in the same way a modern writer does? Moreover, v. 5a connects with the tradition about escape from Egypt in the middle of the night, a tradition whose vestiges remain in J. Verse 5a may be E. But if so, it does not suggest that E had a complete, independent account of the event at the Sea. It suggests rather an effort to show why, in v. 5b, the mind of the Pharaoh changed. It would thus be at best an expansion of J. The same point applies for v. 19. To be sure, the verse refers to the angel of God (*mal'ak hā'elōhîm*), a theologoumenon that belongs to the E source according to classical source analysis. And indeed, v. 19a seems to be a doublet in structure to v. 19b. Thus, it may be likely that v. 19a belongs to E. But if that is the case, it does not give us sufficient evidence to warrant reconstruction of a complete and independent source that might have an independent witness for or against the tradition of Moses as hero.

It is not difficult to isolate P from its J or JE counterpart. P appears in vv. 1-4, 8, 9aβb, 15-18, 21aα, 21b-23, 26-27aα, 28-29. In addition, it seems to me likely that vv. 7, 9aα, and 21a may belong to P.[8] On the other hand, it may be fair to question whether vv. 15-16 fit structurally and in content with the J context more appropriately than with the P narrative. If these verses belong to P, they must hide an original J text that ran very nearly in the same direction. In any case, the only possible contribution to the image of Moses as hero comes in the representation of Mosaic intercession, v. 15. Yet, not all of the intercession tradition belongs to P. Both here and in the murmuring texts cited above, the intercessor is a part of the Yahwistic image of Moses. Moreover, Moses intercedes here not as a part of his office in the Tent of Meeting. He intercedes simply as an act of his leadership. Thus, while the wilderness traditions may suggest a tie between Moses the intercessor and a cultic office in the tent, the connection does not seem consistent enough to the overarching tradition to tie down the Mosaic image to only one office. Moses as intercessor is part of the larger folk hero who resists localization in one particular institution.[9]

In Exodus 15, nothing of the Moses tradition appears in the Song of Miriam or the Song of the Sea. Indeed, the narrative introduction to the Song of Miriam, vv. 19-20, refers to Miriam and Aaron but fails to mention Moses. The next relevant pericope for a study of the Moses traditions is vv. 22-26, the tale of aid for the Israelites at the spring called Marah. The characteristics for this pericope correspond exactly to the one about the event at the Sea. Some limited allusion to the murmuring appears in v. 24. But it is only the larger context, where the verb *lûn* appears so obviously as denoting an act of open rebellion, that suggests a negative layer in this unit. Otherwise, the entire narrative appears to be positive.[10] This point applies also for the question in v. 24b. It is not the standard question in the murmuring tradition. To the contrary, it poses simply a request for water. Moreover, Moses' response to the question is governed by the same verb for intercession used in ch. 14: *wayyiṣ'aq 'el-ʾᵃdōnāy*. Moses meets the crisis posed by thirst as an intercessor for the people. And as a result, God shows him a resolution for the crisis. It is the same image, Moses the heroic leader of the people who intercedes with the Lord and wins the power to meet the crisis. And as in Exodus 14, so here that image belongs to J.

In Exod. 17.1-7 again the same pattern of tradition history emerges from the text. The final form of the text features the murmuring motif with its question of rebellion in v. 3. And the question presented by Moses to the Lord in v. 4 reflects the hostile confrontation: 'What shall I do for this people. In a little while, they will stone me'. But in addition to the hostile content of the murmuring stage, there is also a layer in the tradition's history that is positive. The assumption of this position is that the verb, *rîb*, in v. 2 is not necessarily negative and hostile. It can have hostile connotations, as would be suggested by Gen. 13.7 where the noun form of the root connotes strife. But there is no strife in the request controlled by the verb in v. 2. To the contrary, the request is functionally equivalent to the question in 15.24. Its selection here signifies no greater variance in the form of the tradition than an adjustment to meet the etiology for the place name. And accordingly, Moses' response in v. 4 is introduced with the same key verb for the positive tradition about intercession: *wayyiṣ'aq mōšeh 'el-ᵃdōnāy*. It seems to me, therefore, to beg the question about the tradition if the *rîb* element should be translated with the RSV as 'finding fault'. Moreover, the response of God supports the interpretation that would see a positive dimension in this tale. God gives Moses instructions that will resolve the crisis. He is to take *his* rod (*matteᵉkā*) and strike the rock in Meribah in order to produce water. This is the rod of the exodus traditions. But in this case, it seems to be clear that the rod cannot be defined as an exodus motif, but must be understood as an item of the Moses traditions.[11] With his rod Moses follows the instructions of God and thus provides water to meet the crisis.

This pericope with its traditions of murmuring and aid derives from J. The observation should apply to both vv. 2 and 3. The parallel in the priestly source appears in Numbers 20. The tradition is essentially the same. A crisis confronts Israel. The people respond with the murmuring question, although the verb *lûn* does not appear. Then Moses and Aaron together present the case to the Lord at the Tent of Meeting. And God's instructions follow. Moses, with Aaron, should take the rod, just as in the J counterpart. But then the text reports that God instructs Moses to *tell* the rock to yield its water. The remaining part of the pericope unfolds as in the parallel, at least through v. 11 with the successful production of the water. Indeed, v. 11 emphasizes Moses' deed by noting that he struck the rock twice. But v. 12 imposes divine anger on Moses and Aaron. 'Because you did not believe me to sanctify me before the eyes of the Israelites, therefore you shall not bring this congregation into the land which I gave to them.' The sin of Moses and Aaron is apparently their failure to obey. God told them to speak to the rock. But they struck it instead. Nothing like this tedious sin appears in the J parallel. The priestly narrative has changed the tradition in order to account for the strong facet that remembers Moses and Aaron excluded from the land.[12] For the sake of our interest in the heroic, however, it is important to note that while P preserves old tradition that contains the account of Moses' (and Aaron's) leadership and protection, the peculiar priestly tradition is not heroic. To the contrary, Moses' act, in J a part of the heroic image, here is the occasion of his sin and thus the reason that he would not be able to complete his mission.

Exodus 16 reveals a tradition history similar to the one that emerges from Numbers 20. It is essentially a priestly text, the record of God's gift to Israel of manna and quails together. It is dominated by the perspectives of the murmuring tradition. Thus, vv. 2-3 begin with the verb *lûn* and pose the question of rebellion. Verses 6-12 recount the anticipated response from God, in effect, a concession to the demands of the rebels. Indeed, the oracle to be given to the people, v. 12, sounds in itself far more positive than negative, as if it were in answer to Moses' intercession for aid rather than to the murmuring. Moreover vv. 13-18 recount the gift of the food without negative content. Verses 19-27 have in contrast the anger of Moses regarding disobedience by the people. But even this element seems more directly connected to the etiology for the Sabbath than to the murmuring. Thus, P shows a stage of the tradition which is negative but also signs that a positive stage had a role to play in the tradition's history. But the tradition is hardly heroic. There is no intercession by Moses. There is no Mosaic act that establishes the event. To the contrary, the event is effected entirely by God. Moses and Aaron stand before the congregation simply as interpreters. The measure of manna to be kept as a witness to coming generations would suggest the same perspective. It does not remind the people of Moses' act in concert with God. It was to be placed *before the Lord*, and presumably it would remind generations of the aid given the fathers *by the Lord*.

The J parallel to this tradition in Num. 11.4-34 reflects the same tradition history. But the seams in the narrative have been less carefully polished over. The murmuring stage dominates the received text, although again the verb *lûn* is not used. Verse 4a remembers a problem resident in only a portion of the people. And this element leads to the etiology in v. 34. Verse 4b places the problem with the people of Israel again, with their act defined by the verb 'to weep' (*wayyibkû*). 'Weeping' can be an equivalent to the 'cry' for help. Thus, in Judg. 14.16-17, the wife of Samson wept as she petitioned her husband for aid. The weeping is thus not necessarily negative but rather only an intense presentation of a petition. In Numbers 11, the content of the weeping is a wish, similar or even identical to a petition for meat. And the wish is heightened by the memory of meat in Egypt and the stultifying manna in the wilderness. Moses responds in this case not with intercession for the sake of the people, but in anger (v. 10b). But his speech is nonetheless directed to God. And it looks like a classic complaint. Verses 11-12 give in a negative cast a vision of Moses' positive role with the people.

> Why have you done ill to your servant? And why have I not found favor in your eyes to place the burden of all this people on me? Did I conceive all this people? Did I give birth to them that you should say to me, 'Carry them in your bosom, just as a nurse carries the suckling child, to the land which I swore to their fathers'?[13]

Moreover, just here, the content of the people's weeping comes clear. In v. 13: 'For they weep to me saying, "Give us meat, that we may eat"'. This request is formally identical to the request in 17.2: 'Give us water, that we may drink'. And neither one is in itself negative. Verse 18 constitutes the response to the request, a response now cast in a negative light, but originally, in all probability, positive in content. Thus, the play on abundance in vv. 18-20 makes a punishment out of too much of a good thing. The murmuring stage of the tradition thus influences the shape of the received text. But the primary content of the story is positive and depends on the positive stature of Moses' leadership. The final element in the pericope, vv. 31-34, confirms this point. The local etiology in vv. 33-34 connects with v. 1 as a frame around the unit. In contrast, vv. 31-32 depict a positive scene. God provides food for all the camp in sufficient abundance. This element corresponds to Exod. 16.18. Each family gathered in abundance according to the needs of the family.[14]

The spy story in Numbers 13-14 rounds off the scope of the murmuring stories. In this tale, Moses delegates a member from each tribe to enter the promised land and determine (a) the fortification protecting the land and (b) the quality of the land. Thus, 13.17-20 contains the commission: 'Go up into the Negeb yonder, and go up into the hill country, and see what the land is, and whether the people who dwell in it are strong or weak, whether they are few or many'. The spies return with a positive report about the quality of the land. Thus, 13.23 reports that the men 'cut down from there a branch with a single cluster of grapes, and they carried it on a pole between the two of them'. The point is that the land was so fertile that it produced giant fruit. This motif is confirmed by the formulaic epithet in v. 27: 'We came to the land to which you sent us. It flows with milk and honey. And this is its fruit'.

But the spy report also contains a negative account of the land's fortifications. So, in v. 28, the people of the land appear to be almost as large as the fruit. 'The people who dwell in the land are strong and the cities are fortified and very large, and besides, we saw the descendants of Anak there.' Moreover, after Caleb reassures the people that victory lies within their reach, the other spies emphasize the contrary point. 'The land . . . is a land that devours its inhabitants and all the people that we saw in it are men of great stature. And there we saw the Niphilim . . . and we seemed to ourselves like grasshoppers, and so we seemed to them.' A land that devours its inhabitants is a land caught in the destruction of war.[15] And that would mean that the Canaanites would be prepared for attack. The inhabitants are so large, the cities so well fortified that Israel would have no hope for taking the land.

Chapter 14 describes the response of the people. 'All the congregation raised a cry and lifted their voices, and the people wept that night. And all the Israelites murmured against Moses and Aaron'. The pattern for the murmuring motif is, however, broken here, in comparison to all the other instances that feature the murmuring as an overlay on tales about God's aid in the wilderness. (1) The murmuring does not come here as a response to an explicit crisis in the wilderness. To the contrary, it comes in anticipation of a crisis yet to be faced in the land. (2) It does not appear to be a reinterpretation of a tradition about aid to the Israelites. There is no sign of the typical verb from the aid tradition. In fact, at the point in the narration where the appeal for aid might have been expected, the verb is rather 'to cry out' (*bākâ*). The event is thus parallel to the cry in Num. 11.4b. That verb may belong to the aid pattern. Yet, if such a tradition does in fact lie behind the murmuring, it is masked by the almost total domination of the narrative by the murmuring itself.

Verse 2 sets the dominant theme of the murmuring. Death in Egypt would have been better than the death they now face. Or even death in the wilderness would be preferable to meeting the Canaanites. Thus, the anti-Exodus orientation sounds clearly in the scene.[15] Verse 4 then relates this theme explicitly to the leadership of Moses. 'Let us take a leader, so that we may return to Egypt.' Murmuring means displacement of Moses. Indeed, in the face of efforts to reassure, the people announce their intention to stone those who oppose the rebellion. Thus, the opposition to Moses' leadership reaches its most intense point. And it can be broken only by intervention from the Lord himself. That intervention comes in the form of an appearance of the glory (*kābôd*) of the Lord at the Tent of Meeting. The divine speech constitutes a complete and immediate rejection of the people with an announcement of intention to start all over with Moses as the father of the new people. Verses 13-19 contain Moses' intercession. The warrant for Moses' appeal lies in the character of God. (1) God now has a reputation with the people of Egypt. If the people die in the wilderness, God's reputation with the Egyptians will suffer. (2) The attributes of God for steadfast love (*ḥesed*) and forgiveness undergird the appeal to forgive. On the basis of this intercession, God grants pardon and does not slay the people immediately. But the judgment condemns all but Caleb (or, in P, Caleb and Joshua) to die in the wilderness, not in the promised land.

Thus, in this pericope, the heroic dimension of the text remains apparent, even though the level of tradition about Yahweh's aid does not emerge as clearly as in the other items. Indeed, intercession here comes to meet a crisis posed not by the privations of the wilderness or by Israel's enemies, but by God himself. The reflective character of this intercession, vv. 18-19, suggests that this stage depends on the older form of intercession as an appeal for aid. But in either case, the point remains. Moses leads his people through various stages of wilderness life and enables them to endure despite threats that might spell the end of their experience.

In this pericope, J and P have been integrated, with the dominant structure of the unit provided by J. Thus, J appears in 13.17b-20, 22-24, 26-31; 14.1b, 4, 11-25, 39-45.[16] Some of this material may be secondary in J. But these verses nevertheless distinguish the material of the pericope from P. Thus, commission to the spies, the report to the people about a good land but strong people, the cry of the people in response that constitutes rebellion, and indeed, the specific admonition to replace Moses with a new captain, the judgment against the rebels, and Moses' intercession on their behalf all come from J. P duplicates this form but shows no continuing concern to deal with matters of Mosaic leadership. For P, the issue is simply a matter of rebellion against God (so, 14.3). Again, it seems to be clear that the characteristic lines of the heroic tradition have been drawn from the folk tradition by J, but that by the time of P, the interests in such submerge beneath a more dominant emphasis on the leadership of God.

It is appropriate at this point to consider the hypothesis that the Moses traditions in this sequence belong to an organized body of narrative centered on the spring of Kadesh. Was the Moses tradition originally an account of a hero who led his people during a period of time when they were settled at the oasis at Kadesh?[17] And did the invasion from the south not signal a return to the settled life at Kadesh? Martin Noth observes, in my impression, correctly that this suggestion is not convincing. 'The thesis of Eduard Meyer that his [Moses'] traditio-historical provenance was the cult of Kadesh is certainly wrong. For neither in the Pentateuchal narrative itself nor anywhere else in the Old Testament is there a "Kadesh tradition", and even less a tradition about a cult at Kadesh'.[18]

In summary, I conclude that (1) the traditions about the wilderness period now preserved in the Pentateuch focus on the rebellion of Israel against Moses or Moses and Aaron together, and as a consequence, against God. The issue in the rebellion is explicitly leadership. It was Moses' responsibility to lead the people out of Egypt. It is now his responsibility to meet their needs in the wilderness and finally to bring them to the promised land. The rejection by his own people does not detract from the heroic stature of the leader. To the contrary, it assumes that stature by recognizing the established position of Moses as leader, a position attacked by those who happen not to be king of the hill. Such rejection is, in fact, a stereotypical feature of heroic tradition. In addition, Moses shows himself to be the heroic leader of the people by his faithful defense of them in the face of crises posed by hunger, thirst, and enemies. Indeed, that defense comes to its most poignant expression in Moses' intercession for his people before God. In the murmuring tradition, the image of Moses is fully heroic. He transcends whatever intention the tradition may have for showing the failure of the wilderness generation and thus the rejection by God for that rebellious generation and their descendants.

Moreover, (2) behind the rebellion narratives lay a tradition about the wilderness period that remembered God's aid to his people who received it in faithful obedience. This tradition of aid focuses on God's mighty acts for his people, as would be suggested by Psalm 105. In that recitation, Moses and Aaron are the servants of God. They performed the miracles in Egypt. But the substance of the recitation is only the acts of God. Yet I am not prepared to say that the heroic dimension enters the tradition with the rebellion level. The rebellion level may heighten the heroic dimension. But the heroic has a role to play in the positive form of the wilderness stories. Signs of the positive tradition, such as Exod. 15.22-25, suggest that in the positive tradition Moses plays the part of the leader of the people whose intercession met the privations and dangers of the wilderness. At this point, it seems clear to me that the heroic dimension of the Moses tradition is already intrinsic for the tradition at its earliest level.

For J these traditions remain fundamentally heroic. Moses' style of leadership dominates the full scope of the wilderness theme in J. In P, this point is not so obvious. Not only is the pattern of leadership shared more extensively with Aaron but for both the quality of leadership recedes behind the dominating stature of God himself. In P, it is fair to say that Moses and Aaron are really only supporting characters for stories about God's intervention on behalf of his people and his leadership for those people through the wilderness.

Chapter 6

MOSAIC LEGENDS

In contrast to the heroic tales considered to this point, two legends also present an image of the heroic Moses relevant for this evaluation. By legend, I mean a narrative that emphasizes a particular virtue characteristic for the hero rather than an event accomplished by the hero.[1] The legend is far more static than the tale, lacking a moment of complication or an arc of tension as the center of a plot. And its structure accommodates this focus of intention by constructing points of emphasis on the virtue at one or more key positions in the pericope. The intention of the legend would, under normal circumstances, be the edification of the audience. The virtue characteristic for the hero might become the virtue characteristic for all the audience willing to imitate the model. The legend lends itself to heroic tradition by virtue of its focus on the character of the hero. The heroic tale declares what the hero has done. The heroic legend describes who the hero is. Yet not all legends would fall automatically into the category of the heroic. Again, definitive for the heroic dimension would be the tendency of the narrative to identify the principal with his people and thus to show that the hero serves the best interest of the people. A heroic legend would, then, depict the characteristic virtue of a figure that marks him as a hero *for the people*.

1. *Exod. 17.8-13*
One of the principal areas typical for heroic legend is the military conflict.[2] The pericope in Exod. 17.8-13 describes a military conflict. But significantly, its structural focus does not highlight the battle. It is not a battle report. To the contrary, v. 8 notes that the battle occurred in quite general terms: 'Amalek came and fought with Israel

at Rephidim'. But the story moves beyond the battle to a different interest. In v. 9, Moses instructs Joshua: 'Choose men for us and go out to fight against the Amalekites. Tomorrow I will station myself on the top of the hill and the rod of God will be in my hand'. Verse 10 makes the same division. Verse 10a reports the battle in general terms. But v. 10b turns the attention of the audience to the top of the hill. Verse 11 then makes the concern for the hilltop clear. By his act on the hilltop, Moses influences the rise and fall of the battle. Thus, it is by Moses' act that victory over the Amalekites can be won. Yet, still, the focus of the legend is not simply on Moses' act, delivering the battle to victory for Israel. It is rather on the endurance of the hero in the face of his tiring duty. The endurance, the ability to stick to the task when human strength fades, is the virtue at the center of the legend. Thus, v. 12a reports the problem challenging Moses' ability to endure. Moses' hands grow weary, and his assistants support him. Their support does not detract from the heroic quality of Moses's endurance.[3] Rather, their support simply enables the hero to complete his task. Then, v. 12b confirms the virtue. 'His hands were steady (*ᵉmûnâ*) until the sun set.' In this military encounter, Moses stayed by his post until the job was complete. Moreover, the endurance demonstrated by Moses was not simply a private integrity or even a matter of business ethics. Rather, it served his people. Verse 13 makes this point clear. 'Joshua disabled the Amalekites and their people with the edge of the sword.' Moses' endurance with his faithful hands enabled Joshua to win the victory. This is not a Joshua story, although Joshua fought and won the battle. It is a Moses story.

Moreover, the legendary quality of the virtue is not simply resident in the relationship between Moses and Joshua or even between Moses and people. Moses was a man of integrity. And it is no embarrassment for the tradition to allow that virtue to stand on its own merit. Moses was a man of quality fit for the edification of his people. And perhaps here lies the strongest dimension of the heroic for this legendary figure.

One particular point of interest deserves attention. Verse 9 observes that Moses should go to the hill with the 'rod of God' (*maṭṭēh hā*ᵉ*lōhîm*) in his hand. The rod of God is doubtlessly the same instrument of Mosaic leadership central for the traditions about the plagues and the event at the Sea or the spring from the rock. At those points, I argued that the rod belonged essentially to the Moses traditions, not to the Aaron tradition, and that it represented the authority of Moses before the Pharaoh or before the people. It was the instrument for effecting the signs and miracles. Here the rod functions in exactly the same way. It represents the authority of Moses, his endurance to achieve victory over the enemy. That the rod here is called the 'rod of God' refers the authority of the hero to its divine origin. It is precisely in this combination that the distinctive unity between heroic man and man of God can be seen most clearly. But the combination reminds the audience that this very duality is characteristic for the Moses tradition at various key points, as I have suggested above. Finally, the rod of God in the hand of Moses at this point demonstrates further that the rod cannot be limited to an exodus tradition. It is characteristic for Moses wherever Moses appears.

The pericope closes with two etiological notes. The first puts the emphasis of the unit on a perpetual hostility with Amalek. The second accounts for the origin of an altar, again with focus on hostility toward Amalek. In both cases, the additions change the character and, indeed, the genre of the unit. With these changes, the unit loses sight of its attention to the virtue of Moses and, in its place, concentrates on the relationship of Yahweh with Amalek. But the two seem clearly to be additions to the narrative, not an original part of the legend.

2. *Num. 12.1-15*

This pericope apparently represents another in the collection of traditions about opposition to Moses' leadership. Thus, Aaron and Miriam complain about Moses' exclusive rights as the one to deliver God's word. Behind this stage of formalized and rather general opposition may lie a tradition of Miriam's opposition to Moses because of his marriage to a Cushite woman. Yet, in the present form of the narrative, the oppposition to Moses serves only as the occasion for emphasis on Moses' virtue as leader of the people. It thus qualifies as a Moses legend.[4]

The legendary quality of the pericope appears first in v. 3. 'The man Moses was very "meek", more so than any person on the face of the earth.' The key term for the virtue, 'meek' or 'humble', *'ānāw*, is not, however, a term connoting an inner, private virtue. Nor does it suggest that the leader Moses is reticent or self-effacing. To the contrary, the term connotes integrity in the execution of duty. Moses is the leader above all leaders on the earth who sticks to the responsibilities of his job.

But what, precisely, does it mean for a leader to maintain integrity in his leadership? This pericope makes the point clear. In each element of structure, it underlines the responsibility Moses carries. Thus, following the introduction of the principals in the story in vv. 1-2, v. 3 affirms Moses as 'meek'. The next element describes a confrontation between the Miriam-Aaron axis and God. This element features a Yahweh speech affirming the authority of Moses. And significantly, it describes Moses as responsible. In v. 7, the Lord says: 'Not so for my servant Moses. In all of my house, he is responsible (*ne'ĕmān*)'. This word belongs to the same root as the key term in Exod. 17.12 and thus contributes to the same imagery of a leader whose work can be trusted. Then, in confirmation of Moses' authority to lead the people, and in anger for the rebellion, God strikes Miriam with leprosy, doubtlessly a concession to the older form of the tradition that remembered only Miriam as the subject of the rebellion (see v. 1, with its third-person feminine singular verb).

Yet, still the question remains. In what manner is Moses trustworthy in the house of God? The third element of structure brings Moses' honor into focus. In v. 11 Aaron appeals to Moses for mercy on Miriam. And Moses responds with intercession, rebellious though she was. His responsibility for the one he leads proves stronger than any notion for revenge against her. Thus, he prays for healing. And the response from God brings the confrontation to a happy conclusion. After an appropriate period for cleansing, Miriam returned to the camp and the people continued their journey. It should be noted here that Moses' ability to facilitate healing is tied directly to the issue of his authority among his people.

Both legends belong to the Yahwist, although analysis of Numbers 12 remains problematic.[5] It would nevertheless appear to be clear that the heroic dimension represented by the legends fits into the heroic pattern now clearly documented in the Yahwist. At least it is clear that the priestly source does not employ this genre of narrative for Moses. In both legends, Moses appears as the hero of the people. He demonstrates integrity for completing his responsibilities as leader of the people in the face of physical limitations or community opposition. In such virtue lies the honor of heroic leadership. It is not an honor sought for personal gain or glory. It is an honor of responsible fulfillment of duty. And it is that context that makes greater sense of tradition like Prov. 15.33 and 18.12. The honor of integrity goes before publicly bestowed honor.

Chapter 7

MOSES IN THE SINAI TRADITIONS: EXODUS 19-34

In the present form of the Moses saga, the Sinai traditions do not
represent a distinct segment of narrative tradition. It is possible, for
example, to recognize a narrative shift from the theme of the exodus
out of Egypt to the theme of the wanderings in the wilderness
specifically at 13.17. But the narrative in ch. 19 does not shift from
the theme of the wilderness. To the contrary, it is introduced by an
itinerary formula in v. 2 and a precise date in v. 1. Both serve to bind
the following unit of narrative into the structure of the wilderness
theme. I do not intend to say that there is no traditio-historical
distinction between the wilderness theme and the Sinai traditions. I
mean only to observe that in the present narrative, the Sinai pericope
beginning in ch. 19 is considered as one of the elements embraced by
the wilderness itinerary.[1]

The pericope itself has stimulated extensive discussion in the
circles of Old Testament scholarship.[2] Part of the problem can be
identified by a brief discription of structure. Following the itinerary
and date, the narrative begins without exposition as a report of
Moses' journey up to the mountain of God. Then a divine speech
presents an introduction for the people as a whole to the relationship
with God characterized explicitly as 'covenant'. Verse 4 contains the
precondition for the relationship. God has already acted in the
exodus and the wilderness. It is perhaps significant to note the image
of the eagle's wings as a symbol of God's protective care for his
people in the wilderness (cf. Deut. 32.11-14).

Verses 5-6 then connect the past events with conditions for the
covenant. Verse 6b seems to be an introduction to specific laws:
'These are the words. . . ' The laws would be cast as stipulations for
maintaining a relationship with God already established by his

redemption of the people from the bondage of Egypt. Moses then returns to the people with the laws as yet unspecified by the text. The people respond, v. 8, with agreement. And v. 9a confirms the authority of Moses in the process.

Verses 9b-10 shift to a new process, however, for here the ritual concerns preparation of the people to appear directly before God, not simply before Moses. Moses mediates the words of the people to Yahweh, and the results are instructions from Yahweh for the people to appear at the mountain. In v. 14, Moses goes back down the mountain in order to execute the ritual. The theophany itself begins in v. 15 with storm imagery and a ritual trumpet blast. The people assemble, but the imagery shifts to volcanic patterns. Then God appears at the top of the mountain and summons Moses alone to him. The conversation concerns first a confirmation of the restrictions on the position of the people, with Moses reminding God that the restrictions were already in operation (v. 23). Then instructions to Moses send him back to secure that position, then to return with Aaron.

The decalogue follows in 20.1-17, although it may be out of place. 20.18-20 is an appeal from the people to Moses to serve as mediator, an appeal that might fit more appropriately after 19.25. Verse 21 assumes the position of Moses in vv. 18-20, however, and introduces the Covenant Code. Thus, regardless of the original position of 20.18-20, the function for confirming Mosaic authority for lawgiving remains. The people have asked Moses to represent them in the developing relationship between people and God. And Yahweh gives the Covenant Code directly to Moses (compare Hammurabi).

Chapter 24 then concludes the account of the theophany and reports the agreement of the people to abide by the terms of the law. A sacrificial ritual binds the covenant relationship, with v. 8 as a concluding performative formula. Verses 9-11 report the final theophany and the covenantal meal. Verses 12-18 are related to the scene but seem to be an extension of the account in order to structure the remaining layers of Sinai tradition into this central element. Moses goes up the mountain again in order to receive the law and commandments. The following tradition, Exodus 25-31, contains a relatively late collection of laws and cultic regulations, placed here in order for them to function for Israel under the stamp of Mosaic authority. Exodus 32-34 conclude the longer episode with an account of Israel's apostasy over the Golden Calf, Moses' intercession, and a renewed confirmation of the Mosaic authority. Moses returns to the people, transfigured by his intimate relationship with God. And the transfiguaration motivates creation of a veil so that Moses can continue his work before his people without striking fear in them. The veil would, in a fashion, function as a visible and concrete symbol of Mosaic authority derived from his intimacy with God. The veil might then be defined as a symbol for Mosaic authority, derived from Moses' presence with God, and thus ranked along side the rod as a symbol of Moses' stature. Moreover, that authority stands at the foundation of the covenant.

Brevard Childs has described the character of this narrative:

> Moses is pictured as ascending and descending Mount Sinai at least three times without any apparent purpose. At times the people are pictured as fearful and standing at a great distance from the mountain, whereas at other times there are repeated warnings which are intended to prevent any of them from breaking forth and desecrating the sacred mountain. Again, the description of God seems to fluctuate between his actually dwelling on the mountain and only descending in periodical visits. Finally, the theophany is portrayed both with the imagery of volcanic smoke and fire as well as with that of the clouds and thunder of a rainstorm.[3]

Efforts to resolve this duplicity in the narrative have focused on separation of the patterns into two literary sources. The various proposals, summarized effectively by Childs, have, however, failed to produce a convincing, or even a singular position that might explain the tension. Childs concludes, in my opinion correctly:

> The point of this criticism is not to suggest that there are no literary tensions in the text, but rather that the traditional source division is unable to cope with them in this chapter. It seems quite clear in the earlier part of the chapter that there is repetition—one thinks of the preparation, washing, third day—but the elements of the duplication are so similar as to prevent a sharp division. This leads one to suggest that different traditions were already combined in the oral stage of transmission which accounts for much of the tension. Moreover, even if the literary strands, such as J and E, are present in ch. 19, they share so much of the same oral tradition that a separation is unlikely and without great significance.[4]

The alternative to source divisions for addressing the tensions in the text would thus appear to be a traditio-historical one. Combination of distinct traditions at an oral level must have produced the obvious tensions in the narrative. Thus, the crucial question for this pericope emerges: Is there any indication of complex tradition elements whose characteristics can be traced in recognizable patterns to some common or complementary point of origin? Or does the evidence suggest competing and even contradictory traditions? One possibility for such a pattern would be the one formulated under a hypothesis that the ritual process for covenant renewal can account for the primary characteristics in one facet of the text, while the office connected with the Tent of Meeting might account for the other.[5]

It is obvious that covenant tradition plays some kind of role here. And various kinds of parallels have been advanced in order to substantiate the suggestion.[6] Following McCarthy, Childs argues convincingly that the discussion of tradition in Exodus 19 as a narrative rooted in a treaty covenant pattern is inadequate.

> It would seem, therefore, that Gressmann was correct in suggesting that the covenant form in 19.3-8 reflects a secondary development within the Sinai tradition which received its clearest expression in Deuteronomy. Regardless of how old its roots may be in Israel— the dating of vv. 3-8 is uncertain—it did not play the central role which it has been assigned. Nor does it provide the key to understanding the traditions behind Ex 19.[7]

Rather than the patterns of a treaty document, the tradition in the chapter shows a marked internal tension in its representation of Moses and his relationship to the people. On the one hand, Moses led the people to the base of the mountain in order to establish a covenant between them and God. But the people recoil in fear and appeal to Moses to stand for them before God (20.18-20). On the other hand, the purpose of the theophany was explicitly to legitimate Moses (19.9). Thus, for Childs, the tensions in this pericope arose because two different concepts of Moses' office were joined at an oral level. The one legitimates Moses by reference to the people's request for his mediation. The other accomplishes that goal by referring to God's intention from the beginning. Childs then ties each line of the tradition to a particular office as the setting for the tradition. The concept of the office which depicts Moses legitimated directly by God would derive from the institution of the Tent of Meeting, while the concept of Moses as a mediator established by the appeal of the people to stand for them before God reflects the ritual of covenant renewal.

How can these two images of the Mosaic office be interpreted? It is incorrect, so it seems to me, to relate the one image to J and the other to E. Childs depends in part on older criticism by alluding to the office of Moses as covenant mediator, established by request of the people, as a part of the E source, and to the tradition which sought to legitimate the Mosaic office from the outset as a J formulation. Yet he breaks with the older consensus by suggesting that the two forms of the tradition about the Mosaic office were joined at a pre-literary stage and that this joining accounts for the tensions in the text. 'In sum, although one can at times still distinguish between two literary sources, J and E, there is every reason to suspect that the real tension in the narrative arose from a complex history of tradition lying behind and reflected in both literary strands.'[8]

If Childs's analysis of the Mosaic tradition in this pericope is essentially correct, then this material would contribute substantially to the pattern of the Moses tradition developed to this point. Two images of Moses emerge from the tradition. One has Moses confirmed in his position as leading the people by request of the people after they experienced the awesome presence of God. The other sets Moses before the people as their leader because God chose him for the task. Three questions must, nevertheless, be seriously explored. (1) Are the two conceptions of the Mosaic office in fact contrasting, even contradictory? Or are they in some manner complementary? (2) Must the two be related to two distinct settings in Israel's communal life? Or do they share a common setting and a common intention? Particularly if the two should be complementary, it would be difficult to defend a thesis that they derive from two contrasting settings. If they should be complementary, would the point of their origin not reflect complementary settings, if not a single common setting? And at this point, I would raise a question about the validity of a thesis that must seek the origin of the images for Moses in a sociological institution. Is it not feasible that such images derive from a traditional convention of folkloristic or even literary circles for depicting leaders, any leaders? (3) Do the two reflect the competing interests of two different literary sources? Or does the duplication derive from the process of formulation in the history of the Moses tradition, from the dynamics of storytelling among the folk?

The key texts for substantiating a hypothesis about the two distinct offices for Moses are Exod. 19.9 and 20.18-22. In 19.9, the Lord announces his intentions to legitimate Moses before the people. Indeed, the purpose of the announced coming event is to insure 'that the people may hear when I speak to you and may believe *you* forever'. A similar collocation occurs in Exod. 14.31. In that text an explicit duplicity appears in the tradition. The event occurs in order that the people might believe in the Lord and in Moses. And that act means that the people would follow the leadership of both in obedience and trust. In this text the act is directed explicitly toward Moses and is designed to secure the obedience of the people to Moses' leadership forever. It is appropriate, also, to connect this tradition to the legitimation of Moses with the shining face in Exodus 34 as well as the Mosaic role of intercession for the people. Moses exercises the authority bestowed on him by God when he leads his people under the stamp of this validation.

20.18-20, on the other hand, is controlled by a different perspective. The difference, however, is not qualified primarily by the people's initiative but rather by the goal of the task Moses must face. 'Speak to us and we will obey. But do not let God speak to us, lest we die.' Moses still stands in a relationship of authority-obedience to the people. But the result of the relationship will not secure the people's belief, i.e. obedience to Moses. Rather, Moses places the people into the experience of 'fear of the Lord'. And his task is to elicit an obedience from the people to God. 'Moses said to the people: "Do not fear; for God has come to test you, that the *fear of him* may be before your eyes, that you may not sin".' Here the primary focus is on the relationship between people and God. And Moses facilitates the relationship. I submit, therefore, that the two images are complementary, not contradictory. The one relates a goal for securing the belief of the people in Moses. The other seeks to establish their 'fear' of God. The terms are parallel, just as in Exod. 14.31 the terms are parallel and complementary.

Moreover, the one image appears harmonious with the heroic tradition of Moses, while the other gives expression to the tradition of God's mighty acts. It should be clear now that the tradition is not simply a matter of Moses' acts *vis à vis* God's acts but a matter of Moses' position as leader of his people *vis à vis* Moses' position as representative of God to the people. That tradition which focuses on God's mighty acts on Israel's behalf contributes to the Moses image by painting Moses as a mediate authority for the affairs of the Israelites. Indeed, it is just in this position that the traditional function of Moses as lawgiver comes most to the fore. Moses requires obedience from the people. And the law is the law of Moses. But the law derives from God. Thus, the two cannot be separated into isolated offices. Both the heroic man with his own personal authority calling for belief of the people in him and the mediator for God with the authority of God to call for obedience from the people to God constitute the shape of the Moses image in the Pentateuch.[9] That shape is also the structure of Exodus 19–34. The double image of Moses appears to be fundamental for this section of the Sinai tradition.

Deut. 5.4–5 is a critical text for controlling the adequacy of any hypothesis regarding the image of Moses in Exodus 19–34. Childs describes the linguistic characteristics of these two verses, then poses his formulation of the issue presented by them.

> Verse 4 speaks of Yahweh's direct communication of the Decalogue to the people. The phrase 'face to face' emphasizes especially the lack of any mediation, whereas v. 5 suggests just the opposite. Moses acted as mediator. Moreover, the motivation clause in v. 5b supplies the reason for Moses' role by recalling the people's plea from Exodus 20.18ff.[10]

There can be no doubt that some kind of tension emerges from the juxtaposition of these two verses. In the one God and people speak face to face. And Moses has no apparent role. In the other Moses stands between God and people in order to resolve the break-down among the people in the face of the fire on the mountain. Indeed, Exod. 33.11, a text related to the complex of traditions about Moses, suggests that the 'face to face' relationship describes the Yahweh-Moses bond rather than the Yahweh-people bond. Now, the question must be whether these two apparently contradictory representations do in fact reflect competing images and, ultimately, competing institutions, or whether they stand in some kind of complementary relationship. My hypothesis is that the perspectives of Exod. 19.9 and 20.18-20 facilitate an interpretation. In the one facet of the tradition, the text affirms that the Lord acted so that the people would believe (and obey) him. This facet relates to Deut. 5.4. The other side of the tradition suggests that the events occurred in order to secure belief in Moses. And here Deut. 5.5 finds its point of contact. The two facets would thus function as complements in accord with an extensive portion of Pentateuchal tradition, not as indications of opposing images and institutions.

This explanation of the relationship between two images of tradition regarding people, Moses, and God leaves at least one major problem unattended. The two facets can be represented as images of

God's relationship with the people established through Moses' mediatorial role and God's relationship with the people established without reference to Moses. Is there a tradition about God's mighty acts on behalf of his people that lived quite apart from and independent of Moses? Or does the tradition about God's mighty acts on behalf of his people, designed to secure the people's belief in the Lord, constructed from tradition about a face to face relationship between God and people, embrace Moses as a primary part of the tradition? The question here is not whether Moses belonged originally to the exodus or the wilderness or Sinai. It is whether Moses is secondary to *all* of the themes of tradition about God's mighty acts. In this case, Deut. 5.4 would be representative of a tradition about God's mighty acts that has no contribution to the Moses traditions at all, while Moses the mediator appears in 5.5. In what manner can the tradition of God's mighty acts complement the tradition of Moses as hero? The question is not the same one confronted in consideration of Moses' call to his vocation, in the plague narratives, and again in the account of the event at the sea. The complementary role of the two poles at each point has been observed. This relationship, however, is not simply 'God's acts' in contrast to 'Moses' acts'. It is rather a construction of tradition about Moses' acts designed to elicit the people's faith and obedience in God. Without the one pole, the heroic Moses would tend to exaggerate the stature and work of the hero until the tradition becomes myth and Moses a god. Without the other pole, the man of God would collapse into a docetic image of a tool by an omnipotent God without reference to the freedom and individual contribution of the person. In order to see the full form of the Moses traditions, the two poles must be held in delicate tension. But the question here is whether the tradition about God's mighty acts has pulled Moses secondarily into the field of confessions. The issue relates to the origin of the Moses traditions, specifically to the question about whether the God's mighty acts tradition necessarily requires the figure of Moses. If we observe traditions about God's mighty acts without Moses, is it necessarily true that we must invent a mediator by the same name in order properly to round those traditions out?

This question could be resolved by Childs's thesis about the office of Moses. If we could say that Moses traditions belong from the beginning to some cultic office like the Tent of Meeting or a covenantal mediator, then we would have a basis for affirming that at least here Moses complements the acts of God as a primary part of the tradition. But again, some problem confronts the hypothesis. In what detail can an office for the institution represented by the Tent of Meeting be reconstructed? James Muilenburg sees the role of Moses as intercessor more closely tied to the office of covenant mediator,[11] in contrast to Childs's separation between covenant mediator and the intercessor at the Tent of Meeting. Joshua succeeds Moses, thus suggesting some official capacity handed down from generation to generation. And Joshua 24 has him functioning in the role of covenant mediator. But where is his office of intercession? It is clear that some conscious patterning of the Joshua tradition on the basis of the Moses stories has occurred. But was that done because Joshua or the Joshua traditions belonged to the same institutional office as Moses, the office of covenant mediator? Or was the parallel established by a literary process? Does the image of Moses as intercessor derive from a standing office that traced its lineage to him? Or does it derive from the interests of heroic folk tradition to cast him as a man for his people? Childs cites the cultic flavour of the image as evidence for influence on the image from the office of covenant mediator.[12] There is no doubt that in the traditions Moses mediates the covenant to the people. But what evidence suggests that the image derives from an established cultic office? Where is the *office* at the time of Hezekiah or Josiah? It may be that Josiah himself functions as mediator of a covenant. But is that function an element of responsibility for a standing office? Or does Josiah assume the authority to act this way as an *ad hoc* function, something the leader can do not because of office or institution but because of the necessities confronting the leader. Where is the continuing dimension?

James Muilenburg argued for a continuity of office for the cultic prophet, an office that traced its lineage back to Moses in keeping with Deut. 18.15-18.[13] The cultic prophet had responsibility as covenant mediator. And the mediator was the speaker for the oral recitation of the tradition preserved in Deuteronomy. Yet there are problems. Reconstruction of a cultic prophet is notoriously hypothetical.[14] Moreover, the image of Moses is larger than prophet. Deut. 18.15-18 seems clearly to relate a succession of prophets to Moses. But this text says more about the image of the prophets than it does about a setting or formative influence for the image of Moses. Indeed, Num. 12.6-7 sets Moses in contrast to the prophets. But then one must ask about setting, even for the prophetic dimension in the Moses traditions. Where is the cultic dimension at all? Even in

Joshua 24, Moses' successor does what he does as leader of the people in a unique event.

The issue at stake, however, is not whether there was a cultic prophet or an office of covenant mediator. It is not even whether Moses mediates the covenant to the people. It is whether a standing office has influenced the shape of the Moses traditions. Is a cultic office of covenant mediator the proper *Sitz im Leben* for this facet of the Moses tradition? Or was the tradition shaped basically by a popular literary process as a narrative convention for depicting the leader with at best only tangential contacts with the cult?

The same question must be raised about the office of intercessor at the Tent of Meeting.[15] Exod. 33.7-11, and even more 34.34, do indeed describe habitual action. Childs's remarks about the character of these texts as indicators of a Mosaic office are effective.[16] Yet, the question must be whether they describe action which an official in the cult regularly performed, patterned then as a typical function of Moses. Or do they intend simply to describe the regular, habitual action of Moses? Moses wears the veil following his address to the people because his face shines with the transfiguration effected by God's presence. In what manner is that symbol a symbol of an office that might lie behind the unique work of Moses described in these texts?[17] Is the symbol not peculiar to the Moses image? Does not the fact that the word 'veil' (*masweh*) appears only in this pericope suggest a special Mosaic symbol, not the symbol of an office? The heroic man transfigured by the presence of God, the man whose face shines with the light of God's presence, is uniquely the man of God. The tradition that depicts the shining face, indeed, that emphasizes the veil as a symbol of the hero, presents the hero as a person with divine authority to lead the people (cf. Mt. 17.1-8 and parallels). But that depiction does not arise from a standing office in the cult, just as the image of the transfigured Jesus does not reflect a standing office in the cult. The concern of the transfiguration scene, whether in the Moses tradition or in the Jesus tradition, is to paint a picture of the leader who carries the authority of God for his community.[18] Thus, the question again is not so much whether an office in the institution of the Tent of Meeting existed or whether it exerted influence on the shape of the Moses image. It is rather whether the *Sitz im Leben* for the Moses tradition is the Tent of Meeting as a cultic institution. My impression is that these two facets are not properly to be attributed to two distinct cultic offices as different *Sitze im Leben*, as competing facets, but rather that they should be taken as complementary poles in a common literary, folk tradition. Moses is heroic man. But he is also the man God.

As support for this position, I would argue that the principal shape of the Moses image is not one that would be harmonious with a cultic office, even with the habitual action described in this text. Rather, the primary characteristic of the Moses image in these narratives is his position as leader of the people, the one who acts just as God acts for the benefit of the people. That facet might also be a part of a cultic office. After all, the intercessor or the mediator would work for the boons of the people. But if that were a part of an official figure, set in an institution like the Tent or a covenant renewal ceremony, why would the early texts that might have contact with the cult make no reference to Moses? The Song of Miriam, the Song of Moses, even the historical credos (should they be old and thus relevant to this comment) describe the acts that bring boons to Israel as the acts of God. The earliest references to Moses as such a leader, including the representation of him as a covenant mediator and intercessor, appear in J. I do not intend to suggest that J invented the heroic Moses, much less the historical Moses. The heroic form of Moses may be as old as the confession of the exodus under Yahweh's leadership. But if it is, the evidence for its age must be reconstructed if not simply asserted. The point, however, is that insofar as setting is concerned, Moses as leader in heroic form emerges first in a literary construct. The literary, folkloristic depiction of this tradition about Israel's salvation cannot be imagined without Moses. And indeed, Moses may be implied at all points, even in the cultic forms. But in fact, Moses appears first and strongest in a literary setting. The literature describes him as heroic man and man of God. And it does so not because the image fits any particular office or any particular institution, but because that image was a folkloristic convention for narrating the deeds of past leaders.

If this position is justified, then references to Moses outside the context of the Pentateuchal tradition ought not to undercut it. Martin Noth makes quick reference to the few allusions that might fall into this category.[19] By and large, references to Moses outside the Pentateuch constitute a continuation of the Pentateuchal tradition. Judg. 1.16 and 4.11 might be a distinct, although related allusion to the father-in-law tradition; yet, even if these are old references to Moses, they tell us more about the tradition of a Kenite father-in-law than they tell us about Moses. The allusion to Moses in 2 Kgs 18.4 might be independent of the Pentateuchal form of the tradition, according to Noth. And if it is, some setting for Moses in a cultic context is open.[20] A cultic object owes its origin to Moses. But it takes the narrative elaboration of the tradition according to the patterns of Yahweh's aid and Israel's murmuring to place this tradition in its apparent function as an instrument for healing and thus for authority within the community itself. And the narrative elaboration places the tradition into the patterns of Yahweh's aid and Israel's murmuring, thus, into the larger heroic patterns of the Moses saga. Perhaps the point of origin for this tradition is cultic, not narrative and folkloristic. But the tie remains obscure. Judg. 18.30 suggests that the priesthood of Dan derived from a Mosaic heir. But nothing appears here that might contribute in substance to the Mosaic image itself. Again, some tie to cultic origins might be here. But if so, they remain obscure. Ps. 90.1 identifies Moses as the man of God. But as the ascription to the Psalm, it tells us nothing about what a man of God is. In Deut. 33.4, in the Blessing of Moses, Moses is described as a lawgiver. And this allusion might constitute an independent witness to the early form of Moses in the tradition. But even should it be independent of the Pentateuchal sources, the image of Moses is like the image in the Sinai elements of the tradition. And nothing in the poem itself requires that the image be attached to a cultic provenance. Frank Cross follows Wellhausen in suggesting that 33.8 may also be an allusion to Moses and that the allusion places Moses as a Levite into an institutional position as priest. But this interpretation seems to me to be weak: there is no reference to Moses by name in this verse and the context implies that the subject of the allusion is Levi.[21]

Finally, Josh. 9.24 places Moses into the context of conquest concerns, like the ones described above for Numbers. It would seem to me to be clear, then, that while the literary concerns of J clearly do not account for the origin of the Moses traditions, they nonetheless can give us some insight into the primary setting at least for the heroic shape of the Moses figure. The allusions to Moses defined by Noth as in some manner independent of the Pentateuchal sources offer no single institutional setting for the Moses figure. Contact with an office appears at best minimal. Perhaps Moses traditions do suggest some tie with the cult. But no details emerge. Would the clearest point be the lawgiver of Deut. 33.4? And it may well be that the connection between Moses the lawgiver and the institutional position of the law proclaimer noted above derives not so much from a common cultic tie as from a common folkloristic form for describing both.

It is possible, now, to return to the question about the relationship between Deut. 5.4 and 5.5. Verse 4 represents that facet of the tradition focused on God's mighty acts, a description that makes no reference to Moses. Verse 5 introduces Moses as a complement to the tradition about God's acts. It is not heroic. It represents Moses' role for the tradition about God's great acts.

Thus, two facets in the Moses tradition, reflected by the narrative in Exodus 19–34, seem the better interpreted if they can be related to the two facets of Moses tradition apparent in texts considered earlier. In the one facet, Moses functions as leader of the people. And his deeds inspire belief and obedience from the people for his work. The other presents Moses as the chosen of God whose task is to inspire belief and obedience for God's work. Intercession belongs to the former, although it is not out of place in the latter. Responsibility as lawgiver belongs to the latter, although again it is not out of place for the former. In these two facets, one image is heroic. Moses acts. And the people respond to him in belief and obedience. That facet does not contradict the tradition of God's mighty acts. It is a complement. The other image facilitates belief and obedience from the people for God. That facet does not, so it seems to me at this point, contradict the form and character of the heroic image. It is a complement. But the details of this complement have yet to be worked out.

Two additional points about the Sinai traditions call for some consideration at this position in the discussion:

1. The Sinai traditions include more than Exodus 19–34. The entire scope of the Old Testament law, with all of its layers in tradition history, comes into play under this rubric. The complex thus runs from Exodus 19 through Numbers 10. In this expansive collection of laws, with reformulations and additions attesting the vitality of the law over generations, the focus of attention falls on God's relationship with the people. The contribution of the collection to the Moses tradition is the depiction of Moses as lawgiver. For each generation responsible for formulating the law relative to its own situation, to claim its formulation as Mosaic was primarily an assertion of authority for the formulation. It is an act of veneration for Moses, to be sure. But it is first of all a recognition that each law properly must rest on Mosaic foundation if it is to have authority in the community.[22] Thus, Moses stands as the mediator of God's law. And the law is represented as God's will for the people.

This point is clear for the early levels of legal tradition. For the Covenant Code, for example, Moses receives the law and addresses it to the people. But it is the law of God, and the first person formulation (Exod. 20.22) is the first person of God. Moses speaks the word of Yahweh. Moreover, key terms in the tradition, such as *miṣwâ* or *ḥōq*, tie directly to Yahweh (Exod. 18.16; Deut. 8.1, 2). Yet, the identification of the law suggests a double character. Particularly in the later stages of the tradition, the term *tôrâ* reveals the double character of the law. It is constructed most often in a dependent bond with Yahweh or Elohim (Exod. 13.1; Josh. 24.26; Isa. 5.24; Hos. 4.6; Amos 2.4; Neh. 8.8; *et al.*). But the important role of Moses stands close at hand (see Neh. 8.18; 9.3; 10.29; 2 Chron. 34.14; *et al.*). Indeed, on at least fifteen occasions, the word is also constructed in a dependent bond with the name Moses. In some of these texts, the relationship between the Torah of Moses and the authority of Yahweh is tautological. The Torah of Moses has authority precisely because it is the Lord's Torah (2 Kgs 14.6; 23.25; Neh. 8.1, 14; Ezra 7.6). But on other occasions, the Torah of Moses clearly has authority because it comes from the mouth of Moses (Josh. 8.31, 32). Thus the collocation, *tôrat mōšeh*, becomes an expression for the law itself, the law identified by the contribution, indeed, the creation of Moses (Josh. 23.6; 1 Kgs 2.3; 2 Kgs 14.6; 23.25; Mal. 3.22; 2 Chron. 23.18; 30.16; Ezra 3.2; 7.6; Neh. 8.1, 14; Dan. 9.11, 13). And in a parallel fashion, *miṣwat mōšeh*, in 2 Chron. 8.13 suggests an origin from the lips of Moses. Thus, the two-fold nature of the Moses traditions seems confirmed by the traditional designation of the law, at least in the later stages of tradition elements. Moses the lawgiver mediates the Lord's words to the people. But at the same time tradition remembers the words as distinctively the work of Moses.

In what manner is this double element characteristic for the earlier tradition about Moses? And in what manner can it be related to the heroic image? The answer to this question cannot be formulated as neatly as the answer to the question posed to the Deuteronomistic or later stages of the tradition. The double form of the traditional image about Moses seems more subtly mixed, if not simply cast without reference to Moses as lawgiver. Thus, in Hos. 4.6, the prophet indicts the people for forgetting *tôrat ᵉlōhêkā*. And in Amos 2.4, the indictment condemns Judah for rejecting *tôrat ᵃdōnāy*. It is possible to argue that the intermediate position of Moses is nonetheless present. In Exodus 24, Moses gives the law to his people by oral address. And Moses' act facilitates the obedient response to God by the people. Moreover, Exodus 34 casts the same image. Lawgiving is the external form of implementing the authority exercised by Moses over the community. The law is God's word. And divine authority underwrites its position among the people. But it is the Moses with the shining face who communicates the law to the people. And that double edge, so clearly expressed by the Deuteronomist and the Chronicler, characterizes the Moses image as lawgiver from the earliest levels of the narrative tradition.

2. A second point about the Sinai traditions also requires consideration. It will be helpful at this point to review the overarching structure of the wilderness theme in relationship to the individual tales about God's aid to the Israelites and the corresponding murmuring of the people. It is my contention that the aid narratives lie on a different plane in the tradition's history from the narratives about Israel's murmuring.[23] At the murmuring level of the tradition's history, the Sinai traditions serve a distinctive structural role. The rebellion before Sinai meets no particular punishment, while the rebellion after Sinai consistently provokes God to serious punitive reaction. In the wilderness theme, Sinai serves as a pivotal point marking the moral responsibility of the people and thus the condemnation for their rebellion.[24] This point applies to the final redaction of the narrative rather than to earlier stages in the tradition's history. Thus, Exod. 17.1-7 and Num. 20.1-13 are doublets from the Yahwist and the priestly sources respectively. The judgment element in Numbers 20 is thus a distinctive element in P. In Numbers 11 and 13-14 Yahwistic elements appear. And the judgment element there is distinctive for the Yahwist. The presence of judgmental elements is thus not in itself the work of the redactor of the final text. Yet, the point of the observation is nonetheless effective. Sinai seems to mark the point for moral responsibility imposed on the people. The conclusion to be drawn from this observation is that (a) Sinai seems to be an intrinsic part of the wilderness theme, certainly for the structure of J, clearly in later levels and the final redaction, perhaps for earlier levels in the tradition's history, and (b) in this structure the essential role of Moses as leader controls the dynamics of the narrative. Moses' leadership is confirmed by signs from God at critical points. But it is also confirmed by the law-giving event.

Chapter 8

THE MOSES DEATH TRADITIONS

It seems to me to be an established fact that the figure of Moses cannot be removed from the exodus theme or the wilderness theme as a secondary insertion into the narratives about God's mighty acts. The exodus theme recounts God's redemption of the people from oppressive bondage to the Egyptians. But while some argument might be mounted that the earliest traditions knew no figure such as Moses who effected the event substantially, the argument does not seem to be convincing. At least from the earliest narrative form, Moses is there. And in the same manner, the wilderness tales reflect significant involvement of Moses the leader of the people in relationship to God's care and aid for his people. The Sinai traditions as a part of the wilderness theme would also show this double edge as a distinctive means for describing the critical event. And even if one should agree that at an earlier level in the tradition's history, the Sinai traditions must have represented a distinct theme in the structure of the early traditions of Israel, still it would be difficult to eliminate the Moses figure from the essential composition of the narrative. Moses is the lawgiver. And the law draws its authority not only from God but also from its original character as Mosaic. The Moses figure is the common bond that holds all of these together and shows that from the beginning they were distinct but not independent.

There is, however, another theme of tradition that rounds off the complex unity of Israel's early confessions. In the patriarchal theme, God promised to give his people the land. But that promise is not fulfilled until the Israelites return from Egypt and occupy the land in the place of the Canaanites. The arc of tension from the promise to its fulfillment marks the structure of the Hexateuch with its peculiar cohesion. Thus, the question now to be considered is whether the Moses image relates in any manner to the conquest theme. Particularly, it will be significant to determine whether Moses is in any way as intrinsic to the conquest theme as he is to the exodus or the wilderness with its complement in Sinai.

The first question to consider is the identification of the structural limits of the theme. The assumption in this question is that each of the themes of tradition has explicit structural marks. Gen. 12.1-3, for example, marks the beginning of the partiarchal theme with the leitmotif of promise.[1] Exod. 1.1-14 introduces the exodus theme by emphasizing the oppression of the Israelites by the Egyptians as a negative leitmotif.[2] Exod. 13.17-22 introduces the wilderness theme with a notation about God's leadership through the wilderness.[3] Interestingly enough, the Sinai traditions do not feature such a structural key that might set them aside as a distinctive theme, an element in the structure of the Pentateuch/Hexateuch. In the light of these structural characteristics, then, what can be said about the beginning of a conquest theme?

In the book of Numbers there is no structural marker for the transition between wilderness and conquest. To the contrary, the wilderness itinerary moves through Numbers in order to deposit Israel on the banks of the Jordan in the plains of Moab across from Jericho (cf. Num. 36.13).[4] Moreover, the book of Joshua begins with Israel still encamped but under preparation for the move across the Jordan. Extensive narratives mark this transition rather than simply an introduction of a leitmotif. But the same function nevertheless controls the collection. And a leitmotif comes to the fore. The Canaanites melt in fear (Josh. 2.24). Moreover, the signs of the wilderness leading stop (Josh. 5.10-12). And Joshua is confirmed as leader in the place of Moses (5.13-15). Obviously, the problem with this structural indicator for the beginning of the conquest theme is that Moses would have no role at all in its composition. Joshua is explicitly the successor of Moses and the new leader (Josh. 4.14).[5]

Yet, is it not possible that at some earlier stage in the tradition's history, the Jordan crossing did not function as the line of demarcation? After all, there is an extensive tradition about the occupation of Transjordan. Is it not possible that Moses' role in the conquest theme comes to light within the scope of tradition about Transjordan?[6] Martin Noth argues forcefully for this alternative.[7] Obviously, Moses died before Israel crossed the Jordan. But his death occurred in relationship to Israel's encampment on the plains of

Moab, following the key traditions about conquest of the trans-jordanian territory. On the basis of this observation, he concludes that the Moses tradition must have been rooted in the theme of the conquest originally. What firmer location for the tradition can be found than the memory of the death of the leader? Indeed, this firm rootage provides some key for Noth's historical concern. The firm historical memory about Moses is that he died. And as a consequence, tradition about his death reveals the point of entry for Moses traditions into the Pentateuchal themes.

An examination of the texts, however, fails to support Noth's thesis. It is true that conquest traditions appear within the structure of the wilderness theme. Thus, Num. 21 recounts the conquest of territory from Sihon and Og. Num. 22–24 report events associated with the conquest but focused on the Moabite side of the struggle. And with Num. 25, a sequence of tradition begins. These traditions, especially Num. 21, are associated in one degree with the conquest of land. But the role of Moses in them is extraneous (Num. 25) or non-existent (Num. 21–24). Indeed, the conquest story in Num. 21.21-30 parallels the story in Num. 20 rather closely. In the Num. 20 story, Moses does not lead the people in conquest but moves around the territory in question, avoiding the conflict. In the Num. 21 Sihon story, Israel does not move around the conflict but rather enters the battle and takes the land. But Moses does not lead (cf. vv. 21, 23, 24, 25). It is as if Moses is intentionally withheld from the conquest story.[8]

There is an exception to this observation. In Num. 27, Moses functions as judge, responsible for deciding a legal question of inheritance procedures. Num. 30 presents a similar legal problem, although it does not concern the distribution of land. In Num. 32, the issue is more directly a matter of conquest, concerned specifically with the question of land distribution in the transjordanian territory. And Moses decides the matter in a way that is binding on the tribes involved. In Num. 34, it is Moses who determines the territory to be given to each of the tribes even in Cannan. And finally, in Num. 35, Moses defines the territory for Levi and the cities of refuge in Canaan. This material may be primarily late, although Noth suggests some older traditions in the earliest sources. 'There can be no doubt that the old sources culminated with the narration in one way or another of the occupation of the preeminently important land west of the Jordan.'[9] The tradition here is at best fragmentary. And contribution to the image of the Moses figure must remain tenuous.

Yet, if some hypothetical constructions can be advanced with good cause, it would appear that this tradition represents Moses as the one with authority to decide matters of civil concern. The lawgiver image thus extends beyond the strict lines of mediation for the covenant to validate the boundaries and inheritance procedures for west-bank land. Israel receives the land from God. Indeed, God instructs Moses for the act of distribution. But the division itself, the act that establishes districts to be occupied by the tribal groups, comes from Moses. Thus, again, the two-fold nature of the tradition seems confirmed. God acts for his people. He gives them the land. But the act is implemented for practical purposes by Moses. Moreover, at this point the Moses figure appears as intrinsic for the tradition as in the other parts of the wilderness theme. If there was a conquest theme in this early, pre-Deuteronomistic stage, it would have required the Moses figure for its completion. But the role of Moses in these conquest traditions does not feature the topic of Moses' death and burial. It is rather his authority to distribute the land.

The key traditon for consideration in this section, however, is the narrative about the death of Moses. On the surface of the discussion, this topos would not appear to be evidence of primary location for the Moses' tradition *vis à vis* the exodus, the wilderness, or Sinai. There is no indication in the narrative units that the tradition is connected to the conquest of Transjordan or the topic of land distribution. Rather, the position of the unit is more closely tied to the wilderness theme with its report of the death of the wilderness generation.

Three pericopae compose this topos: a. Num. 27.12-33. b. Deut. 31.1-23. c. Deut. 34.1-12. In these three units, three stages in the tradition's history come to light.[10] (1) The tradition relates Moses' death to the sin of both Moses and Aaron at Meribah in Kadesh. (2) It also relates Moses' death to the sin of the people at Meribah and other places of the theme. (3) It offers no rationale for the death of Moses. It simply reports that at the time for death, Moses died. And unfortunately, it was at a time when his people still needed his leadership, as well as a time when physically he could still have fulfilled the task with power.

a. Num. 27.12-14 introduces the topos with instructions to Moses to climb the mountain and view the land promised to the people. Viewing the land is cast as a substitute for entering the land, a privilege denied Moses just as it was denied Aaron. It is significant for placing the narrative in its proper position in the tradition's history that the text makes the parallel with Aaron explicit. Thus, the rationale for the early death before entry is established as the violation at the water. Verse 14b makes this connection explicitly the violation at Meribah, reported in Num. 20. This text therefore depends on the priestly account of the event, or at least on the tradition reflex that sought to explain the fact of Moses' exclusion by reference to a violation at Meribah. This reflex is not present in the early form of the Meribah tradition. And it is explicitly not heroic.

The introduction of a succession motif in v. 15, however, moves beyond the topos of death and, incidentally, does suggest something about the heroic image of Moses characteristic for the earlier traditions. Moses petitions Yahweh to appoint a successor as leader of the people ('*îš 'al-hā'ēdâ*). Verse 17 then describes the responsibility of the leader. And that responsibility depicts the character of leadership at the heart of the heroic image: '... who will go out before them and come in before them, who will lead them out and bring them in. So the congregation of the Lord will not be like sheep for whom there is no shepherd'. The idiom, 'to go out and come in', is rather general and supports the contention that the heroic image is inclusive of various offices. Thus, the idiom can refer to the activities of the priest (Exod. 28.35), the king (2 Kgs 11.8; Jer. 17.19), indeed, specifically the activities of David (1 Sam. 18.13, 16) and Solomon (1 Kgs 3.7), the prophet Jeremiah (Jer. 37.4) or the prince (Ezek. 44.3-10). In Josh. 14.11, the idiom describes the general activity of Joshua, Moses' successor, just as in Deut. 31.2 it refers to the general activity Moses can no longer fulfill. This part of the description would not appear to be distinctively heroic, then, but rather a general and inclusive term for the activity of the leader. Indeed, the Hiph'il form of the idiom in Num. 27.17 suggests that the people generally engage in the activity connected with the idiom.

But the Hiph'il form of the idiom does suggest something distinctive about Moses. This unique formulation of the idiom avers that Moses enables the general activity of the people to occur. He causes them to go out and come in. This image of the leader who facilitates the very life of the people opens the way for the simile in v. 17b. The people without a leader are like sheep without a shepherd. The shepherd image, with its ranges of attachment between people and leader, sheep and shepherd, of stability and life in his presence in contrast to chaos and death in his absence, of facility offered by the shepherd to the sheep for their very lives in normal flow, thus comes sharply to the front as an artistic symbol for the hero. The suggestion of Moses as shepherd contrasts significantly with the definition of Moses in Exod. 3.1, at the beginning of the vocation account, as shepherd. The full range of this image comes to light in detail in Ezekiel 34, although at that point the image is applied in a negative way to David. Thus, the leader feeds the sheep, heals them, defends the weak and crippled, seeks out the lost, and rules them with care, not with harsh oppression. The Lord announces that he will himself become Israel's shepherd. Then he will bring out his people, an allusion to the exile rather than the exodus although certainly the imagery derives from exodus language. He will feed his sheep, make them lie down in security, bind the crippled, strengthen the weak, watch over the strong, and give them justice. Verse 28 defines the human shepherd for these duties as David. But the imagery is also relevant to the configurations in a portrait of Moses. Is it not possible just here to see the use of the image in a traditional definition of leadership, formed not by a particular office in an institution, but by popular conception of traditional leaders?[11]

In response to Moses' plea for a successor, the Lord instructs Moses to ordain Joshua. The symbol represented by the act of laying hands on the successor is explicitly an act of validation in the office (v. 19). But it seems important to me to observe that the validation involves transfer of authority. It is explicitly the Mosaic dimension of authority given to Joshua that facilitates the obedience of the congregation to the new leader (cf. Josh. 1.16-17). But still this tradition stands within the structure of the heroic Moses. Verse 20 affirms explicitly that only a part of the authority of Moses will validate the leadership of Joshua: *wᵉnātattâ mēhôdᵉkā 'ālāyw lᵉma'an yišmᵉ'û kol-ᵃdat bᵉnê yiśrā'ēl*. The partitive *mem* with the noun *hôd* is crucial. The successor cannot carry all of the authority of the hero. The same pattern appears in the account of the succession of Elisha to the position of leadership occupied by Elijah in 2 Kgs 2.9. Is this request more properly understood as a petition for a fraction rather than a multiple of Elijah's spirit?[12] The same sense of succession is apparent in Num. 11.17, 25. The intention is to lighten the load on Moses. Yahweh took part of Moses' spirit. Again a partitive *min* controls the image: *wayyā'ṣel min-hārûaḥ ᵃšer 'ālāyw*. And that part served to authorize seventy elders. Moreover, that same spirit promoted ecstatic prophecy among the elders and even extended beyond them to Eldad and Medad in the camp. The spirit of Moses is greater than the total of all who work as his successors. But, nonetheless, Num. 27.21 makes it clear that Joshua will give to the people the same kind of leadership fulfilled by Moses. At his behest, the people will be able to carry on their regular activity. They will go out and come in. Thus, the Joshua image shares a heroic dimension with the Moses traditions. Verses 22-23 then complete the transfer of authority to Joshua. And the pericope comes to its end without a report of Moses' death. The initial structural direction of the unit fades into the account of Joshua's ordination. It is clear that the final redaction of the unit presupposes the priestly account of Moses' sin at Meribah, Num. 20.1-13. And the Moses' sin tradition is not consistent with the heroic image, or, I might add, the authority of Moses depicted by v. 20. Yet, it seems likely that behind the allusion to Numbers 20 represented in this unit by v. 14 and perhaps the universal perspective about Yahweh in v. 15, or the references to Eleazer the priest in vv. 21 and 22, older tradition about Moses dominates the unit. I do not want to deny the pericope in its present form to P, a source that tends to gloss over the heroic dimension in the Moses tradition. I simply want to recognize that the priestly source commonly preserves older tradition. And in this case, contrary to the general tendency in P, some heroic elements of the older tradition remain. Moses is the leader who has authority to facilitate the life of the people. And the authority is passed down to Joshua.

b. In Deuteronomy 34, the image of Moses is a remarkable complement to the one in Numbers 27. It begins in exactly the same fashion as Numbers 27. The land to be taken by Israel in conquest lies before the eyes of Moses who stands on the top of a mountain. But as in Num. 27.13, so here in v. 4, Moses is denied entry into the promise. Verse 14 of the Numbers text explains the denial by reference to the sin of Moses and Aaron at Meribah, an allusion that demonstrates the position of the text in the final form of the Pentateuch, if not also in P. In the Deuteronomy text, no explanation for the denial to Moses is given. There is no allusion to P and thus no fundamental reason to attribute this text to P. The assumption of the unit is simply that Moses now has reached the time of his death. And he must necessarily obey that time. Verses 5-8 then move beyond the Numbers complement with an explicit death report. Moses died in accord with the word of Yahweh.

Verse 6 is crucial for the heroic dimension of the report. Moses died alone, apart from his people. No person would know the place of his burial. But the isolation was not absolute. The antecedent for the subject of the verb in v. 6, *wayyiqbōr*, must be Yahweh. Yahweh alone attended the death of this hero. And Yahweh alone buried him. This presence of God at the death of the hero confirms the life and ministry as acceptance for God. This hero belonged to God in life. And in his death he also belongs to God. At this critical point in the heroic story, intimacy between the hero and God is apparent. But in the death away from the people, intimacy between hero and people is broken. In the past he also belonged to his people. Now his people are absent. The death of the hero is thus typically tragic: 'No man knows the place of his burial to this day'. Verse 7 heightens the tragedy. Moses was one hundred twenty years old. That age is the time for death (contrast Deut. 31.1). But for Moses the vigor of his heroic life remained. 'His eye was not dim, nor his vigor abated.' He could have continued his leadership. He was in physical form if not in chronological age a young man. And he left his people when he would have still been able to lead them.[12]

c. In contrast, Deuteronomy 31 depicts Moses at the point of his death as an old man, one hundred and twenty years but no longer able to lead. Thus, in v. 2, Moses confesses that he cannot go out and come in. Justification for the death of Moses before the completion of his leadership for his people to the land is thus in part chronological age, debilitating loss of vigor.

In addition to this non-heroic image, v. 2b refers to the word of the Lord, almost an exact parallel to Deut. 34.4. Moses will not go over the Jordan. But then in a fashion parallel with Numbers 27, the narration shifts to the question of leadership for the people after the Jordan crossing. The first affirmation is in keeping with the two-fold character of the Moses traditions generally: Now God himself will lead the people. And it will be his leadership that gives victory over the Canaanites. But this divine deed will be translated into practical forms of community leadership by Joshua. Verse 7 makes this point explicit: 'You shall go with this people into the land which the Lord has sworn to their fathers to give them. And you shall cause them to inherit it' (*we'attâ tanḥîlennâ 'ôtām*) Verse 14 returns to Joshua as the successor of Moses. But in this case, contrary to Num. 27.23, it is the Lord who ordains Joshua. It would appear to me, then, that this succession story, non-heroic in its depiction of Moses, is in fact a Joshua tradition. And it opens the door to heroic construction for the Joshua figure.

One final point must be made about the Moses death tradition. Num. 27.14 explains the necessity for the death of Moses before entry into the land by reference to his sin. Deut. 34.4 and 31.2 explain the untimely death of Moses, not by reference to sin for which the death is a punishment, but by reference to age. The death is thus in some sense a tragedy.[14] There is one further explanation in the history of the tradition. In Deut. 1.37 and 3.26, as well as Ps. 106.32, the tradition avers that Moses fails to enter the land because of the people. This collocation does not suggest that Moses suffers exclusion in the place of his people who then may be free of their guilt and enter the land. But it does suggest that Moses suffers exclusion because of the sin of his people. The preposition in Deuteronomy, *lᵉma'an*, appears also in Genesis 18 as indicator of agency. For the sake of fifty righteous, Sodom would not be destroyed. A second preposition also enters this tradition field. In Deut. 1.37, the text avers: 'Against me also the Lord was angry on your account' (*biglalᵉkem*). In Gen. 39.5, the same preposition suggests that Potiphar's house was blessed for the sake of Joseph. And in Ps. 106.32, the tradition observes that it went ill for Moses on their account (*ba'ᵃbûrām*). In Gen. 3.17, the same preposition connotes agency: 'The ground is cursed for your sake'. Thus, in the tradition, as an indicator of agency, the prepositions affirm that for the sake of the people, Moses must remain outside the land. This is not yet a vicarious death, although it may be moving in that direction.[14] The vicarious suffering of the servant in Second Isaiah is different from this expression only by virtue of its affirmation that the suffering of the servant for his people effected healing. But the real point of this tradition lies in the identification of Moses with his people. The parallel in older sources, though not related to the death tradition, is in the intercession of Moses, especially Exod. 32.32.

The tradition about Moses' death thus sets the stage for Moses' successor, an element which in itself can have heroic overtones. But the heroic dimension comes the more sharply to the fore in the emphasis of this topos on leadership with vigor and ability even at an advanced age, on the death while his leadership was still vigorous, and on the explanation of the death by reference to the people. Because of the people, Moses died. And even though no healing occurs as a result of this death, the door is open to the vicarious tones of the Servant in the second Isaiah.

Chapter 9

HEROIC MAN AND MAN OF GOD

The working hypothesis for this probe of the Moses traditions suggests that two complementary structures representing two complementary bodies of tradition merge in order to form the present Hexateuch: the heroic saga of Moses and the confessional themes about God's mighty acts. Moreover, the contrast between Hexateuch and Pentateuch can most adequately be explained by recognizing that one of these, the structure for the Moses traditions, accounts for the Pentateuch, while the other, the structure for the themes about God's mighty acts, accounts for the Hexateuch. The one body about Moses appears now as heroic saga, featuring narratives about the mighty deeds of Moses in his leadership of the people and the people's response in faith (or rebellion) to that leadership. The other body affirms the importance, both theologically and in the history of the tradition, of God's mighty acts on behalf of his people. At times this body of tradition complements the heroic accounts of Moses' mighty deeds, and at times it conflicts with those accounts.

In this part of my probe of the Moses traditions, I intend to examine the facet of the Pentateuchal narratives embracing the confessions of God's acts. I do not intend, however, to explore the tradition history of the various themes in this structure. Such a task would move too far afield, for although issues such as the relationship between the patriarchs in Canaan and Moses in Egypt are certainly relevant to a history of the Moses traditions, they involve problems of wider concern than the one at the heart of this monograph. The task of this part of my probe is therefore limited to a definition of the contribution the traditions about God's mighty acts make to the Moses image. In what way do the confessions about God's care for his people influence the shape of the Old Testament portrait of Moses?

In order to explore this facet of the task, I propose the following addition to the working hypothesis: *The heroic saga about Moses' deeds of leadership for his people merges with the narrative themes, confessional in context, that recount God's acts on behalf of Israel.*[1] *These narrative themes contribute to the Moses traditions insofar as they represent Moses as the one who facilitates God's acts.*

This facet can obviously present Moses in the form of covenant mediator or even lawgiver. But it is not simply a repetition of the hypothesis discussed above. And it does not suggest that the image belongs to a sociological setting such as the cult, the subject of a cultic celebration of covenant renewal or intercession. Rather, it is broader. It considers the fact that the entire range of the Moses traditions embraces several images and touches various sociological settings. And it functions as a necessary complement for the heroic saga, designed to insure that the Moses narration should never move beyond its commitment to describe a human creature who works for the commitment of his people to God. Thus an initial problem would be to account for the move for the traditions from their cultic confessional setting to function as a complement for the literary, folkloristic character of the heroic saga. Does this move provide the context for interpreting the fact that particularly in the pre-exilic tradition Moses appears so rarely outside of the Pentateuchal sources? And another question: Does the move alter the form and genre of the Moses narrative? Or does it simply expand the intrinsic lines of form at home in the heroic saga?

But the question has still another side. Is there integrity in the themes of confession about God's mighty acts apart from the Moses saga? To be sure, reference to the themes appears in the Old Testament without incorporating Moses into the confessions. The articles of faith in the little historical credo illustrate the point. But does that mean that some levels of the tradition report God's mighty acts without having any necessary contacts or formative position for the Moses traditions? Was the exodus tradition ever in circulation in a form that was completely independent of Moses? Can tradition about Israel in the wilderness reveal signs of formulation that give no position to Moses? Can Sinai tradition be identified apart from the Lawgiver?

The structure of the Hexateuch reflects a system of organization in the early history of Israel composed of five major themes of tradition about God's mighty acts. These themes reflect a tradition history which, according to the analysis of von Rad, derived from confessional articles about God's mighty acts. But the confessional articles reveal in themselves a problem of unity. Exodus, wilderness, and conquest belong to one set of traditions, summarized by the 'little historical credo', while the Sinai event belongs to a quite different setting and reflects a quite distinct history.[2] In both cases, the tradition themes would derive from a cultic setting.

The credo traditions, moreover, represent a particular problem for the Moses figure, for at their earliest levels, they have no apparent role for Moses. But when the themes become the subject of narrative expansion in the baroque form now present in the Hexateuchal narratives, Moses entered the field and indeed dominated the sequence of scenes. The observation is not intended to deny that Moses was a part of the tradition from the beginning. It is intended rather to observe that at the earliest levels, Moses appears in a narrative, folkloristic setting, not in a cultic setting. As a part of such a folkloristic setting, Moses functioned in order to facilitate the belief of the people in God. This thesis must now be tested.

1. *The Exodus Theme: Moses, the Liberator*

The most fundamental confession of Israel's faith connects Yahweh with the exodus event. This confession can be documented in the earliest prophecy (Hos. 11.1; Mic. 6.4) as well as in older narratives (Exod. 19.1; 20.2; Judg. 6.13; 2 Sam. 7.23).[3] Indeed, the confession develops quickly into formulaic sentences. 'I am the Lord your God who brought you out of the land of Egypt, out of the house of bondage.' In these earlier references to the event, however, there is no allusion to Moses. It is quite clear that the confession affirms an act of God on Israel's behalf without any reference to a human agent who facilitated the event. Thus, the formula is regularly constructed with a Hiph'il form of the verbs *yāṣa'* or *'ālâ*, a phrase with *'ereṣ miṣrayim* controlled by the preposition *min*, and some indication of Yahweh as the subject.[4] Where, then, does the tradition indicate involvement for Moses in a way that contributes to the image of Moses in the larger narrative unit?

Although the dominant form of the tradition outside of the narratives of the Pentateuch clearly shows Yahweh as the subject for the exodus event, the tradition can be constructed in particular situations with Moses as the subject. These occasions are essentially negative; nonetheless, they indicate something about an image of Moses functional for the tradition. Thus, in the Golden Calf episode, Exod. 32.1, the people address a speech to Aaron. The speech is constructed in a narrative frame. It represents the apostasy of the people by having them request Aaron to make gods. The key term here is *ᵉlōhîm*. However, this term is followed by an *ᵃšer* clause with a *plural* verb: *ᵃšer yēlᵉkû lᵉpānênû*. Then the explanation for this apostate request, constructed as a *kî* clause, refers to Moses as the one who accomplished the exodus: *zeh mōšeh hā'îš ᵃšer heᵉlānû mē'ereṣ miṣrayim*. In effect, the golden calf would replace Moses, not Yahweh, as the leader of the exodus. And it would do so in terms of position for the deity. The request thus assumes Moses' position in the place of God. But nonetheless, it assumes an occasion that views Moses as the author of the exodus event. In this particular case, then, Moses competes with Yahweh for a role in the tradition. And the two forms of the tradition are not clearly complementary but would appear to be in conflict.

In the same pericope, Yahweh addresses Moses who is on top of the mountain with new instructions to return to his people, who have already attached themselves to the golden calf. Verse 7 identifies those people in terms of the exodus event. *šiḥēt 'ammᵉkā ᵃšer heᵉlîtā mē'ereṣ miṣrāyim*. 'Your people, whom you brought up from the land of Egypt, have corrupted themselves.' The setting is still negative. Indeed, Moses' response in v. 11 uses the same formula (although it employs the alternate verb) to describe the people as the ones Yahweh brought out of Egypt. But the point remains that the formulaic allusion to the exodus event can construct Moses as the subject. The parallel in Deut. 9.12 would doubtlessly be simply dependent on this Exodus text. Yet, it too shows that although the circumstances are negative, the tradition can conceive Moses as the author of the event. And when this happens, it happens in a narrative setting, not a cultic one.

The golden calf pericope implies that Moses stood in the place of God as the author of the event. The tradition can, however, construct Moses' place in the event in a different, more positive manner. The key text here is Hos. 12.14: 'By a prophet, he was preserved'. In this case Yahweh is still the author of the event. But Yahweh accomplishes his event by means of a prophet: *ûbᵉnābî' heᵉlā ᵃdōnāy 'et-yiśrā'ēl mimmiṣrāyim ûbᵉnābî' nišmār*. This text does not suggest, so it seems to me, that Moses has been conceived in the narrow, more limited institutional office of prophet, just as Gen. 20.7 cannot place Abraham into the institutional role of prophet. Rather, in both cases, the term connotes a broad role of leadership (cf. Judg. 6.8). But the critical element for the image of Moses represented by this text is the preposition, a *bet* of instrument, that controls the noun. 'By means of a prophet...' Yahweh is the author of the event. But the prophet is the agent that enables the event to occur. Moses facilitates the intention of God to bring Israel out of Egypt. 2 Sam. 3.18; 11.14; 12.25; 18.2 provide a selection of texts to illustrate the common idiom. The idiom can connote the relationship between messenger and the one who commissions the message (so, 2 Sam. 16.8). But the thrust of the idiom is to highlight authority for an action (so, 2 Sam. 18.2). 1 Kgs 8.53-56 expands this image for the Moses tradition. Verse 53 reports that Yahweh separated Israel from all the other people of the earth as his own possession. But this separation was announced—and it thus occurred—by the hand of Moses: *bᵉyad mōšeh 'abdekā*. Moses is the instrument that facilitates the event. But he is more than mere instrument. He is the mediator of authority. And it is by this act that the authority of Yahweh is made public. In 1 Kgs 8.56, this wide range of Mosaic act is affirmed. 'Not one word from all of his good words which he spoke by the hand of Moses his servant (*bᵉyad mōšeh 'abdô*) has fallen.' Moses facilitates proclamation of Yahweh's words and events (cf. Num. 12.2; Josh. 14.2; 20.2, 8; 22.9; Judg. 3.4; Neh. 8.14; 9.14; 10.30; 2 Chron. 33.8; 34.4; 35.6).

It is just at this point, however, that the Moses traditions must be carefully interpreted. On the basis of this review of allusions to Moses' work in the tradition of God's mighty acts, we might well conclude that Moses is nothing but an instrument. These traditions are not really about the work of Moses. They do not hold him in any particular esteem. The Lord might have chosen some other instrument. In fact, the instrument is of little value or importance. Indeed, when importance is attached to the instrument, it occurs in a negative context. And it implies an exalted position for Moses as a person that detracts from God's position as the Lord of the community. But the full range of the exodus traditions never facilitates that conclusion. The image of Moses as the instrument for facilitating God's intentions is always held in tension for the scope of the tradition with the image of Moses as hero. To hold the one image as separate from the other would distort the biblical portrait of Moses.

This point is substantiated by the narrative display of the exodus tradition. The leitmotif for the narrative theme is the oppression of the Egyptians that provokes the cry of the Israelites for help. The structure of the theme builds on an arc of tension from the introduction of the crisis represented by the leitmotif to the resolution of the crisis in Israel's escape from the house of bondage. It is God's intention to redeem his people from their oppressive slavery. The narrative then describes the execution of those divine intentions by the introduction of Moses. The two-fold characteristic noted above serves this combination of divine act and Mosaic involvement well and should not be separated into the emphases of two different sources. Thus, in Exod. 3.7-8, Yahweh announces his own intention to redeem his people from the Egyptians in response to their cry. But vv. 9-10 implement that intention by sending Moses to the Pharaoh. That tension is the key formulation for the Moses traditions. In order to see Moses fully, but also in order to understand the character of God's mighty act, the tension must not be broken. To break it would produce a transcendental divine history unencumbered even by the instrumentality of human involvement, or a human history devoid of divine involvement or even focused on elevating human involvement to the world of the divine (so, Exod. 32.1).

This point is also attested in the narratives about the plagues. The plagues are God's events. But they are effected by Moses (and Aaron). They are also Moses' events (so, Deut. 34.11-12). The combination is captured in the dual image defined above. Moses acts. But in fact, it is God (see Exod. 7.17, 25). The same two-fold picture of the plagues appears in Ps. 105. 26-36. Verses 26-27 remember that God sent Moses and Aaron together in order to do the signs. But then vv. 28-36 celebrate each sign as God's act. And indeed, v. 37 brings the series to its climax with the exodus as God's act. The point at issue, however, is not that God here is celebrated as the author of the event. It is that God and Moses-Aaron are held in tension. God acts. But it is in fact Moses (and Aaron) who acts. The description here does not appear to be in conflict. Rather, the combination holds the two in tension as mutually complementary.

Finally, the exodus event itself, according to the tradition, knows the event to be uniquely the event of God, the one that marks his greatest revelation of himself to his people. Yet, the event belongs in a special way to Moses. This facet is not apparent in the Passover tradition or the descriptions of the exodus event associated with it. But in the tradition about the exodus describing the event as a secret escape, the double edge is clear. Ps. 105.37, for example, depicts this tradition as Yahweh's act: 'He [Yahweh: see v. 7] brought them out with silver and gold'. Exod. 11.3a relates the foundation for this event to the act of God: 'The Lord gave the people favor in the eyes of the Egyptians'. But v. 3b combines God's act with the stature of Moses: 'Also the man Moses was very great in the eyes of the servants of the Pharaoh and in the eyes of the people'. The exodus occurred because God gave the people favor in the eyes of their captors. But it also occurred because the man Moses commanded the respect of the Egyptians. By the time of the priestly description of the exodus as the central Passover event, this combination has been lost. Moses is simply the speaker for the ritual. But for the early tradition, the exodus tradition appears with two natures bound together in a unique balance.

2. *The Wilderness Theme: Moses, the Shepherd*

The wilderness theme is secondary to the central confessions about Yahweh's mighty acts in the exodus and his gift to Israel of the promised land.[5] This conception of the wilderness traditions organized into some kind of systematic presentation assumes the overarching thesis that exodus theme, conquest theme, patriarchal theme, and especially the Sinai theme were originally independent confessions, each hiding its own tradition history and its own peculiar origin. The thesis does not provide an adequate control, however, for the position of the Moses traditions that cut through all of the topics. If the wilderness theme had its origin in a secondary combination of the exodus and the conquest, in what manner does the Moses figure enter the picture?

The history of the wilderness theme resembles the pattern described for the exodus theme. Some of the earliest witnesses to the event of the wilderness allude to God's acts on behalf of his people. And there is no role in these allusions for the figure of Moses. Particularly in the earlier tradition, the topic about the event at the Sea belongs to the general structure and theology of the theme.[6] Its tradition makes sense only in terms of the confessions associated with God's acts in the wilderness. The hymn of praise called the Song of Miriam thus provides an early celebration of the keystone in the theme: 'Sing to the Lord, for he has triumphed gloriously. Horse and chariotry he has thrown into the sea'. This hymn, which certainly has its setting in the early cult, describes Yahweh's victory over the enemy at the sea in mythopoeic terms.[7] Moses has no role in the event at all. Indeed, the later expansion of the poem in the hymn of praise called the Song of the Sea recites the details of the event without reference to Moses.[8] In both cases, this key event in the series organized under the theme of Yahweh's leadership and protection glorifies the event as an act of God. It was God's intervention that protected the people that day at the Sea from the threat of death represented by the horse and chariotry.

The same perspective can be documented at various stages in the history of the wilderness traditions. Thus, in Ps. 78.13, the poem remembers the event at the Sea as God's event. But then a broad scope of wilderness events composes the period, each cast as God's event. Ps. 74.12-17 uses the same kind of mythopoeic language to describe the event at the Sea. And again the image functions as descriptive patterns for the entire range of wilderness traditions: food, water, protection. Ps. 77.16 personifies the Sea, so that it responds to God as if itself the enemy. Ps. 114.1-8 features the same personification. And in both cases, the event is cast entirely as God's mighty act. Creation, represented by the Sea, responds to God. And in the response, the tradition of Israel's early history comes to expression. The second Isaiah alludes to the event at the Sea as God's event without reference to Moses (Isa. 51.9-11) and even the recitation of the tradition in Neh. 9.9-12 makes the same point. It was God who saved his people at the Sea. In the narrative, Exod. 14.25 ties into the same mythopoeic conception of God's act in the wilderness for the sake of his people. The event occurs because the Lord fights for Israel.

Other elements in the wilderness theme seem to reveal the same kind of tradition history. Thus Ps. 78.14-16 and 23-29 describe the events of aid for Israel in the wilderness without reference to Moses who interceded in the face of the crisis and facilitated the rescue of the people. Pss. 105.37-41, 106.7-15, and Neh. 9.9-22 fit the same pattern. But perhaps the most significant text to depict God's act in the wilderness is the Song of Moses, Deut. 32.1-43, a poem that recalls Yahweh's special act of election as an act that occurred not in the exodus from Egypt but in the protection and aid of the wilderness. Indeed, the assumption is that the relationship between Israel and Yahweh began when Yahweh 'found' his people in the wilderness: 'He found him in the land of the wilderness; in the howling waste, he was nourished. He encircled him and cared for him and guarded him like the center of his eye'.[9] God established his relationship with Israel in the wilderness. And in this description Moses is not present.

Thus, again the question must arise: Under what circumstances does Moses enter the tradition, and what does his function here suggest about the configurations of the Moses image? Ps. 106.16 alludes to the leadership of Moses and Aaron under attack by the jealous Dathan and Abiram. But the allusion derives from the narrative in Numbers 16. Ps. 77.21 places Moses and Aaron together as instruments of the leadership of the Lord through the wilderness. The key, *nāḥâ*, controls the allusion. And the image of the shepherd is the obvious model. But the subject of the verb is second person, a reference to God rather than to the two leaders (cf. v. 17). Moses and Aaron enter the picture in v. 21b as agents of God's act. 'You led your people like a flock, by the hand of Moses and Aaron.' Ps. 78.53-54 uses the verb also in the sense of a shepherd. But the subject is God. Neh. 9.12 and 19 employ Hiph'il forms of the verb to refer to the leadership of Yahweh symbolized by the pillar of fire and cloud. As in Exod. 13.21, Deut. 32.12 sets Yahweh as the subject of a Hiph'il form of the verb. And the eagle image for God, brooding over its young, is the form of the leadership. But the pattern with the verb is not consistent. In Exod. 32.34, a second-person formulation of the verb refers to Moses. Thus, the verb for describing leadership in the wilderness, clearly used as the act of God, can also denote the act of Moses. And the shepherd image, the form of the agent who serves a superior, can also describe God's act.

In the narrative about the event at the Sea, it is still quite clear that the event belongs to Yahweh. Verse 24, a J passage, affirms that 'it came to pass in the morning watch that the Lord looked down into the camp of the Egyptians from the pillar of fire and cloud, and he discomfited the camp of the Egyptians'. Indeed, the Egyptians respond to the event with a cry of retreat: 'Let me flee from before the Israelites, for the Lord fights for them against the Egyptians'. Thus, the narrative stands in line with the mythopoeic descriptions noted above. But the narrative combines this mythopoeic dimension with an explicit role for Moses. In the pattern of the episodes about Yahweh's aid to Israel, the Israelites see the drawing crisis. Then in a fashion that is now clearly typical for the Moses traditions, the text reports: 'The Israelites lifted up their eyes, and behold the Egyptians were marching after them. And they were exceedingly afraid. And the Israelites cried out to the Lord. And they said to Moses. . . ' The double nature of the Israelite's act depicts a problem in the tradition's history. The appeal goes first to God, then to Moses. But does the problem not belong to the double edge in the tradition noted above? To appeal to God is to appeal to Moses. The two are not the same. But the act is the same. To rebel against Moses is to rebel against God.

Then Moses acts, first in the intercession to the Lord for his people, then in execution of the instructions for their delivery. The execution features the rod, defined above as distinctive for the Moses tradition, used now in parallel with Moses' own hand. Both symbols function in the account of the event itself. Thus, just here the tradition affirms both poles as complements (compare Isa. 63.11-14; Ps. 77.21). The event occurs because the Lord fights for Israel. But it occurs in fact when Moses acts. For this narrative, the two cannot be separated into distinct traditions or sources. They belong together as a single affirmation about the event. Moreover, they come together when the cultic, mythopoeic tradition must be transposed into narrative, descriptive form. The cultic image may be shaped heavily by the image of holy war, with the charismatic leader who initiates the action in the name of the Lord. But the image comes together with the various other images for Moses in the narrative, literary setting of storytelling. Moses enters the tradition complex as the central agent of Israel's story.

The image of Moses in that story can have negative overtones. In Numbers 11, Moses responds to the request of the people for food. His response is hostile, although the text does not clarify whether the hostility mentioned in v. 10b is directed toward the people who weep at the doors of their tents or the Lord whose anger was hot. The speech implies that Moses was angry with the Lord, for it begins with an accusation against Yahweh: 'Why have you dealt ill with your servant?' The second line of the accusation identifies the problem in an infinitive clause: 'Why have I not found favor in your eyes, to place the burden, all this people, on me'. The evidence of failure to find favor in God's eyes is the burden on Moses by God.

But the important point is that here Moses defines the people as a burden. Thus, the following questions have a negative cast. In v. 12: 'Did I conceive all this people, or did I give birth to them that you should say: "Carry them in your bosom as a wet-nurse carries a suckling child to the land which you swore to their fathers"?' The question implies a negative answer. Moses did not conceive the people. Yahweh did. Therefore, Moses should not carry the people as a wet-nurse carries a child. The formulation is negative. Yet, it witnesses a conception of the Moses involvement that is consistent with the pattern described above. God conceived the people. And as a matter of fact, Moses must now carry them like a wet-nurse. The noun is generally feminine in form, obviously. The one occasion of a masculine formulation of the noun is here. And the negative allusion to Moses is ironic. But it does imply a functional and applicable image for Moses' role with the people. Though used in a negative context, it connotes precisely the image of the facilitator suggested in the working hypothesis for this section of the probe.[10]

Again, in the wilderness theme, Moses brings the people to Meribah. Exod. 17.1-7 affirms that by the direction of the Lord, Moses takes the rod symbolic of his leadership and moves to the rock. At the proper moment, he strikes the rock with the rod and produces water for the needs of his people. The rod itself belongs to the double edge in the Moses traditions, clearly a symbol of his leadership and yet named in 17.9 as the rod of God. Moses the hero acts by the power of God, a unique union symbolized by the Mosaic rod. Moreover, the same perspective can be uncovered in the tradition's history. Moses acts decisively in order to establish the event—and his authority—before the people. But the same event appears in Pss. 78.20 and 105.14 strictly as an act of God. And Deut. 32.13 doubtlessly has the same tradition in view. For the wilderness traditions, then, it seems clear that Moses appears in the narrative elaboration of typical episodes. And his role is the role of the facilitator for God's acts. God aids his people in the crises they face. And the aid comes by the hand of Moses.

3. *The Sinai Traditions: Moses, the Lawgiver*

As a part of the wilderness theme, the Sinai events involve Moses and the people in a unique relationship with God. A review of the Mosaic figure in the Sinai events recalls the two-fold character of the tradition noted above. Exod. 19.9 establishes the authority of Moses to speak before the people and to expect their response. But Exod. 20.18-20 affirms that the Mosaic authority facilitates the fear of God in the eyes of the people. Moses' position is a position that enables the people to 'fear' the Lord. Thus, to stand in proper awe and intimacy with God is to recognize the authority of Moses. This position is precisely the position that underwrites the proclamation of the law. And finally, the authority of Moses in the proclamation of the law bears fruit for the people in his corresponding authority to intercede with Yahweh for the sake of the people. It is in this context that the image of covenant mediator makes sense for the Moses tradition. But the point remains that covenant mediator imagery belongs to a considerably larger complex that sets Moses for the people before God. (For the details of this position, see the comments above.)

4. *The Conquest Theme: Joshua, the Warrior*

As a part of the wilderness theme, Moses' involvement in the distribution of the land rests on the traditional role of his authority in the community. Because he said, according to the tradition, that the land should be distributed in a particular way, the traditional distribution carried authority in the community. But the foundation of the authority is the relationship of Moses' proclamation and God's instruction (Num. 34.1). It is distinctive that in this complex of traditions, Moses has a significant role in non-narrative forms. But there is no narrative presentation featuring a role of Moses in the distribution of land. It does not seem to me to be correct, therefore, to conclude that Moses belonged originally to the theme of the conquest or to the early memories of distribution for the land taken from the Canaanites. To the contrary, the position of Moses in these traditions seems to be an extension of the position of authority established for Moses in the Sinai events. In the same manner, the Moses death tradition belongs to the wilderness theme, at least insofar as the itinerary structure is concerned. Moses does not tie primarily to the conquest theme in any clear manner.[11]

Moreover, it is clear that the history of the conquest traditions follows much the same pattern as the history for the exodus and the wilderness. Thus, early allusions to the topic confess Yahweh's act without reference to Moses. This point is clear in the themes of the credo. But in other texts, it is also clear. In Josh. 2.10-11:

> For we have heard that the Lord dried up the waters of the Sea of Reeds before you when you came out from Egypt and what you did to the two kings of the Amorites in Transjordan, to Sihon and Og, that you destroyed them. When we heard, our hearts melted and courage did not rise up for any man because of you. For the Lord is God in heaven above and on the earth beneath.

And in the Song of the Sea:

> The people have heard. They tremble. Pain seizes the inhabitants

> of Philistia. Then the chiefs of Edom are dismayed. The leaders of Moab, trembling seizes them. All the inhabitants of Canaan have melted. Terror and fear fall on them. Because of the greatness of your arm, they are dumb like stones, until your people, O Lord, pass over, until this people whom you purchased pass over. You will bring them in and you will plant them in the mountain of your inheritance.

In this dimension of the examination, nothing appears that controverts the thesis about Moses' position in the themes of tradition about God's mighty acts. It seems to me more likely that the uneven pattern of involvement for Moses results from the combination of heroic saga tradition with the structure of the confessions about Israel's early history with Yahweh.

Thus, in both the exodus theme and the wilderness theme, along with the related topos about events of the conquest of Canaan, Moses appears as the one who enables his people to believe in Yahweh. Moses has authority, but the authority derives ultimately from Yahweh. Moses' role in the themes that depict God's mighty acts complements the role apparent in the heroic tradition by depicting his acts as acts that inspire obedience not only to him as the heroic leader of the people, but also to God. His acts enable God's acts to be seen by the community. In most cases, his acts are God's acts. And the narrative elaboration of that tradition conflicts with the God's mighty acts tradition only insofar as it claims the same acts recited in the confessions as God's acts for the narratives about Moses. God's acts are in some cases really Moses' acts. This facet of the tradition develops essentially as a narrative elaboration of the cultic confessions about God's acts. None of the early confessions mentions Moses in any role. It would appear to me, therefore, that the shift from cultic confession of God's mighty acts to the tradition of Moses' role in those acts is a shift that occurred when the confessions expanded to elaborate narrative detail. Even in this facet of the tradition, the Moses image is the product of literary art, storytelling that can use cultic forms or military forms, royal forms or political forms, but nonetheless storytelling whose setting is primarily popular. Moses tradition is old, no doubt. But in the form now preserved by the Old Testament, its old form was preserved in popular storytelling rather than in cultic or political institutions.

Moreover, it is clear that the depiction of Moses in this facet of the tradition complements the heroic saga of Moses. The heroic man acts so that his acts make public the acts of God. The tradition thus does not alter the form and genre of the heroic saga. Even with the image of Moses as man of God, and the themes that depict God's mighty acts, the form of the Moses narration remains as it was. Heroic saga is the narrative display of the hero as the man of God. And this display belongs to the exquisite art of Israel's storytelling.

Provenance of the Moses Traditions

From the perspective of the heroic saga, the Moses traditions cut across the distinctive lines of the confessional themes. In the narrative elaboration of those themes to complementary content for the saga, Moses belongs to the exodus or the wilderness at the same level as the one represented by his position in the Sinai traditons. The conquest represents a problematic area for this position since the Moses involvement never produces an extensive narrative elaboration but rather remains rather peripheral, even in accounts of conquest in Transjordan. The exception to this observation is Moses' involvement in distribution of the land. But this image seems to draw on the depiction of Moses with authority drawn from the Sinai complex. Thus, from the perspective of the heroic saga, Moses cannot be assigned originally to any one topos in contrast to all others.[12]

When the question is put from the other direction, however, the tradition history looks somewhat different. It is obviously the case that the exodus and the wilderness themes developed from the earliest points without reference to Moses. Moses may have been assumed by the early confessions. But in fact, Moses does not appear in the explicit formulations of the events. Rather, mythopoeic imagery features God acting directly for the sake of his people. The conclusion to be drawn, according to the hypothesis defended above, is that Moses enters the field of tradition in these themes when the topos shifts from cultic confession with its mythopoeic imagery to popular narrative elaboration, with its historical imagery. The issues are somewhat different but the same conclusion applies to the conquest theme. Yahweh gives the land to his people. And although Moses may be represented as the chief agent of authority for distribution of the land, he is nonetheless held at a distance from narrative elaboration of the theme. Thus, even though Moses does not enter the narrative display of the theme in an extensive role, the minimal role he occupies for the theme suggests that the Moses image generally requires a narrative setting. Would the same observation not apply for an evaluation of the Joshua traditions in the conquest theme?

When one explores this pattern for the history of the Sinai traditions, however, a different image emerges. It is possible to see allusions to Sinai as the home of Yahweh, with no reference to Moses who comes to this divine abode. Thus, Ps. 68.8-9 avers: 'O God, when you went out before your people, when you marched through the wilderness, the earth quaked. The heavens rained in the presence of God, this Sinai, in the presence of God, the God of Israel'. And in the Song of Deborah, Judg. 5.4-5 avers: 'O Lord, when you went forth from Seir, when you marched from the region of Edom, the earth trembled. Also the heavens rained. Also the clouds rained water. The mountains quaked before the Lord, this Sinai, before the Lord, the God of Israel'. These poems may assume the exodus and wilderness traditions. And they thus set the allusion to Sinai into the context of the central confessional themes. Thus, the allusion to God's 'going out' from Seir or simply before the people employs the traditional verb for the exodus, *yāṣā'*. And certainly the psalm uses wilderness vocabulary to describe God's leadership. Yet, these allusions to Sinai, which are heavily laden with mythopoeic imagery, make no reference to Sinai in terms of law or authority. Sinai is simply the abode of God.

When the fundamental content of the Sinai complex features the law, however, the mythopoeic imagery tends to drop away. To be sure, theophany still provides the context for the event. And the narrative description of theophany employs descriptions of nature in upheaval.[13] But with the law, the focus of the tradition shifts from mythopoeic imagery to the exchange between Yahweh and Moses. There is no law tradition without Moses. To be sure, specific sets of law, such as the Covenant Code, can be identified. And internally, the Covenant Code has little to do with Moses. But the Code becomes the words of Moses as soon as it is given a narrative setting. Thus, von Rad can observe with critical insight: 'The decisive and pre-eminent factor in the coalescing and aggregation of the many traditions was their common attachment to a place (Sinai) and to a person (Moses)'.[14]

But would this process not be the same tradition history observed for the exodus or the wilderness? Does any evidence suggest that with the proclamation of the law at Sinai, we have discovered that point where Moses was originally at home? Did Moses as a literary figure spread to the exodus and the wilderness when Sinai was combined with the credo traditions and all of them were elaborated into a pan-Israel, mighty acts of God narrative? The implications of this question must be clear. I want to determine whether at its earliest levels the Sinai tradition already involved Moses. But I want to raise that question not simply in terms of an institutional office. I have suggested above that the appearance of Moses in the office of the mediator or the intercessor would seem to be a literary, folkloristic phenomenon rather than a sociologically grounded, institutionally shaped one. Does Moses appear in the Sinai narrative as an intrinsic figure? But then the question is whether Moses has traditio-historical rootage behind the Sinai narrative that would account for his role in both the Sinai collection of traditions and in the narrative about God's mighty acts. Does the Sinai tradition contain the origin of the Moses figure as a literary, narrative phenomenon?

The answer to this question lies in a careful evaluation of Exodus 19–34. I suggested above that in my opinion this narrative unit cannot account for the origin of the Moses traditions in terms of institutional office from some particular sector of Israelite society. But that conclusion does not preclude the possibility that the setting for the Moses tradition lies hidden in the narrative process represented by these chapters.

The first structural element in the unit prepares for a theophany as the critical event for the narrative. The preparation involves first an announcement about God's past act and an appeal for obedience in future action. 19.5 is critical. Obedience is tantamount to life in the covenant. And the focus here is on the community in covenant. As obedient members, Israel will carry the title, 'a kingdom of priests' (*mamleket kōhᵃnîm*) and a 'holy nation' (*gōy qādôš*), the construction of v. 6a. Moses fits here simply as messenger, the point of v. 6b. Verses 7-8 then document that the message was delivered and that the people agreed to abide by its terms.

Verse 9 strikes a new tone in the description, however, for here Moses' authority before the people is established. The relationship between God and people will parallel the relationship between Moses and people. And the issue is explicitly obedience. The goal of the event announced at this point will be 'belief' in Moses. Obedience will occur when the people see God's presence with Moses 'in a mass of cloud' (*bᵉ'ab he'ānān*). When the people hear God speaking to Moses, they will respond in obedience to his word. The imagery here is not simply messenger, but one who speaks out of authority that establishes his own creative role in the community.

The next element of structure features the theophany, with Moses moving up and down the mountain in order to secure the proper position of the people for the event. The results of the preparation lead to the people's appeal in 29.18-20 for Moses to mediate God's word so that they will not of necessity stand directly in the presence of God. Moses' response establishes, not his own authority for the people, but rather the proper worshipful relationship between people and God.

Laws now intervene. The decalogue interrupts the exchange between people and Moses and is perhaps out of place. Significantly, there is no effort to show that Moses reported the words of the decalogue to the people. This point increases the impression that 20.18-20 belongs more tightly with ch. 19 as a concluding and complementary element. Moreover, 20.21 implies fulfillment of the conditions announced in 19.9, although a different term serves to depict the thick cloud (*hā^ᶜrāpel*). And with this notation, the Covenant Code begins. Specifically, the Code is addressed by God to Moses.

Exodus 24 constitutes the response to the Code and to the appeal for obedience. Verses 1-2 anticipate vv. 9-11 in the pericope, a designation of authority for Moses specifically in relationship to Aaronic groups and the seventy elders (see Num. 11.24-25), perhaps a distinct tradition about a covenant that rests on a sacral meal. The key elements for continuation of the unit appear in vv. 3-8. Again the people commit themselves for obedience to the law according to Moses. And Moses seals the commitment in writing and ritual. Verses 12-18 recall Moses to the mountain. The law will be given to Moses on tablets of stone. And thus, the primary image for Moses in this narrative is established. He will receive the law. But the event itself is yet to come. God then appears. The cloud again serves the narrative as a motif for depicting the presence of God. But in this case, the 'glory of the Lord' serves that function as well. And here the people see the presence. So, in v. 17b: 'the appearance of the glory of the Lord was like a consuming fire on the top of the mountain before the eyes of the Israelites'. And the validation of Mosaic authority can occur. The people see Moses and Yahweh together.

Thus the covenant relationship grounds on the people's commitment to obedience both to the Lord and to Moses. But the unit does not properly end here, at least insofar as the final form of the text is concerned. Moses leaves his people in order to enter the cloud.

And the text leaves its audience waiting for the validation of Mosaic authority as anticipated by 19.9: *ba⁽ᵃbûr yišma' hā'ām bᵉdabbᵉrî 'immāk wᵉgam-bᵉkā yaᵃminû lᵉ'ôlām*.

The narrative sequence continues in Exodus 32–34. Chapter 32 recounts Israel's apostasy with the golden calf (vv. 1-29) and the beginning of Moses' intercession. A principal motif in the intercession is Moses' identification with his people. The intercession dialogue continues into ch. 33. It is interrupted, however, by vv. 7-11, recounting something about the typical activity of Moses' intercourse with God. This interlude functions structurally to prepare for the intercession speech in vv. 12-23. But it also provides the validation for Moses anticipated by 19.9. Thus, the scene notes the regular position of Moses for mediating the people's inquiry of God at the Tent of Meeting. But vv. 8-9 shift the focus from mediation to the relationship between God and Moses. Moses would enter the tent. Then God, symbolized by the cloud, would also enter the tent. Verse 9b is then the key: 'He would speak with Moses'. Verse 10 confirms the event and, accordingly, the authority of Moses. 'Then all the people would see the pillar of cloud standing at the door of the tent, and all the people would rise and worship, each man at the door of his tent'. The correspondence between this scene and 19.9 cannot be accidental. The regular event in the career of Moses establishes his authority to function in the community with the belief of the people and thus with their obedience. It is out of that correspondence that I would argue that though described as a regular event in the career of Moses, the description is something that is peculiar to Mosaic imagery rather than typical for an office that derives from an on-going institution in Israel's cult.

Verse 11 summarizes the event validating Moses' authority. It features a description of the relationship between Moses and God with two parts. (1) The Lord would speak with Moses 'face to face'. This point is supportive for the validation. But the definition of the event specifically is 'face to face' (*wᵉdibber ᵃdōnāy 'el-mōšeh pānîm 'el-pānîm*). The idiom itself connotes intimacy (cf. Gen. 32.3; Exod. 25.30; Deut. 34.10; Judg. 6.22; Ezek. 20.35). And this same connotation is at the heart of the validation for Moses. (2) The Lord relates to Moses 'just as a man speaks to his friend (*rē'ēhû*)'. To be a friend with God, or even to relate to God on the basis of an analogy of human friend with human friend, is to enjoy a remarkable intimacy. This definition of the relationship between Moses and

Yahweh is not secondary in this narrative. To the contrary, it connects with 19.9 in an arc of narration that focuses on Mosaic authority. Moreover, it sets the stage for the intercession in 33.12-16. The basic warrant for Moses' appeal is sharing that intimacy with his people. The Moses speech in these verses also features the importance of intimacy. 'You say to me, "Bring this people up". But you have not made me know whom you will send with me.' The issue here is presence. But then the appeal continues. 'You say, "I know you by name, and also you have found favor in my eyes".' To know someone by name is a warm act of intimacy (cf. 33.17. Contrast Josh. 23.7).

The exchange in vv. 14-15 is somewhat obscure. Verse 14 appears to commit the presence of God for the people in contrast to the previous announcement of punishment by refusing the presence. But v. 15 assumes the contrary. Moses appeals again for the presence of God in the exodus as the distinctive characteristic of Israel. Intimacy with God is the essence for both Moses and people. Thus, v. 16 marks Moses as a figure who relates both to God but at the same time identifies with his people. 'Is it not when you go with us that we are separated, I and your people, from all the people on the face of the earth?' This appeal for reaffirmation of intentions must be similar to the process for establishing relationships in Josh. 24.16-20. The people in that case appear to commit themselves in loyalty to the Lord. Verses 16-18 make the commitment quite explicit. But Joshua's speech, vv. 19-20, assumes a negative response. And the assumption brings a renewed commitment. The final fruit of the commitment is intimacy with God (cf. v. 25). In the Exodus text, the dialogue produces commitment from God and then reveals the presence of God to Moses. The vision of God intensifies the intimacy of the relationship. In particular, this event repeats the name of God to Moses, and it defines the name with an *idem per idem* construction similar to the one in Exodus 3. This theology of God's presence in a particular way must be very near the heart of the tradition about Moses in the Old Testament.

Exodus 34 then relates this scene to the apostasy of ch. 32 by having Moses reconstruct the tablets of stone and then reform the commandments. Verses 29-35 conclude the pericope with the Mosaic transfiguration. This distinctive event marks Moses' special relationship with God and thus grounds the authority by which he speaks. Thus, in v. 32, the relationship between Moses and people comes to the front: 'Moses commanded them all which the Lord had spoken with him on the Mountain of Sinai'. The fruit of the intimacy, the consequence of Mosaic authority, was the lawgiving so characteristic for the portrait of Moses in much of the tradition outside of the Pentateuch.

In the light of this focus, the narrative then marks the Moses figure in its intimacy with God, transfigured with a shining face, with the veil. It is important to observe that the veil does not function as the vestment of an office. When Moses speaks with God, he does not wear it. When he receives inquiry from the people, he does not wear it. Rather, it marks the regular and normal intercourse of his life by rendering the signs of his intimacy with God palatable to his people. It functions, then, as a sign of Mosaic daily activity rather than the activity of an institutional office. And thus it would appear to me to be a motif for narrative description of the hero who is at the same time the man of God.

One final comment about this scene is in order. The present form of the text clearly marks the golden calf as an item of apostasy, initiated by Aaron in the absence of Moses. Indeed, the accusation by Moses against Aaron, 32.21, defines the act symbolized by the construction of the calf as a great sin ($h^a\dot{t}\bar{a}$'$\hat{a}$ $g^ed\bar{o}l\hat{a}$). But again, it is important to note that the act is defined as a replacement for Moses, not for God. And the construction of the performative ritual, 32.4, denotes with irony that the replacement involves Israel not only with idols falsely credited as gods with the execution of the exodus, but also with a plurality of gods, *polytheism*. The parallel with the act of Jeroboam when he constructed a new sanctuary to replace Jerusalem is obvious (cf. 1 Kgs 12.25-33).[15] But at this point, one must consider the possibility that the polemic against the golden calf derives not from the primary shape of the Moses traditions, but rather from the Jerusalem court in reaction to the rebellion of Jeroboam. If that interpretation is correct, then the way would be open to consider the possibility that the golden calf was originally positive, a symbol of Yahweh's presence with his people and with Moses. Could the difficult text about the shining face have indeed intended to depict Moses as horned (see the Vulgate)?[16] Would the horns connect Moses to a bovine element in the Yahweh religion?[17] Was the Calf in fact a symbol of Moses rather than an idol or even a symbol of God? An analogy between this proposition and the cross in Christian churches, the symbol of the presence of Jesus to the church, comes readily to mind. If this hypothesis has merit, then it would suggest that the Moses tradition was at home primarily in the north, a competitor for the Davidic tradition in the south.

It is my contention that the core of Mosaic tradition lies embedded in this narrative. To be sure, the narrative is now expansive. It carries theological reflection of some sophisticated advancement (33.19). Yet, in these lines, basic Mosaic tradition provides the foundation from which the narrative grows. (1) Moses identifies himself with his people, particularly by his commitment of himself in intercession. (2) He enjoys intimacy with God, the basis for his intercession for his people. (3) He commands the people in accord with the intimacy he shares with God. The commandment with authority seems to me to be the basis of the tradition out of which the whole scope of Mosaic narrative grows. It is, moreover, a narrative tradition which gives context to traditions of law that develop from generation to generation. The kernel of the Moses tradition, then, clearly at home in the Sinai complex, is the image of Moses as one who comes to his people with authority. And his leadership, including the portrait of Moses as a shepherd (cf. Zech. 11.16), develops from the basic tenet of authority. Indeed, many of the images derive from or serve secondarily as tools for the depiction of divine authority at home with Moses.

Moreover, this depiction of Moses rests essentially on tradition that derives from a folkloristic, narrative setting, not tradition whose setting is cult or court. It is a tradition about Moses that grows from storytelling, with the primary form of the Mosaic figure conceived as the lawgiver. It is a tradition depicting God (and Moses) loving the people and the people responding in obedience.

Yet, a problem confronts defense of this hypothesis. I have argued to this point that the themes of tradition defined by von Rad and Noth cannot serve a hypothesis about the origin of the Moses traditions if the hypothesis rests on an assumption that Moses roots in only one theme, the other four being originally distinct and independent of the one supporting Moses and of each other. Does this view of provenance for the Moses tradition not argue against that position? Does it not support von Rad's construction that sees Sinai as distinct and independent of the other four? Resolution of questions about the origin and roots for the Moses traditions depends apparently on a final resolution of the question about the relationship of the Sinai complex with the remaining themes of tradition.

One should bear in mind, however, that there is no necessity, given the analysis of structure in the Pentateuch, to conclude that the elements in that structure were originally independent of each other.

The analysis is not of necessity disintegrative. To the contrary, identification of the parts in the composition of the Pentateuch helps clarify the significance in the relationship of the parts. Moreover, the complementary relationship of the elements carrying the confessional themes with the elements of the heroic saga strengthens the unity characteristic for the whole. What sense can be found, then, in the impression that the Moses traditions root fundamentally in Sinai? Would it not be logical to conclude that, rooted in Sinai, they spread secondarily to the other themes of tradition when the heroic saga developed?

That conclusion makes sense only if the hypothesis about the original independence of Sinai from the other themes could be substantiated. But there is an alternative to that hypothesis. The body of legal tradition in the Sinai complex, with Moses depicted as lawgiver, relates to the event of theophany in Exodus 19 in a very particular way. The theophany itself precedes presentation of the law through Moses. Chapter 19 describes the theophany in striking detail. And the theophany, witnessed on behalf of the people by Moses, leads to the proclamation of the law. It is as if proclamation of the law were a logical, or better, a theological consequence of the event of the theophany. The relationship is explicit in vv. 4-6: 'You have seen what I did to the Egyptians, and how I bore you on eagles' wings and brought you to myself. Now therefore, if you will obey my voice and keep my covenant, you shall be my own possession among all peoples, for all the earth is mine, and you shall be to me a kingdom of priests and a holy nation'. The law is built into the event that makes God's graceful act of salvation visible. 'Because I have done this, you shall do that.' Thus, Moses the lawgiver gives the law as the essential content of the event he announces. To announce the event is to give the law. In terms of traditional law/Gospel dialogue, the point is that the Gospel assumes the law. The law defines the ways and means for the faithful to respond to the Gospel. The implication of the paradigm is that the redemption at the center of God's act requires the response defined by the center of God's law.

Given this dialectic, Moses' role as lawgiver rests not simply in the Sinai complex, but equally in the other themes as well. The element of law is not worked out as systematically in the exodus theme as it is in the Sinai traditions of the wilderness theme. But it is there. 'I am the Lord your God, who brought you out of the land of Egypt, out of the house of bondage. You shall have no other gods before me.' 'You shall not pervert the justice due to the sojourner, or to the fatherless, or take a widow's garment in pledge, but you shall remember that you were a slave in Egypt and the Lord your God redeemed you from there; therefore, I command you to do this.'

Thus, I would argue, the primary role of Moses as lawgiver does not limit Moses to the Sinai traditions. That role can be seen clearly in the Sinai complex. But to the contrary, the primary role of Moses as lawgiver recognizes that Moses proclaims law as a natural consequence of the Gospel. To have Gospel without law, to have the themes of God's mighty acts, revealing his graceful redemption for his people, without the law to show his people how to respond would open the Gospel in the Old Testament to heresy. The people could be forever takers, taking God's goodness, his redemption, without being at the same time givers, giving that goodness to the stranger, the widow, the fatherless who live in their midst. To call Moses lawgiver does not mean that Moses has no fundamental role in the exodus, the wilderness, or the conquest. It means rather that the mythopoeic confessions of God's mighty acts necessarily call for Moses, the lawgiver, when they are elaborated into narratives. At the same level, the exodus, the wilderness, the theophany at Sinai all call for the ministry of Moses in order to make the full range of meaning each carries as clear as revelation.

Deuteronomy makes this hermeneutic even more explicit:

> When your son asks you in time to come, 'What is the meaning of the testimonies and the statutes and the ordinances which the Lord our God has commanded you?' then you shall say to your son, 'We were Pharaoh's slaves in Egypt; and the Lord brought us out of Egypt with a mighty hand, and the Lord showed signs and wonders, great and grievous, against Egypt and against Pharaoh and all his household, before our eyes; and he brought us out from there, that he might bring us in and give us the land which he swore to give our fathers. And the Lord commanded us to do all these statutes, to fear the Lord our God for our good always, that he might preserve us alive, as at this day' (Deut. 6.20-24).

Thus, I conclude that the fundamental function of Moses as lawgiver defines the essence if not the origin of the Moses tradition. It does not mean that Moses roots in the Sinai traditions and then spreads secondarily to the other themes. It means rather that Moses as lawgiver uncovers the basic theological character of each theme in the same way. The fundamental theological confession for Israel is not 'I am the Lord, your God, who brought you out of the land of Egypt'. It is: 'Because I am the Lord, your God, who brought you out of the land of Egypt, you shall therefore obey my voice'.

But Christians might object just here. Grace and redemption represent the free gift of God. Does that mean that God through Jesus Christ has no expectation for response from the redeemed?

> And a ruler asked him, 'Good Teacher, what shall I do to inherit eternal life?' and Jesus said to him, 'Why do you call me good? No one is good but God alone. You know the commandments. "Do not commit adultery. Do not kill. Do not steal. Do not bear false witness. Honor your father and mother"'. And he said, 'All these things I have observed from my youth'. And when Jesus heard it, he said to him, 'One thing you still lack. Sell all that you have and distribute to the poor. And you will have treasure in heaven. And come, follow me'. But when he heard this, he became very sad, for he was rich. Jesus looking at him said, 'How hard it is. . .' (Luke 18.18ff.).

I conclude that Moses, like Jesus, is the lawgiver who interprets the mighty acts of God not only as signs of God's redemption, but also as imperatives for the moral response of the audience. That role is unique in each theme of tradition about God's mighty acts, yet the common element that binds the confessional themes into the unity of the heroic saga.[18]

Excursus A

EPITHETS FOR THE MOSAIC FIGURE

The picture of the heroic man, marked by a duplicity that affirms both the importance of the hero's deeds and the relationship of those deeds to God, can be sharpened by reference to two titles for Moses, both functioning in the history of the tradition as classical epithets.

1. *The Man of God* (*'îš hā*ʷ*lōhîm*)

On the surface, the title seems to indicate nothing more than a relationship. The one who carries the title is one who belongs to God (see the numerous construct bonds that set the noun in relationship to some other noun, as e.g. *'îš yiśrā'ēl* in Josh. 9.6; 10.24; Judg. 7.14; 20.22; or 1 Sam. 17.25). Thus, the title *'îš hā*ʷ*lōhîm* connotes some kind of relationship between the man of God and God himself. Moreover, the title can function as a narrative epithet, a shorthand reference to the principal of a story (so, 1 Kings 13). On six occasions, Moses carries the title: Deut. 33.1; Josh. 14.6; Ps. 90.1; 1 Chron. 23.14; 2 Chron. 30.10; Ezra 3.2. None of these references is clearly earlier than the Deuteronomistic Historian, although Josh. 14.6 may hide an earlier use of the title.[19] Two of these texts, Deut. 33.1 and Ps. 90.1, are simply ascriptions for poems and thus tell little about the character of Moses or the shape of the image that portrays him. At most they suggest that Moses was a famous man who therefore might have been responsible for a poem, i.e. eligible for credit in the ascription of a pseudonymous poem. In these cases, the title indicates nothing more than a relationship between Moses and God. In 1 Chron. 23.14, the title places Moses' sons among the Levites. But the value for defining Moses as 'man of God' does not appear to be strong. Indeed, in the contrast between the sons of Moses and the sons of Aaron, the Aaronides seem to be the more highly exalted. Thus, it would appear to me that the term is a general element of tradition, an epithet which in these contexts has no specific qualification for the Moses figure.

The other two references to Moses as man of God in the Chronicler (2 Chron. 30.16 and Ezra 3.3) plus the reference in the Deuteronomistic Historian (Josh. 14.6) are more substantial for defining the shape of the overall picture of Moses. The Chronicler's view of Moses as the man of God resides with the general patterns of Moses as lawgiver. 2 Chron. 30.16 refers to the law that controls the operation of 'priests and Levites' in the House of the Lord at Passover as the law of Moses, the man of God. The allusion seems to me clearly to be an attribution of authority for the law by reference to Moses. But the qualification of the attribution by the title is not clear. Is it not an effort to claim that the Mosaic authority validating the law facilitates an appeal beyond Moses to an authority that ultimately derives from God? In Ezra 3.2, the same point can be made. The subject of the narrative is construction of the altar for burnt offerings in the restoration of the Temple. The authority for the construction lay in the law of Moses, the man of God. Thus, construction of the altar in a particular way was validated by reference to Moses. And the validation has a twofold character: (a) Moses (b) who is known as the man of God. The twofold character suggests that Moses facilitates a final authority beyond himself. Moreover, this twofold character is precisely the character of the heroic image defined above. The authority of the law resides in its origin in Moses. But in fact, Mosaic authority is valid because of his relationship with God. It does not affirm that validation is not really in Moses, but rather in God. It affirms that validation is in the double edge. The image is thus quite complementary to the heroic shape of the Moses tradition. It adds to the shape of the image the conviction that Moses, in some particular manner, belongs to God.

The Deuteronomistic Historian gives further expression to this point. In Josh. 14.6, Yahweh is cited as the author of a decision concerning Caleb, a decision which has practical consequences in the distribution of land taken from the Canaanites. Again, the concern is for authority. Moses proclaimed that Caleb should inherit the land he explored in his spying mission. But here it is clear that the decision pronounced by Moses derived from God. Moses simply mediated that decision to his people. It should be clear, however, that this act of mediation is not the same as the function of the covenant mediator. Covenant mediator would have had a very specific task to perform. Here, the image of Moses as mediator applies not only to the proclamation of law, thus the view of the Chronicler, but to a wider area of responsibility in the life of the people. In effect, here Moses facilitates the distribution of the promised land to a portion of the people (see Num. 34–35). And that event is finally the fulfillment of the promise of God to his people. It is God's act. Thus, Josh. 14.6 depicts Caleb's speech to Joshua: 'You know the word which the Lord spoke to Moses, the man of God, concerning me and you in Kadesh-barnea'. Thus, the title functions here in a manner that is consistent for the heroic form of the people's leader. He proclaims a decision that establishes a portion of the people on the land. The unique element of this allusion *vis à vis* the heroic is an explicit definition of the relationship between Moses and God with the epithet. The authority for the life of the people is the Moses who belongs to God. And belonging to God means just here that Moses implements God's decision about the land.

It would be helpful at this point to define more precisely the content and function of the title. Fortunately, the title itself is broadly attested in the scope of Old Testament narration: For Elijah, 1 Kgs 17.18, 24; 20.28; 2 Kgs 1.9, 10, 11, 12, 13. For Elisha, 2 Kgs 4.7, 9, 16, 21, 22, 25, 27, 40, 42; 5.8, 14, 15, 20; 6.6, 9, 10, 15; 7.2, 17, 18, 19; 8.2, 4, 7, 8, 11; 13.19. It can also function for unnamed figures: Judg. 13.6, 8; 1 Sam. 2.27; 1 Kgs 13; 20.28; 2 Kgs 23.17; Jer. 35.4. And finally it can refer to such diverse leaders as Samuel (1 Sam. 9.6-10) and David (2 Chron. 8.14; Neh. 12.24, 26). Werner Lemke surveys these occurrences, concluding that since most appear in Deuterono-mistic contexts, and since the heaviest concentration appears in the Elijah–Elisha tradition and in the story about the unnamed man of God in 1 Kings 13, 'it would appear that the term originated in northern prophetic circles and that it was characteristic of those prophetic traditions which were remembered and handed down among those circles'.[20] Yet, it seems to me necessary to urge caution in drawing similar conclusions about Moses, the man of God. It is true that the vast majority of occurrences for this title refers to a prophet. But I am not convinced that such an observation warrrants a conclusion that wherever the title occurs, it suggests that the principal was understood as a prophet or even that the narrative about the principal was handed down in prophetic circles. There can be no doubt that Moses was remembered on occasion as a prophet. And Hosea's allusion to the prophet who led Israel out of Egypt (12.13) would place that memory in the northern kingdom. But I do doubt that the prophetic circles of the north were substantially involved in the formation of the Moses portrait as a man of God in order to place Moses in line with the prophetic office. It seems to me necessary to consider another alternative. The term functions as an epithet in narrative or general references to Moses. Moreover, its widest use is in saga material about the deeds and victories or failures of its subject. Such a narrative function would account for the use of the term for principals that cannot fit the mold of the northern prophet, such as David. The observation does not mean that the term is used inappropriately for prophetic figures. Nor does it mean that the term could not have been used in northern prophetic circles. It means that the term must have had a wider circulation and broader meaning than that kind of limited setting would suggest. And it means that that setting must be defined as folkloristic, popular narrative, as storytelling which certainly occurred in northern prophetic circles, but which occurred at other places as well.

If such an observation about the title is substantially correct, then it would be relevant to observe that the title 'man of God' which says something about the intrinsic relationship between the principal who bears the title and God belongs to the same setting as the heroic saga.

2. *The Servant of the Lord* (*'ebed ᵃdōnāy*)

This title builds primarily on the combination of the noun, *'ebed*, with a name for God or a suffix that refers to God. The most common form of the expression is *'ebed ᵃdōnāy*, although on three occasions, the title for Moses is *'ebed hā'ᵉlōhîm* (Dan. 9.11; Neh. 10.30; 1 Chron. 6.34). Moreover, the title stands as synonymous for *'îš hā'ᵉlōhîm* in at least one clear case in the Moses series. In Josh. 14.6, Caleb refers to Moses as the man of God who defined the territory for Calebite inheritance, while in v. 7, the same speech refers to Moses as the servant of the Lord who sent Caleb on the spying mission in the first place. In this case, the two terms refer in the same way to the man who has authority for pronouncing decisions about land to the community of the people.

Walther Zimmerli discussed almost forty references to Moses qualified by some form of this title in a larger evaluation of the title through the Old Testament.[21] He demonstrated that the collocation, *'ebed ᵃdōnāy*, or some adjusted form of it such as *'abdî*, refers primarily to the relationship between the principal and God, not to the work which the principal will accomplish as the servant of God. Thus, as for the title, 'man of God', so for the title, 'servant of God', the term does not connote one single, limited office, identified by its peculiar work. A large complex of occurrences for this title applies its qualification to David. But the title does not warrant a conclusion that the qualification of Moses conceives of Moses as king or even that the title was limited to polite, courtly speech. The title is not necessarily messianic. Rather, it can refer to various famous people who enjoyed an intimate relationship with God. Thus, Josh. 24.29 shows the title as a qualification of Joshua, Num. 14.24 for Caleb, 1 Kgs 14.18 and 15.29 for Ahijah, 2 Kgs 14.25 for Jonah, and Job 1.8 and 2.3 or 19.16 and 43.7, 8 for Job. Particularly, the Jonah and Job texts suggest that the title is a general epithet available for describing traditionally famous and pious persons of the past.

In the Moses traditions, the title appears at least on three occasions in pre-deuteronomistic sources: Exod. 14.31; Num. 12.7, 8; Deut. 34.5. In accord with the suggestion by Zimmerli, I would contend that in each case the title functions to emphasize the relationship between Moses and God. Indeed, in Exod. 14.31 and Num. 12.7 and 8, it facilitates expression of the twofold character of the Moses image. The heroic man is at center stage. In Exod. 14.31, the event at the Sea promotes belief of the people in Moses. And in Num. 12.7 and 8, Yahweh confirms the position of Moses as leader of the people *vis à vis* the opposition of Miriam and Aaron. But at the same time, the event affirms that Yahweh acted. The same event that promotes belief in Moses promotes belief in Yahweh. It is the same demonstration of authority. To refer to this leadership of the people as servant of the Lord is to recognize the validation of his authority in God.

> But in what he [Moses] powerfully accomplished Yahweh was so obviously present that the people's responsive faith submits to Moses and to Yahweh in him. An essential feature of the biblical revelation comes out here. God's history is not transcendental heavenly history. It stoops to earth and appoints men with their deeds and words as signs.[22]

It is precisely the heroic deeds of the man Moses that become the signs of God's presence. Heroic deeds and the mighty acts of God merge. And the merger enables the mighty acts of God to be translated from a transcendental heavenly history into human history. Human history demonstrates the authority of God to compel belief and thus obedience.

Deut. 34.5 is also in my opinion a pre-deuteronomistic allusion to

Moses as servant of God. It is the key element in the death report. Thus, at a point calling for a summary statement of Moses' career, the title identifies the great leader, who dies according to the word of the Lord and, appropriately, in the presence of the Lord, as the servant of the Lord. The relationship is a key element. And the relationship shows the intimate contact between the heroic man and the presence of God that transforms the transcendental history of God into concrete human terms. The heroic man is no god. But the heroic man is no mean creature either, forgotten at death by his creator. In the servant of the Lord, human event is transformed by divine presence into an act of God. As a matter of fact, it is precisely in the death topos of the tradition that the use of the title as an epithet can be seen most clearly, In Josh. 1.1 and 2, the title functions in an allusion to the dead Moses. And in Josh. 24.29 and Judg. 2.8, the title describes Joshua at his death.

The title appears most frequently as an epithet for Moses in the book of Joshua. Here it qualifies Moses in allusions to various topoi in the Moses saga. But its most common function is to validate the authority of Moses to require obedience from his people or to establish the order of life in which the people must live (Josh. 1.7, 13, 15; 8.31, 33; 9.24; 11.12, 15; 12.6; 13.8; 14.7; 22.2, 4, 5). The deuteronomistic elements in 1 Kgs 8.53 and 2 Kgs 18.12 and 21.8 round out this pattern. And the title with Moses in Mal. 3.22 belongs to the same image. The distinctive element that emerges from this series is an affirmation of the authority of Moses in distribution of the land, not only the Transjordanian territory, but also the land of Canaan. It is perhaps significant to observe the distinction between this representation of Moses and the one represented by the Yahwist, for while the heroic element may not be so sharply distinctive in this deuteronomistic layer, the authority of the hero to establish possession of the land is. 1 Kgs 8.56 stands out from this collection of references to Moses as a general summary. God spoke various words to his people, all of which he fulfilled. But those words, or promises (RSV), were translated into a form understandable for the people by Moses, the servant. Moses functions here as mediator. But clearly his mediation is not limited to covenant renewal or the work of a single office. *All* the promises came through his mouth. And all the promises were fulfilled. This reference to the promises of God as words spoken by Moses shows the kind of intimate relationship between hero and God characteristic for the heroic tradition.

In the writings, the pattern for reference to Moses with this title is similar. Dan. 9.11 sets the pace by identifying the law as the law of Moses, the servant of God. The title validates the authority of the law. In Ps. 105.26, the title qualifies Moses in an allusion to the divine commission marking Moses' vocation. The allusion may be simply dependent on the Pentateuchal foundation. Yet even if this were so, it would provide an allusion to the tradition which now employs the title. And in the Chronicler, the title functions again with Moses as a general appeal to authority (1 Chron. 6.34; Neh. 1.8; 9.14; 10.30) or an appeal for authority in particular cultic institutions. 2 Chron. 1.3 shows that Moses established the Tent of Meeting and 2 Chron. 24.6 and 9 refer to the tax levied by Moses for support of the Tent. Thus, it is clear that while the heroic man of authority held central importance for the Yahwist, and while the later narrative sources seem to reduce the heroic element by emphasizing the acts of God, the tradition of the heroic source of authority did not die. The title does not place Moses in any one particular office. It does not define the setting for the Moses tradition in any one particular cultic institution even though the Tent might be a possibility. Rather, the title seems again to be a term from the popular world, an epithet within the dynamics of folk narrative for referring to a hero in the narrative, regardless of his office.

The epithets in the Moses tradition appear, therefore, to support the contention in the working hypothesis for this project that the tradition depicts Moses, not in terms of prophet, priest, or king, portraits drawn from institutional offices operative in the time of the storyteller, but as the hero of the story, Israel's story. And as hero, Moses casts an image that embraces many offices, many forms, many responsibilities. It would be precisely this diversity that opens the door for development of the Moses image with two natures, the heroic man and the man of God.

Excursus B

MOSES PARAPHERNALIA

References to Moses paraphernalia appear at scattered points in the previous sections of this probe. The purpose of this excursus is to bring those observations together for a more pointed evaluation. By paraphernalia, I mean those items described in the narratives that function in one way or another as symbols of the Moses tradition. In the same way that the cross represents tradition about Jesus' crucifixion and resurrection, but in addition gains inclusive significance for the entire scope of the tradition, so in the Moses traditions various symbols represent various items of critical importance for the shape of the Moses image.

1. The rod (*māṭṭeh*). Perhaps the most important symbol for Moses in the construction of traditions as heroic saga is the rod. A person carrying a rod for use as a handy, personal tool is not in itself unusual (cf. 1 Sam. 14.27, 43; Isa. 28.27). Indeed, the tool can stand for the character of the person whom it symbolizes (cf. Gen. 38.8, 18, 25). The term can also denote the larger family unit that gives meaning and identity to all of its members (Num. 31.34, 36). This category is, of course, distinct from the denotation for a tool; yet, it marks the place of symbol for personal reference.

In the hands of a particular leader, the tool carries the weight of power (Ps. 110.2). The same point about the rod as a symbol of power can be established from negative contexts (Isa. 9.3; 10.24-26; 14.5; Jer. 48.17). The rod can appear in the hand of a shepherd (Exod. 4.2) but it is not peculiar to shepherds (Exod. 7.12). It can in fact refer to the reputation and authority of a person and his family as a symbol preserved as witness to that position for future generations. Num. 17.16-28 describes the rod of Aaron as a symbol of his position of authority *vis à vis* those who would murmur against him and thus challenge his authority in the community. In the test designed to determine the validity of Aaron's leadership, Aaron's rod blossomed. And that fact functioned as validation. But perhaps the more important point in this pericope is not the sign represented by the vitality of the rod, but the function of the rod with its blossom as a perpetual symbol of Aaron's position (17.25-26). The rod is clearly an item in the paraphernalia of Aaron, preserved as a witness to Aaron's position for coming generations.[23]

For Moses, the rod functions clearly as a symbol of power. The point is established in the confrontation between Moses and the magicians of Egypt. Both sides wield rods. And both possess the power to turn the rods into serpents (*tannîn*). When, however, the sign was first given to Moses on the Mountain, the text reports that the rod became a snake. The word for the reptile produced by the rod is different (*nāḥāš*). The rod then functions as the sign of Moses' power. In the confrontation with the Pharaoh, the rod serves Moses at the moment of power, the moment when Moses effects a sign. The tie between the rod and the sign is strong (Exod. 7.9-12; 15-20; 8.1; 13; 9.23; 10.13). And the sign before the Pharaoh functions as evidence for imposing authority over the Pharaoh, just as it does in the scene depicting Moses before the Israelites (Exod. 4.30-31). To be sure, the Pharaoh rejects the claim of power for the sign because of his hard heart. But the function of the sign is to establish the authority of the wielder. The symbol reveals a double nature in the plague series, however. The rod obviously belongs to Moses. But on occasion, Aaron wields it before the common foe. This element reflects the particular history of the Aaron tradition and should not detract from the perception of the object as a symbol of Moses' position.

It is important to note, however, that the rod functions more broadly for the Moses traditions than simply in the confrontation with the Pharaoh. Exod. 17.9 presents Moses with the rod of authority in his hand, responsible for the success of the battle against the Amalekites. One should remember just here, however, that the rod has a dual nature. It is both the rod of Moses and the rod of God (cf. 7.25). And indeed, the same dual nature characterizes the image of Moses generally. The rod symbolizes both the authority of Moses and the authority of God. The one is tantamount to the other. In the event at Meribah, Exod. 17.1-7, the rod functions as the tool in Moses' hand, effective for producing water for the community from the rock. The priestly parallel in Numbers 20 cuts the heroic character of the scene down to human size by depicting Moses and Aaron as sinners before God. But the rod is not in itself the sin, as if wielding it would be usurpation of divine power. Even the designation of the rod as the rod of Moses does not imply that Moses grasped power in his hand that belonged to God. The rod remains a symbol of the appropriate power of Moses, a symbol effective for the tradition in depicting the authority and power of the hero.

A problem remains, however, for the definition of the rod as an effective symbol for the position of Moses in the community. If the challenge against Moses' authority functions as a motif in the tradition on the analogy with the challenge to Aaron's authority, and if the rod serves as a witness to the validated authority of Moses as it does for Aaron, if both the rod of Aaron and the rod of Moses function for the tradition as efficacious symbols for the authority and power of the one who wields the symbol, then why does the tradition report that the rod of Aaron was preserved as a testimony to his position *vis à vis* the rebels against Aaron? Why does the tradition not also report that Moses' rod was preserved as symbol for Moses' position *vis à vis* his rebels? Why would it not have been presented dramatically as a sign of Moses' power and authority for all generations to come?

Perhaps the answer to this question lies in the hypothesis that the rod as a symbol of Moses' position and power changes its shape in some of the wilderness tales. In Exod. 15.22-26, for example, the Israelites face a crisis in the wilderness. They arrive at Marah, obviously expecting water to drink. But they could not drink the water because it was bitter. And the bitter pun points to the intention of the tale. But the Moses tradition moves the simple etiology to a tale about Yahweh's aid in the wilderness for his people. God showed Moses a tree ('ēṣ) and Moses throws the tree into the water in order to make the water palatable. The tree is not the rod. Yet, it fulfills the same function as the rod. It is the instrument by which Moses effected the event and met the needs of his people. That is precisely the function of the rod.

But one more point of connection can be made. What is the connection between the rod-tree symbolism and the statute-ordinance in vv. 25b-26? It is the tradition of Old Testament scholarship to label these verses as a Deuteronomistic expansion of the Yahwistic tale about Marah.[24] And perhaps the definition of these verses as Deuteronomistic is in order. But the intrinsic connection between them and the tale about bitter water turned to sweet should not be missed. Yahweh obliges Israel to obey the statute and ordinance, a part of his test for Israel (*nissāhû*). The implication of the aid is that in response to the aid, Israel will obey the Lord.[25] The event of the aid already contains the proclamation of the law. But still a further point is in order. Obedience to the law will protect Israel from the diseases (*hammaḥªlâ*) Yahweh put on the Egyptians. The diseases obviously refer to the signs effected by Moses with the help of the rod. And now obedience to the law constitutes the antidote to the power of the rod to bring disease. Significantly, the process is defined in v. 26 by an epithet for Yahweh. He is Israel's healer (*rōpᵉ'ekā*). Would not, in fact, the power to 'heal' the bitter water by a tree reflect the same power?

Even if, however, the 'tree' that heals bitter water is in some manner related to the rod that brings diseases on the Egyptians and, according to the hypothesis, wards those diseases away from the Israelites, the question about preservation of the symbol as a witness to the power and authority of Moses for future generations is not yet answered. If the rod changes its shape within the scope of the Moses traditions, does it emerge in still another form? Num. 21.4-9 narrates an event in the wilderness journey that threatened the lives of the Israelites under Moses' care. Fiery serpents (*hannᵉḥāšîm haśśᵉrāpîm*) attacked the Israelites because of the rebellion against both God and Moses. And some of the Israelites died from the bites. The remaining population confessed their sin, and as a result Moses interceded for them and received instruction for the remedy. A bronze serpent (*nᵉḥaš nᵉḥōšet*) on a pole (*nēs*) would reverse the fatal quality of the serpents' bite. Those stricken by the attack would need only to see the bronze serpent in order to survive the fate inflicted by the serpents.

Again, there is no explicit connection between the rod (*maṭṭeh*) and the bronze serpent (*nᵉḥaš nᵉḥōšet*). Yet it is significant that in the first scene pitting Moses against the Pharaoh, the rod turned into a serpent. Indeed, the initial account of the deed, Exod. 7.10, named the serpent *tannîn*. But the same scene shifts the vocabulary (7.15) to *nāḥāš* (cf. also 4.3). And when the Pharaoh's magicians throw their rods (*maṭṭeh*) before the Pharaoh, they become *tannîn*. The rod of Moses then swallows the serpent of the Egyptian magicians, anticipating a final victory by Moses over their skills. But the foreboding character of the scene is heightened by reference to Moses' serpent with a different noun. His serpent is a *nāḥāš*. Does the change in the vocabulary not anticipate the bronze serpent of Num. 21.4-9?

Moreover, the bronze serpent was preserved in the Temple, the Nehushtan of popular tradition. Indeed, 2 Kgs 18.4 reports not only that incense was burned before the Nehushtan in the Temple during the days of Hezekiah, but also that the figure had been made by Moses.[26] Hezekiah's reform that broke the bronze serpent into pieces would thus have an anti-Moses cast about it. The description of an act of reverence addressed to the bronze serpent, the act of burning incense before it, may be intended in this text as a polemic, a definition of the act as worship, or at least very high reverence paid to an object that compromised absolute reverence to Yahweh. In that case, the interpretation would be like the interpretation of the golden calf. From the perspective of the south, the bronze serpent compromised loyalty to Yahweh. Its pro-Mosaic character suggests a pro-northern quality in the tradition. But the symbol, with its quality of healing power, connected in some manner to the symbol of Mosaic authority, may constitute the most significant object of Mosaic tradition within the scope of the heroic saga.[27]

In the legend in Numbers 12, Miriam suffers the punishment from God for her challenge to Moses' position in the form of leprosy. There is no reference to the rod here, no Nehushtan. There is no note that Moses laid his hands on the leprous Miriam. He prays for the healing. And the healing occurs. It is important, nonetheless, to note that healing constitutes a role for Moses in the heroic tradition.

2. According to tradition now preserved in the MT, the golden calf was a violation of covenantal loyalty to Yahweh. Yet the calf was created not as a replacement for Yahweh, but as a replacement for Moses. And indeed, behind that show of weakness in anticipating the return of Moses from the Mountain may be a traditional symbol for the leadership of Moses. If, then, the depiction of Moses as horned connected with the symbol of the golden calf, the function of the symbol would be not only a representation of Moses, but specifically a depiction of Mosaic authority. The transfiguration of Moses, a tradition that focuses on Mosaic authority, would support this contention.[28] Moreover, the veil would provide the means for communicating that authority to the public. Would the rod not support the impression that symbols such as these functioned as signs of authority for the community (Jer. 48.17)?

But the golden calf was reduced to a sign of apostasy and rejected as an effective sign of Yahweh's (and Moses'?) presence in the community. The fate of the golden calf and the bronze serpent reflects the strong anti-Moses (anti-northern?) bias in the tradition. Would this element not reflect the same tendency as the murmuring motif, a tendency to show that the wilderness generation lost its unique relationship with Yahweh because of its rebellion? Would it not show a tendency in the form of the tradition now preserved in the MT to undercut the Moses position? Would this too not be a pro-David factor effecting the shape of the tradition originally at home in the north?[29]

3. In the priestly tradition, the ark of the covenant functions as a Mosaic symbol. But in the typical priestly fashion, it is not heroic in quality. It was constructed by Moses. But it functions, not as a symbol of Moses' presence for his people, but as a symbol of God's presence. Its character as a war palladium (Josh. 3) certainly reflects its function as a symbol of God and his presence for the army (1 Sam. 4). But in the earlier tradition, particularly in the heroic tradition, there is no role for the ark in the Moses story.[30]

4. Num. 27.12-23 depicts Moses laying hands on Joshua to mark him as his successor. The act symbolizes transfer of power and authority. But it also reminds the audience that the hands of Moses parallel the rod as instruments to effect the power of God/Moses for the people. Laying hands on Joshua marks not simply a transfer of power and authority, but even more, a transfer of spirit that characterizes Moses, a recognition of divine presence, the defining quality of Moses as man of God, now passed to the successor. And perhaps in the process is the element of cleansing/healing.[31] In order for one confronted by God to accept a divine commission, the cleansing/healing process was necessary (cf. Isa. 6.6-7; Jer. 1.9; Ezek. 2.9). But the process of transfer opens the door to a new symbol of Moses for the community. In Joshua appears a new Moses, one shaped by tradition and experience as a disciple of the teacher, a new form of the ideal model.

Chapter 10

SETTING AND INTENTION FOR THE SAGA

The hypothesis about the Moses traditions as heroic saga, complemented by the structure of confessional themes depicting God's
mighty acts to save his people, may now be tested by exploring the
setting and intention for each stage in the history of those
traditions.

1. The final form of the Pentateuch preserves the Moses story in
narratives and laws from Exodus through Deuteronomy. It is
obvious that at the canonical level, the Moses story contains a
delicate balance between the tales, legends, anecdotes, and reports of
the Moses saga and the laws in the Sinai tradition. At the canonical
level, the Moses story narrates the great events initiated by God and
Moses in the redemption of Israel and proclaims the great laws
detailing God's will for Israel's response to those events. Indeed, the
one builds on the foundation provided by the other. The dialectic
between the two works on the following pattern: 'Because when you
were slaves in Egypt I delivered you from Egyptian bondage, you
shall therefore hear my laws and obey my will'. To have the one
without the other distorts the character of the Moses traditions as
they are preserved in the MT.

Moreover, the canonical level of the story depicts Moses as both
heroic man and non-heroic man. That portrait paints Moses as a
man who can take initiative in the events that save his people, and at
the same time as a man who witnesses God's action that saved his
people. The heroic man is active. The non-heroic form of the man
shows him as passive. Moses knows that the critical events that effect
the shape of the people's destiny come from God. And he simply
facilitates the process. Yet Moses also knows that the leader of the

people cannot simply wait and watch, allowing opportunity to slip away with time. As leader of the people, he must seize the moment, as in the exodus by secret escape, and follow that moment to whatever fate may be at its end. This dialectic centers the Moses tradition in a dynamic process, not in a static ideal of human form. To be an ideal hero, always the same, yesterday, today, tomorrow, and forever, is not the shape of the Moses image cast by the final form of the story. Moses, the hero, can be just as effective in proclamation of God's salvation for his people as Moses, the non-hero, who simply mirrors the events of God's salvation. That combination can be confusing. Is the model a form that calls people to action, willing to accept the consequences of the action? Or is the model a form that calls people to a meek confession that all action, particularly if it is good and helpful, comes from God? The dialectic between images of Moses the hero who acts for his people and Moses the non-hero who is simply a tool in the hands of God also characterizes the canonical level of the Moses traditions. The canonical shape of the Moses story insists that the two belong together in a delicate balance. To have one without the other distorts the character of the Moses tradition.

But still a third dialectic characterizes the canonical shape of the Moses figure. Moses, the hero, the leader of the people who identifies with the people but also steps out at their head, the liberator who defends the people against the acts of various enemies, the lawgiver who tells the people what God expects of them, is at the same time the man of God, the servant of the Lord who himself obeys God's commands, follows his commission even when doubts arise, even submits to his judgment in the face of apparent tragedy. To be heroic man without the imperatives attached to his role as man of God would make Moses God. Final authority would rest with the hero until wrested from him by the next hero. To be man of God without the confidence and ego of the heroic would make Moses a puppet, unable to obey the will of God because, having no will or ego of his own, he would have no decisions to make. Obedience in a person who has no opportunity to be otherwise is no virtue.

Thus, the combination of various traditions about Moses that produced the final picture of the horned leader builds on dialectic between various, at times contrasting poles. Gospel: Law. Heroic: Non-heroic. Heroic Man: Man of God. And those opposing fields of dialectic give the portrait of Moses the character of a collage. Yet, I submit, the diversity in the collage does not render the portrait a surrealistic jumble of mutually exclusive norms. Even the final portrait, the heroic and non-heroic together, captures an experience of humans who shoulder the responsibilities of leadership. Why must the leader look the same today as he looked yesterday? Could the same man who said, 'Father, forgive them, for they know not what they do', also say, 'It is written. "My house shall be called a house of prayer". But you make it a den of robbers', and then drive all who sold and bought in the temple to the streets? This Moses rises to the heights of heroism, defends his people even against God, but also falls to the depths of despair and witnesses a purge of his opposition. This Moses effects the signs and wonders that lead to the exodus, but also submits to the authority of the God who sent him. This Moses is meek and strong, a man of integrity and a man of commitment to people who often had no integrity, a defender of his people even when they were ready to stone him. The canonical picture of Moses, a man caught in the torrents of life and leadership, is in all of its contradiction, its competing images, a remarkably effective portrait of human form. I am unable to conclude that the juxtaposition of competing poles in the picture of this giant is the result of haphazard combination of originally independent sources. I believe that the juxtaposition of these poles is in fact the result of a combination of sources. Moreover, the two principal sources that comprise this picture were apparently independent, at least in the sense of developing quite distinct goals. And yet, the combination of heroic and non-heroic creates an image that, in its surrealism, captures a genuine facet of human experience. The hero is at times necessarily balanced by the non-heroic. The leader who bears the weight of all the people as a nursing father might must on occasion give that people back to God. 'Today is vacation. O God, today, they belong to you.'

The combination of the competing poles in the Moses picture reflects a redactional setting, an age concerned to preserve the traditions from the past. But it does not reflect a nonsensical commitment to preservation, as if the only goal were preservation. The shape of the preserved reflects the struggle with contradictions in public as well as private life characteristic for the setting of the redactor. The age is no longer heroic. Its post-heroic view reflects the concern to survive, as well as a concern, having survived, to make sense out of the form of the survival. That stance fits, so it seems to me, in the period classically defined as the period of redaction for the

Pentateuch. It was an age of new beginning, an age of consolidation, an age of search for new identity. In the swing from captivity to new land with a new law of Moses, could Ezra not be depicted as a New Moses?

In the priestly source, the image of Moses is non-heroic. Two points about setting play a role in the defining of significance for this observation. (1) The priestly source derives from a period of time when no Israelite state provided identity for the people who remembered Moses. No kingship provided leaders who might model their administration after the form of Moses, the hero. The leaders of the people were rather vassals to a controlling state outside the geographical boundaries of the promised land. The ideal image for the period, then, does not develop forms calling for action from the leader, initiative to throw off the yoke of slavery. Rather, the ideal is the lawgiver who proclaims to the community the forms of morality and ritual that will make the community holy before God and, indeed, will effect both that holiness and the events of redemption that provide identity. Again, no king provides the incarnation of the ideal. Rather, identity derives from the ritual. Indeed, the event of salvation itself is the result of the ritual. God comes to the community when the community prepares for the event by the priestly patterns that set the community at worship. In such a community, with the ritual at center stage, could the priestly cast of Moses not offer identity for those who drew life from the execution of the ritual?

2. In a period marked by pressure from outside, the priestly cast of leadership can profit from the virtues of ancient models who depend on God and in their dependency defer to his time. Moses does what he does because God calls him to do it at God's moment. That moment may be effected by the ritual. But the ritual itself belongs to God. If Moses should pervert the ritual, then God's time might be delayed. But Moses succeeds with the ritual, and the success marks the season of God's advent. God comes to Sinai. And so must Israel. In the moment of the ritual, could the tradition not see the New Moses in Jeshua, the priest?

The second part of the definition about significance in the observation focuses on intention. The priestly vision of Moses places value beyond Moses himself, beyond the work of Moses, fully if not exclusively on the work of God. Moses merely facilitates the work as a tool in the hands of the savior. And that facility comes to expression foremost in the law. Moses proclaims God's standards to the community. And the proclamation overshadows the stature of the proclaimer.[1]

In the book of Deuteronomy and in the Deuteronomistic Historian, the operative image for Moses builds on the issues of power and authority.[2] Moses is the lawgiver. The second law draws its authority from its source in Moses. And, indeed, the Deuteronomistic Historian develops a construction of the history of Israel and Judah built on the authority assumed from the position of Moses.[3]

In the Yahwist, the image of Moses is fully heroic. Two points about setting demand attention here also. (1) The portrait of Moses as hero derives from a heroic age. Heroic age assumes a period of kingship, not a period when kingship has become simply a shadow of the past, a stage never again to be set before the audience of the saga.[4] (2) The age reflects a period when, despite pressures from the outside, the model for identity in the community lay within the community. Moses resisted pressure from the outside; indeed, he fought against that pressure and destroyed it. Pressures from the outside, affecting the period from which the saga derives, could also be defeated. With the help of God, the hero can meet the challenges of the day.

The classical definition of setting for the Yahwist in the court of the Davidic king fits this picture of a heroic age. A new kingship under the pressures of foreign threat, under the sign of failure in the efforts to establish kingship by Saul and even by Abimelech called for visions of the heroic. Definition of the Moses narratives as heroic saga supports the traditional conclusions that the Yahwist must come from the time of Solomon or perhaps even from the court of David.[5]

Yet, a major problem confronts this definition of setting for the heroic saga. A strong disjunction between the traditions of Moses and the traditions of David emerges from the Old Testament traditions.[6] In what manner could the Moses traditions as heroic saga have any role at all to play in a court that called on its own traditions about a son of David as the model for identity and leadership? Why would a son of David be concerned about images of heroic leadership associated with Moses?

Observations about intention in the saga for the Yahwist open some insight into the problem. The Moses saga presents a model for judging the quality of leadership established by any son of David at any point in the history of Israel. Even within the Davidic court, Israel's theologians were concerned to establish standards for judging the quality of their kings. This point is already expressed in the Yahwist's presentation of the Garden of Eden as the court of Adam, the first king. The model places limits around the first man, and as a sign to the king, the first man shows the distinct difference between king and God.[7]

The Moses traditions also show what the king should look like. David should exhibit the qualities of Moses in his administration of the kingdom. Otherwise, he might confuse himself and think that he was more than the Son of God. For David and Solomon to be judged by the standards of the New Moses was to prevent abuse by David, Solomon, or any other king of royal power. But at the same time, the Moses traditions show a positive side of the king. The king may be a messenger commissioned by God, a man called to a specific task. But the king is no mean creature, as if by nature he must be a sinner in the sight of God. God calls the king to perfection according to both the model of David and the model of Moses. And that perfection enables the king to perform the tasks for which he carries God's commission. There are no excuses for missing the mark.

Thus, Ezekiel 34 brings the standards of Moses tradition to bear explicitly on the qualities of the Davidic kings. Verses 1-6, the first half of the oracle, describe the abuse of royal power, the abuse of the power of the shepherd. The duties of the shepherds match the elements of tradition in the Moses saga: (1) Feed the sheep. (2) Strengthen the weak. (3) Heal the sick. (4) Bind the crippled. (5) Bring back the strayed. (6) Search for the lost. (7) Rule the sheep with the opposite of force and harshness, i.e. with justice (cf. v. 16). These verses set the responsibilities in a negative cast. The shepherds of God's people fail in these tasks. The burden of Ezekiel's oracle is that the shepherds who have failed will be replaced by one shepherd, 'my servant David'.[8] But this David is a shepherd whose characteristics are Mosaic. Is Ezekiel's vision of the New David not dominated by the characteristics of the New Moses? Is the union not already the fulfillment of the sign act in Ezek. 37.15-28?

To be sure, the time of Ezekiel is not the same as the time for the Yahwist, at least given the traditional definition of the time for the Yahwist's activity. My contention is nonetheless that this element of judgment on the standards and activity of the leadership of God's people, this unique combination of characteristics that belonged to

Moses with the power and authority that belonged to David was present from the beginning of Davidic monarchy, at least from the time of the united monarchy. In fact, since signs of position for the Mosaic tradition in the north have been uncovered, perhaps it was precisely the moment that united the monarchy that brought Moses tradition into contact with Davidic tradition. The images of Moses fit precisely with this pattern: the Liberator, the Shepherd, the Lawgiver who makes the expectations of God for response to his mighty acts explicit. The new Moses is the new David who rules by the way of the Torah, the laws given from Sinai that define the righteousness of David by the justice of Moses.

Could the shape of the Moses tradition as heroic saga be earlier than the period of the kingship? Could the tradition inherited by the Yahwist already have had the heroic element about Moses? The earliest picture of Moses available, perhaps the only picture of Moses from the period before the monarchy, depicts Moses as lawgiver (Deut. 33.4).[9] The focus of the event described by this text highlights God's act. He came from Sinai. He came to his people. He loved (*ḥōbēb*) his people. Indeed, the love he gave to his people was the love of a nursing father (cf. Job 31.33, where *ḥōb* is that part of one's body where security is certain). And that love recalls the image of Moses as the nursing father. The result of God's action was obedience from the people. And then the expression of that divine act is translated to the realm of humans by the act of Moses, the lawgiver. At a pre-Yahwistic level, Moses enters the depiction of God's mighty act as the means for elaborating that act in a narrative of human experience. Indeed, the emphasis on law at just this point suggests that the connection between law and event described above is the fundamental crucible that gives life to the Moses tradition, perhaps even the womb that gives birth to the Moses story as a life-giving tradition for Israel. Moses leads his people from Egypt to the Jordan, meeting each crisis as it comes. And the process provokes Israel's response in faith. To spell that response out, the tradition employs the images of Moses, the lawgiver, and all the rich diversity that accompanies that shape.[10]

The Elohist's image of Moses, like the Elohist source itself, remains too fragmentary to describe in detail. At most, I would conclude that the Elohist pulls the Moses image away from its heroic qualities in order to place greater emphasis on the pictures of God. But that appears to be the work of an editor, expanding the Yahwist's narrative, rather than the work of an independent storyteller.

Chapter 11

THE MOSES TRADITIONS BEYOND THE SAGA

Robert Polzin's treatment of the Moses traditions in the Deuteronomist introduces a significant methodological orientation for evaluating
the function of Mosaic image outside the heroic saga.[1] He reviews the
merits of the historical and literary alternatives in an approach to the
Moses traditions, concluding that for his own work, the focus of his
probe will fall on an exploration of the literature about Moses in the
Deuteronomistic History, but that that exploration cannot stand
isolated from historical critical evaluations. His concern is clearly
not to reconstruct Moses as he really was, not even to reconstruct
Moses as the Deuteronomistic Historian thought he really was. His
concern is rather to describe the manner of imaging Moses reflected
by the Deuteronomistic History. 'The principal role of Moses as seen
in the Book of Deuteronomy is hermeneutic: he is the book's primary
declarer (*maggîd*) and teacher (*mᵉlammēd*) of God's word'.[2] Moreover,
this depiction emphasizes the *authority* of Moses to declare or teach
the word of God, not in the sense of a modern interpreter who stands
to some degree removed from the subject of his work, uninvolved in
the process of interpretation already under way in the text, but rather
in the sense of an involved witness of the power resident in the
tradition. The authority of Moses is then the key item that
underwrites transmission of the Mosaic tradition into the future. The
Deuteronomistic Historian then becomes the interpreter of God's
word in the same history of tradition as Moses. Indeed, the authority
he wields to interpret the post-Mosaic period of history is the same
authority that Moses wields in interpreting the post-exodus history.
It stands in continuity with the authority of Moses to interpret God's
word for the exodus and wilderness generation.

Polzin raises a serious question about the Moses figure in the

Deuteronomistic tradition, however. In order to show that the Deuteronomistic Historian wields the authority appropriate for interpreting the Word of God, the tradition must first diminish the authority of Moses.[3] According to the tradition received by the Deuteronomistic Historian in Deut. 34.1-12, for example, Moses' voice is exalted at the expense of other voices, including the 'author' of the book. But at the same time a second voice appears in the book that exalts the narrator at the expense of Moses' *unique* position of authority, a voice heard in various comments from the narrator that breaks into the body of the text, such as Deut. 1.37; 3.26-27; 4.21-22. This voice is also the center of the tradition as reflected in Deut. 18.15-18, a text that sees another prophet who will do what Moses has done and thus a text that diminishes the unique quality of Moses' leadership.

Yet, some objection from the perspective of a tradition history of the Moses narratives is in order. The tradition about the death of Moses cannot be taken in itself as an indication of a reflex in the tradition designed to diminish the importance of Moses. Perhaps to attribute Moses' failure to enter the land to a sin at the spring of Meribah and thus to God's explicit denial of Moses' right is to be understood as an effort to diminish the authority of Moses. But significantly, the statement about Moses' sin comes from the priestly source with its tendency to non-heroic forms of the Moses tradition. The Yahwist reports nothing of Moses' sin at Meribah. Those texts in Deuteronomy that emphasize Moses' sin and the consequent denial of right for Moses to enter the land show the sin to be heroic. Moses did what he did 'because of you', because of his people.

Moreover, the texts that undercut the unique status of Moses, Deuteronomy 18 and 31, do so by announcing that a new prophet will appear. But the new prophet does not compromise the authority of Moses in the community, but only his singular position. Indeed, the authority of the new prophet to announce the Word of God, and in fact, the authority of the Deuteronomistic Historian to interpret the history of Israel are explicitly Mosaic. They stand in the succession of authority for prophets, teachers, and proclaimers, interpreters of the Word, that roots ultimately in Moses. To diminish the authority of Moses would be to diminish the authority from which the narrator himself speaks. I cannot see, then, the cogency of the interpretation that constructs two voices in conflict with each other, with the result that the voice of Moses is diminished in authority.

It is, I believe, nonetheless significant that two voices appear in the tradition as preserved by the Deuteronomistic Historian. The one voice clearly does exalt Moses as the principal spokesman for the Word of God in the process of the exodus. The other voice complements the voice of Mosaic authority by showing that the power of the Word of God proclaimed by Moses resides outside of Moses' own personal leadership style. To make the claim diminishes Mosaic authority only insofar as the authority roots in Moses alone, in Moses as a single and final judge over all issues. It is just this position that the Old Testament dialectic between heroic man, the paragon of virtue and the administrator of Power, and the man of God, the servant who does what he does as obedient creature to a superior power, comes into play. The dialectic gives expression to the role for the two voices without forcing a showdown between them that would require the exegete to label the one or the other as supreme.

For the history of the Moses traditions, the most important point in Polzin's review is perhaps the observation that the Deuteronomistic Historian speaks with the authority that once belonged to Moses. A similar kind of hermeneutic can be found within the content of the Deuteronomistic history. But at this point the issue is not simply that the Deuteronomistic Historian speaks with the authority of Moses. It is that the Deuteronomistic Historian paints new leaders in Israel's history with images drawn from the Moses traditions. It is as if the Historian wants to describe some leaders in Israel's past as New Moses. The point here is not that the Historian would think that in any one of the subsequent leaders, Moses was reincarnated. There is no theology of reincarnation, indeed, no theology of resurrection here. Rather, the traditions about Moses' leadership become hermeneutical tools for explaining to his people the peculiar style of leadership he found in subsequent leaders of the people. The most obvious point for applying the term of Mosaic leadership to a new leader in Israel is the Deuteronomistic interpretation of Joshua. There is, for example, not only the explicit commission that sets Joshua in the line of Mosaic leadership, Josh. 1.5 and the following address from Joshua to the people confirming the promise of Moses (so, Josh. 1.15), but also the response of the people to Joshua in terms of their previous fidelity to Moses (Josh. 1.17). Moreover, the appearance of 'a man' to Joshua at a critical moment of leadership, an appearance that is marked by the introduction and following instructions ('Put off the shoes from your feet, for the place where you stand is holy'.) as theophany, recalls the confrontation Moses experienced with God at the burning bush. The character of Joshua's relationship with the people is like the character of Moses' relationship with the people: He must lead the people to a particular place. And indeed, the leadership will not be easy. Thus, in Josh. 7.1-26, the effort to take Ai fails. And Joshua laments the failure to God, just as Moses laments the failure of his leadership in Num. 11.14 and Israel laments the loss of Yahweh's presence in Num. 11.42. Moreover, the concluding ceremony for the capture of Ai describes Joshua building an alter according to the description of Moses. And the preparation for the battle at Jericho reports Joshua's confrontation with a man, the commander of the army of the Lord. Joshua's response is identical to Moses' response to confrontation with the Lord at the burning bush. And the stranger instructs Joshua to remove his shoes from his feet, 'for the place where you stand is holy' (Josh. 5.15; cf. Exod. 3.5). As Moses' successor, Joshua is represented by the tradition as a New Moses.

This point is clear in the description of Joshua's position in Josh. 1.5: 'No man shall stand before you all the days of your life. Just as I was with Moses, I shall be with you. I will not fail you or forsake you'. And Josh. 1.16 describes Israel's response to Joshua: 'They answered Joshua saying "All that you command us we will do, and everywhere you send us we will go. Just as we obeyed Moses, so we will obey you. Only may the Lord your God be with you just as he was with Moses"'. In both texts, the intention of the speech clearly sets Joshua's leadership for his people in the mold of Moses. Joshua is Moses' successor. But the text does not imply that Joshua simply fills Moses' office, that a line of succession in a particular office emerges. To the contrary, Joshua is his own figure. He has his own task. But the task merits Mosaic imagery for description of relationships between the leader and the led, and indeed, between the leader and God. Insofar as the imagery is concerned, Joshua is a New Moses.

Mosaic office appears to surface in Deuteronomy. In ch. 34, Moses lays hands on Joshua. And the process marks the 'spirit of wisdom' for Joshua. The result of that ordination is obedience to the commands of Joshua from the people. But the obedience is explicitly a response to Moses. Moreover, Moses is the head of a series of prophets to appear in Israel. In Deut. 18.15, Moses reports that 'the Lord your God shall raise for you a prophet from your midst, from your brothers like me, and you shall obey him'. But the issue is again not an office. The issue is not a prophetic voice or a prophetic tradition. The issue is obedience to leadership. And the leadership fits the model of Moses, not an institutional office that might be Mosaic, but a heroic figure who calls the people to respond. The image is relationship between the leader and the led, not the constitution of a permanent prophetic office.

In this sense, then, Joshua must be seen, not as a prophet in the line of Mosaic prophets, but as a leader whose image is 'New Moses'. The point is that the Mosaic dimension in the Joshua tradition is not institutional. The setting for the Joshua tradition is not the Mosaic office. Rather, the point is that the imagery available to the tradition for describing Joshua and what he did is hermeneutic. The Mosaic quality of the imagery enables the audience to interpret who Joshua is. And since the Mosaic imagery fits the Joshua forms, Joshua must be described explicitly as a New Moses.

One must be careful at just this point. It is important not to interpret any leader whose tradition appears in the form of a heroic saga as a New Moses, just because the form happens to be the same as the form used by tradition for describing Moses. Not every hero of Israelite tradition is by that fact a New Moses. To the contrary, to speak of some figure in tradition as New Moses means to recognize that the tradition interprets the figure in terms and categories that belong in the first order to Moses. Thus, in the relevant Joshua texts, the tradition makes the connection explicit. In Josh. 1.17: 'Just as we obeyed Moses in everything, so we shall obey you. Only may the Lord your God be with you just as he was with Moses'.

The Deuteronomistic Historian clearly interprets the acts of leadership by Jeroboam I as apostasy. Yet, it seems a strong possibility to suggest that from the perspective of the northern empire, from the bias of supporters for Jeroboam I, the model of his leadership must have been Mosaic. An obvious point of contact with Mosaic tradition is the cultic act instigated by Jeroboam in establishing the golden calves in Dan and Bethel. It is well known that the negative interpretation of the golden calves, now obviously at the center stage of the Deuteronomistic History, reflects the bias of the southern tradition. In Exodus 32, Aaron's act falls under the condemnation of Moses as a violation of the newly formed covenant with Yahweh. But it is at least a highly probable conclusion that the tradition in the Yahwist interprets as apostasy an event that was seen

originally as an act of faith in Yahweh.[4] The bulls would not have
been interpreted as idols, actual images of Yahweh, any more than
the cherubim in Jerusalem were. Rather, they would have symbolized
the presence of Yahweh by depicting the seat of his power, a Yahweh
invisibly enthroned on the bulls.[5] For Jeroboam to institute the
symbols in Dan and Bethel, then, would not have been an act of
innovative apostasy, but rather an act of reformation, a call for Israel
to return to the form of worship originally associated with Moses and
Aaron. A part of that positive tradition might be preserved in the
description of the creation of the bulls by Aaron. In his defense to
Moses, he reports that he threw the gold into the fire and the bulls
came out automatically, miraculously (Exod. 32.34). This proposition
is not explicit in the text. The Deuteronomistic Historian casts
Jeroboam's act as an event of simple innovation. The feast for
celebrating the cult of the calves was celebrated 'on the fifteenth day
in the eighth month in the month which he had devised from his own
heart'. But the configuration of the event with its calves is in some
sense Mosaic. And it seems likely that in trying to establish an
alternative to Jerusalem, he would appeal to a tradition that was
sacred to his people, perhaps a tradition that had been displaced by
David's move to Jerusalem.[4]

The Deuteronomistic Historian, perhaps even earlier prophetic
tradition, interprets the prophet Elijah as a New Moses. This
proposition is not built on the fact that Elijah was a prophet and thus
the son of the great father of the prophets. There is no indication that
Elijah simply stands in the succession of prophets that traces its
origin to Moses. To the contrary, the Elijah tradition interprets the
prophet as a Mosaic figure. Thus, Elijah stands before a king in order
to impose the command of Yahweh concerning total filial loyalty.
And the natural process supports the authority of the figure. By
divine aids, Elijah eats and drinks in the wilderness east of the
Jordan. And by God's presence in particular acts, the cruse of oil, the
son of the widow, Elijah's audience declares: 'Now, this I know: You
are a man of God, and the Word of the Lord is truth in your mouth'.
Indeed, a major part of the Elijah tradition documents Yahweh's
preeminence over Baal. And in the face of discouragement in
completing that task, Elijah retreats from the battle to Horeb. The
ensuing theophany involves the wind, an earthquake, a fire. But
finally, a voice identifies God's presence to the figure (cf. Exod.
33.17-23). The presence of God, and particularly the location of

theophany on Horeb, recall the patterns of Mosaic tradition with its promise of presence to Israel through Moses.

Josiah was obviously in the Davidic succession, a king in Jerusalem. Yet, if the association of Josiah's law book (2 Kgs 23.1-3) with Deuteronomy is sound, then Josiah places himself into a Mosaic structure. Indeed, with his official act instituting reform based in the Book, he opens the door for the Deuteronomistic Historian to cast him as a New Moses, a proclaimer of Law and defender of loyalty to the Lord according to the principles of Moses' farewell address to his people. Josiah's concern to extend obedience to the principles of his reform to all of his kingdom receives explicitly a stamp of approval from the Mosaic tradition. 'Before him, there was no king like him who turned to the Lord with all his heart and with all his soul and with all his might, according to all the law of Moses. . . ' Moreover, the design for Mosaic order leads to an effort by Josiah to reconcile the people of God. Josiah launched an extensive campaign to establish control of the north, the people who would have been concerned about Mosaic tradition. It would appear to be clear that had he been successful, his political hegemony over the region of Samaria would have reflected a concern to reunite the divided people of God, a concern that would have brought New Moses and New David tradition together (cf. Ezek. 37.15-28). It was, of course, a tragedy in that great design that his untimely death at Megiddo brought those designs to ruin. Josiah could see the promised land. But he died before he entered the promise.

The prophet Isaiah anticipates an event in the succession on the throne of David that would establish in peace the security of the kingdom of God for all of God's people (Isa. 9.6). The child announced would be for Isaiah a New David. The Second Isaiah also anticipates an event with a distinctive leader. Old Testament scholars have debated the identity of Second Isaiah's servant of the Lord. Could the servant described by the prophet have been Josiah, perhaps the poet-prophet himself? But to find a name identity is misleading. The general content of the prophet's message of hope to the exiles is that a new exodus would constitute God's act of salvation for the people caught by foreign rule. And the leader of the new exodus would be a New Moses. The first of the servant poems identifies that leader as Yahweh's servant, a principal epithet for Moses. His leadership will face trials but will not provoke complaint.[5] Instead, all the earth will await his justice (*mišpāṭ*) and his law (*tôrâ*).

The argument is not that the second Isaiah expects Moses to return. The servant is not Moses raised from the past to lead the present. To the contrary, the leader is a new figure, unnamed by the prophet. But his form, his work, his identity are defined by the Moses traditions. The servant is the New Moses, just as for the first Isaiah the leader is the New David.[6]

In the second poem, the servant title continues. In 49.3, moreover, the leader is named 'my servant Israel'. But even that communal identity has a place in the Mosaic tradition. In the role of Moses as intercessor, Moses makes his identity with his people crucial in his position before God, so much so that the fate defined for the people by God becomes the fate claimed by Moses for himself (Exod. 32.32). But even more, the servant figure receives a universal dimension, like the comment about the torah in 42.4. The third poem catches the tradition of rebellion against Moses, a rebellion that challenges the authority of Mosaic leadership. And the response of the poet is to affirm the authority of the servant in the face of the rebellion. The fourth poem emphasizes the suffering of the leader in the process of his work with the people of God, *for the sake of the people of God*. The vicarious element, only implicit in the Mosaic tradition, is now explicit for the servant. Yet the pattern is clear. Moses was denied the fruit of the land, the goal of his work, *because of the people*. The servant also faced frustrations in completing his mission. 'They made his grave with the wicked and with the rich man in his death, although he had done no violence, and there was no deceit in his mouth.' The analogy may not be exact. The violation of Moses in the later stages of the tradition suggests rash words, some kind of violation with his mouth. Yet, this element does not appear to be a part of the earlier levels in the Mosaic tradition. Thus, the prophet who speaks to exiled Israel of a new exodus describes the servant who effects that exodus as a New Moses.

The same split in the tradition, obvious in the New David of the Isaiah from Jerusalem and the New Moses of the Second Isaiah, can be seen in other forms. Zerubbabel was a member of the house of David, potentially a New David for the new community in Jerusalem. Perhaps Jeshua, the priest, could be interpreted by the new community as a New Moses (Ezra 3.1). Ezra brought a new law for the new community. And his law carried the authority of Moses (Ezra 7.6). Could Nehemiah stand in the position of a New David? Indeed, figures at the center of different genres in Old Testament narrative might be interpreted by the same categories. Could Esther not be understood as a New Moses?[7] Perhaps Ruth could be seen as a New Abraham or, since she stands as ancestress to David, perhaps the storyteller sees her as pre-David, a figure to be interpreted by the standards of the Davidic tradition. Indeed, the connection between David and Abraham might suggest a type of relationship that models Ruth as New Abraham and Pre-David.[8] Ruth, a New Abraham, sets the pattern for David.

The key to the hermeneutic is that the shape of the tradition about David and, for that matter, the shape of the tradition about Moses function heuristically in the process of understanding new figures. Who is Zerrubbabel? Could he not be more clearly understood in terms of the Davidic tradition? Who is Ezra? Could he not be more clearly understood in terms of the Mosaic traditions? Who for Isaiah of Jerusalem is the Messiah? Could he not be more easily identified in terms of the Davidic traditions? Who for the Second Isaiah is the Suffering Servant? Could he not be more easily identified in terms of the Mosaic traditions?

Perhaps the greatest tragedy in the history of these traditions is the fact that the Davidic traditions were not only distinct from and independent of the Mosaic tradition, but they were also the fierce competitor of the Mosaic tradition. The Davidic tradition belonged to Judah. Mosaic tradition belonged in a similar way to Samaria. And the two symbolized the war between the north and the south. Why could the Moses people not recognize the claim of authority from the David people? Why could the David people not submit to the priority of Moses? The tragedy of the split thus posed a pressing question: Could the David people and the Moses people ever be reconciled? Ezekiel dreamed that dream (37.15-28). But where in the history of the tradition did reconciliation ever occur?

In many respects, the pattern of union is apparent in the examples cited above. Ezra-Nehemiah. Zerubbabel-Jeshua. But can the reconciliation of the traditions be found in one figure? Does any one figure in the history of the tradition qualify as both New David and New Moses? The remarkable item about Josiah's career is that he functioned not only as the son of David on the throne in Jerusalem, and thus potentially the New David, but in the reform founded on the principles of Deuteronomy, he functioned as the New Moses, the one who proclaimed the new law for the life of the people of God. Moreover, a major part of his campaign to ground his political reform was to reassert political hegemony over the north. The peace proffered by that prospect would facilitate the rule of a Messiah who would be both New David and New Moses. And the tradition would have helped his subjects understand who he was and what he was doing. But unfortunately, like Moses, his task was cut short, before it could be completed. Har-Meggido proved to be the last battle in the campaign to unite Moses and David. And the disciples of the two must have struggled in order to look beyond Josiah to a future completion of the task.

The New Testament clearly interprets Jesus as a New David.[9] Thus, Jesus was born in Bethlehem, the city of David (Lk. 2.4, 11). Joseph belonged to the house of David (Mt. 1.20). Indeed, the 'Benedictus' identifies the house of David as the source for the horn of God's salvation. But the tradition also employs images from the Moses traditions to depict Jesus. The argument that Jesus is presented as New Moses is not new.[10] The Mount of Beatitudes sets the proclamation of this new lawgiver before his disciples and, thus, before the world. And indeed, the announcement of his salvation by the grace of God does not void the law of Moses. To the contrary, it fulfills it (Mt. 5.17). As Moses enters the world under threat from the Pharaoh, Jesus enters the world under the threat from Herod (Mt. 2.16). As Moses was transfigured before God, an event witnessed subsequently by his people through the shining face, so Jesus transfigured before God, an event witnessed by his disciples and attended by Moses and Elijah, another Moses figure. And as the transfiguration symbolizes the authority of Moses, so it symbolizes the authority of Jesus. The address to the disciples, Mt. 17.5, makes this point clear: 'This is my beloved Son, with whom I am well pleased. *Listen to him*'. As Moses the shepherd feeds his sheep, so Jesus feeds his own and calls his disciples to follow suit (Jn 21.15-19). As Moses heals the pain of his people at the face of death from the serpents and even brings his sister back from the edge of death (Num. 12.12), so Jesus heals the sick and calls the dead to life. Indeed, the untimely death of Jesus, the Suffering Servant, draws fuller meaning from the tradition that sets Jesus in the line of the suffering servant in the Second Isaiah. And like Moses, his death is for the sake of the people. The oppressed are redeemed. The lost are sought out. The weak are strengthened. The crippled are bound up. And Jesus the Good Shepherd leads them.

Yet, these parallels do not suggest that Jesus is cast by the tradition simply as a New Moses.[11] In Jesus, the tradition finds an occasion when the warring factions of leadership unite. This was the man who spoke of Jews and Samaritans together. This was a New Moses and a New David. But like Josiah, he died before the task was complete. As for Moses, the promised land remained a vision of the future. The followers of this New David/New Moses would of necessity look to the future for the completion of the task defined by the tradition of the Messiah and the Suffering Servant. To unify those traditions required more than a lifetime. It would require a new life, a new creation, a New Adam.[12]

Chapter 12

CONCLUSION

The working hypothesis for this probe of the Moses traditions, refined at several points, states: 'The Moses narratives, structured as heroic saga, merge with narrative tradition about Yahweh's mighty acts, structured around confessional themes'. An elaboration of the first element in the assertion emphasizes a particular point about heroic tradition: 'This heroic tradition binds the hero with his people. Either by military might, or by skillful intercession, or by familiarity with surroundings and conditions, he defends and aids his own. He brings "boons" to his people'. On the basis of the examination, I conclude that the hypothesis as refined is sustained. The Moses traditions do not derive from a single office within one institution of Israel's society. They derive from the folk. They therefore employ a wide diversity of images that depict a diversity of facets from the complex figure of Moses. The description of that complex as heroic allows for the diversity, yet emphasizes that in each facet Moses appears as a leader *for the people*. He identifies with their woes. He experiences their crisis. And with the help of God, he acts to resolve their problems. But he is also the man of God who represents God's imperatives to the people. In fact, he is in the first order the one who gives those imperatives a voice. He is the lawgiver. In the dialectic between those two poles, he emerges as an authentic creature, the one who is intimate with God and people, the one who in his intimacy facilitates the intimacy of his people with each other and with God. But he is at the same time a tragic model. His people reject him, despite his intercession for them before God, in spite of his sacrifice for them all along the way. In the heroic tradition, he maintained his intimacy with God and people despite the tragedy. And in that integrity, he calls his people to follow his pattern. Moses, the hero, the authentic man, the suffering servant of the Lord, combines two natures to display the image of the human being available for us all.

NOTES

Notes to Chapter 1

1. In addition to this obvious point of contact in the tradition, see Wayne A. Meeks, *The Prophet-King. Moses Traditions and the Johannine Christology*, NTSup 14 (Leiden: Brill, 1967).

2. The following survey of a Moses bibliography provides context for my work. It is not intended to be exhaustive. For a critical assessment of the discussion about Moses, see Eva Osswald, *Das Bild des Mose in der kritischen alttestamentlichen Wissenschaft seit Julius Wellhausen*, Theologische Arbeiten 18 (Berlin: Evangelische Verlagsanstalt, 1962); Rudolph Smend, *Das Mosebild von Heinrich Ewald bis Martin Noth*, Beiträge zur Geschichte der biblischen Exegese, 3 (Tübingen: Mohr, 1959). For a more recent survey of the Moses discussion, see Herbert Schmid, 'Der Stand der Moseforschung', *Judaica* 21 (1965), pp. 194-221, and C.A. Keller, 'Von Stand und Aufgabe der Moseforschung', *ThZ* 13 (1957), pp. 430-41.

3. John Bright, *A History of Israel* (Philadelphia: Westminster, 1972) p. 124. See also Edward F. Campbell, 'Moses and the Foundation of Israel', *Interp* 29 (1975), pp. 141-54; W. Söderblom, *Das Werden des Gottesglaubens. Untersuchungen über die Anfänge der Religion* (Leipzig: Hinrichs, 1915), p. 310.

4. W.F. Albright, 'Moses in Historical and Theological Perspective', *Magnalia Dei. The Mighty Acts of God*, ed. Frank M. Cross, Werner F. Lemke, Patrick D. Miller (Garden City: Doubleday, 1976), pp. 129-31; *idem*, 'From the Patriarchs to Moses. II. Moses out of Egypt', *BA* 36 (1973), pp. 48-76.

5. Albright, 'Moses in Historical and Theological Perspective', p. 120.

6. Bright, p. 124.

7. Dewey M. Beegle, *Moses, the Servant of Yahweh* (Grand Rapids: Eerdmans, 1972). For greater detail in the following critique, see my review, 'What do we Know of Moses?', *Interp* 28 (1974), pp. 91-94.

8. Beegle, p. 82.

9. Greta Hort, 'The Plagues of Egypt', *ZAW* 69 (1957), pp. 84-102.

10. Beegle, p. 96.

11. Beegle, pp. 347-48. See also Gerhard von Rad, *Moses*, World Christian Books 32 (London: Lutterworth, 1960), pp. 8-9.

> But we have not yet come to the most important point of all. Not a single one of all these stories, in which Moses is the central figure, was really written about Moses. Great as was the veneration of the writers for this man to whom God had been pleased to reveal himself, in all stories it is not Moses himself, Moses the man, but God who is the central figure. *God's* words and *God's* deeds, these are the things that the writers intend to set forth.

See also my comments about this point in 'Moses Versus Amalek: Aetiology and Legend in Exod. 17.8-16', *VTSup* 28 (1975), pp. 29-41.

12. Elias Auerbach, *Moses* (Detroit: Wayne State University, 1975), p. 7.

13. Auerbach, p. 8.

14. Auerbach, p. 8.

15. Martin Noth, *A History of Pentateuchal Traditions*, trans. Bernhard W. Anderson (Englewood Cliffs: Prentice-Hall, 1972), pp. 156-75. See also the critical evaluation of Noth's work by Robert M. Polzin, 'Martin Noth's *A History of Pentateuchal Traditions*', in *Biblical Structuralism. Method and Subjectivity in the Study of Ancient Texts* (Philadelphia: Fortress, 1977), pp. 174-201.

16. Gerhard von Rad, *Old Testament Theology*, trans. D.M.G. Stalker (New York: Harper, 1962), I, p. 14. See also the critical evaluation of von Rad's work by Robert M. Polzin, 'Gerhard von Rad's *The Form-Critical Problem of the Hexateuch*', in *Biblical Structuralism. Method and Subjectivity in the Study of Ancient Texts* (Philadelphia: Fortress, 1977), pp. 150-73.

17. Von Rad, *Theology*, I, p. 289 n. 1.

18. Walther Eichrodt, *Theology of the Old Testament*, trans. J.A. Baker (Philadelphia: Westminster, 1961), I, p. 512.

19. Franz Hesse, 'Kerygma oder geschichtliche Wirklichkeit? Kritische Fragen zu Gerhard von Rads "Theologie des Alten Testaments", I. Teil', *ZThK* 57 (1960), p. 24.

20. Walter C. Kaiser, Jr, *Toward an Old Testament Theology* (Grand Rapids: Zondervan, 1978), p. 26.

21. Roland de Vaux, *The Early History of Israel*, trans. David Smith (Philadelphia: Westminster, 1978), p. 371.

24. James S. Ackerman, 'The Literary Context of the Moses Birth Story (Exodus 1-2)', in *Literary Interpretations of Biblical Narratives*, ed. Kenneth R.R. Gros Louis, James S. Ackerman, and Thayer S. Warshaw (Nashville: Abingdon, 1974), p. 75.

25. For details of this discussion, see Sigmund Mowinckel, *Psalms in Israel's Worship*, trans. D.R. Ap-Thomas (Nashville: Abingdon, 1962), pp. 1-22.

26. Bright, p. 124.

27. Klaus Koch, 'Der Tod des Religionsstifters', *KuD* 8 (1962), p. 105. For a critical review of Koch's position, see Friedrich Baumgärtel, 'Der Tod des Religionsstifters', *KuD* 9 (1963), pp. 223-33; S. Herrmann, 'Mose', *EvT* 28 (1968), pp. 301-28; Rolf Rendtorff, 'Moses als Religionsstifter? Ein Beitrag

zur Diskussion über die Anfänge der israelitischen Religion', in *Gesammelte Studien zum Alten Testament* (München: Kaiser, 1975), pp. 152-71.

28. Koch, p. 105.

29. J.R. Porter, *Moses and the Monarchy. A Study in the Biblical Tradition of Moses* (Oxford: Blackwell, 1963), pp. 8-9.

30. J. Jeremias, *Moses und Hammurabi* (Leipzig: J.C. Hinrichs, 1903).

31. See the argument for this definition in my essay, 'Humility and Honor; A Moses Legend in Numbers 12', in *Art and Meaning: Rhetoric in Biblical Literature*, JSOT Supplement 19 (Sheffield: JSOT, 1982), pp. 97-107.

32. Porter, p. 16. See also Ivan Engnell, *A Rigid Scrutiny. Critical Essays on the Old Testament*, trans. John T. Willis (Nashville: Vanderbilt, 1969), p. 60.

33. See the discussion by Albert Gerlin, *The Poor of Yahweh*, trans. Mother Kathryn Sullivan (Collegeville: Liturgical Press, 1964).

34. So, the argument in my essay, 'Humility and Honor'.

35. Murray Lee Newman, *The People of the Covenant. A Study of Israel from Moses to the Monarchy* (Nashville: Abingdon, 1962), pp. 156-87. This point appears forcefully in Walter Brueggemann, *The Prophetic Imagination* (Philadelphia: Fortress, 1978).

36. Trent C. Butler, 'An Anti-Moses Tradition', *JSOT* 12 (1979), pp. 9-15.

37. Butler does not connect the anti-Moses tradition to the cult in Jerusalem. Indeed, some of the pro-Moses tradition may belong there. My point is simple. If an anti-Moses tradition exists, what relationship did it have to the covenant tradition in Jerusalem? Would Murray Newman's arguments about conflict between Mosaic covenant and Davidic covenant not become decisive for the discussion?

38. Brevard S. Childs, *The Book of Exodus. A Critical, Theological Commentary*, OTL (Philadelphia: Westminster, 1974), pp. 35-36.

39. Childs, p. 353.

40. Childs, p. 353. See also James Muilenburg, 'The Form and Structure of the Covenantal Formulations', *VT* 9 (1959), pp. 347-65.

41. Childs, p. 356.

42. Rudolf Smend, *Yahweh War and Tribal Confederation. Reflections upon Israel's Earliest History*, trans. Max Rogers (Nashville: Abingdon, 1970), p. 120.

43. Smend, *Yahweh War*, pp. 122-24. See also Franz Schnutenhaus, 'Die Entstehung der Mosetraditionen' (Heidelberg: Unpublished dissertation, 1958).

44. Smend, *Yahweh War*, p. 127.

45. Smend, *Yahweh War*, p. 128.

46. Ann M. Vater, 'The Communication of Messages and Oracles as a Narration Medium in the Old Testament' (New Haven: Unpublished dissertation, 1976), p. 137. See also J. Kenneth Eakins, 'Moses', *RevEx* 74 (1977), pp. 461-71.

47. Maurice Luker, 'The Figure of Moses in the Plague Traditions' (Madison: Unpublished dissertation, 1968).

48. James Muilenburg, 'The "Office" of the Prophet in Ancient Israel', in *The Bible in Modern Scholarship*, ed. J. Phillip Hyatt (Nashville: Abingdon, 1965), p. 87.

49. Lothar Perlitt, 'Moses als Prophet', *EvT* 31 (1971), p. 606.

50. Von Rad, *Theology*, I, p. 292.

51. Von Rad, *Theology*, I, p. 293.

52. Von Rad, *Theology*, I, p. 294.

53. Von Rad, *Theology*, I, p. 294.

54. Von Rad, *Theology*, I, p. 296.

55. Von Rad, *Theology*, I, p. 291.

56. A.H.J. Gunneweg, *Leviten und Priester. Hauptlinien der Traditionsbildung und Geschichte des israelitisch-jüdischen Kultpersonals*, FRLANT 89 (Göttingen: Vandenhoeck & Ruprecht, 1965), p. 66.

57. Gunneweg, p. 68: 'Wie man auch immer über die Historizität Moses als einer Person und über die überlieferungsgeschichtliche Herkunft Moses als einer Überlieferungsgestalt urteilen will, sicher dürfte auf jeden Fall dies sein, dass die Mosegestalt ihre überragende, zentrale Bedeutung im jetzigen Gesamtgefüge der Pentateucherzählung erlangt hat nur als der Mittler zwischen Jahwe und Israel, als Bundesmittler, als Formulator des Gesetzes und in der von Mose ausgeübten Funktion der Gesetzesvermahnung.'

58. Hugo Gressmann, *Mose und seine Zeit. Ein Kommentar zu den Mose Sagen*, FRLANT 18 (Göttingen: Vandenhoeck & Ruprecht, 1918), p. 392.

59. Geo Widengren, 'What do we know about Moses?' in *Proclamation and Presence. Old Testament Essays in honor of Gwynne Henton Davies*, ed. John I. Durham and J.R. Porter (Richmond: John Knox, 1970), p. 43.

60. There is, of course, a problem in reading the text. A variant suggests, not Moses, but Manasseh. Yet, regardless of the resolution in the textual problem, the form of the text as it is now received suggests Moses. At some stage in the history of the text, and thus, the history of the tradition, this priesthood follows a lineage to Moses. See my comments in *Rebellion in the Wilderness. The Murmuring Motif in the Wilderness Traditions of the Old Testament* (Nashville: Abingdon, 1968), p. 264. See also Herbert Schmid, *Mose. Überlieferung und Geschichte*, BZAW 110 (Berlin: Töpelmann, 1968), pp. 98-99.

61. Eichrodt, I, p. 289. He then emphasizes 'charisma' as the key factor in understanding the Moses image.

62. Thomas L. Thompson, 'The Joseph and Moses Narrratives', in *Israelite and Judean History*, ed. John H. Hayes and J. Maxwell Miller (Philadelphia: Westminster, 1977), p. 178.

63. Vater, p. 138, asks a similar question: 'What underlying or all-pervasive Moses image realizes, i.e., actualizes the role(s) of history and tradition according to our witness?' The question could be better formulated,

I think, by asking what underlying or all-pervasive Moses image actualizes the story. Her remaining questions follow: 'Then, what is the historical probability of that image? Next, what are the narration patterns and other formal elements which carry the image? Then, what is the narration use of those patterns and elements? And finally, what story do the patterns which carry the image really tell?' These questions leave us with a methodological problem. If I ask about the historical probability of the image, what kind of answer might I expect? Would it be a literary one? In that case, the image would reflect a significant degree of historical verisimilitude. Or is it a historical or sociological one? In that case, the image would lead us to the historical Moses or at least to the 'office' related to Moses.

64. Gressmann, pp. 345-92.

65. Gressmann, p. 360. The German term 'Sagen' is not appropriately translated by the English (Scandinavian) term '*Saga*'. *Sagen* refers to a genre told for the sake of entertainment or indoctrination. Various genres might appear under this more general term. In this particular case, however, the English term 'tale' seems the more appropriate.

66. Gressmann, p. 364.

67. Gressmann, p. 367.

68. Gressmann, p. 378.

69. Gressmann, pp. 387-88.

70. See the discussion of Noth's position, above.

71. Noth, pp. 172-73. Noth formulates this position by asserting that Moses was originally fixed in the grave tradition and not broadly to a conquest theme.

72. Childs, pp. 353-60.

73. Schnutenhaus, pp. 151-52; also Smend, p. 123.

74. Schmid, pp. 112-13.

75. This conclusion does not mean that the division of the narrative into distinct themes also rests on sand. It is quite clear that a unit of narrative about the exodus appears under the stamp of a leitmotif, the oppression in Egypt. And the narrative ranges from its introduction in Exodus 1 to an account of an exodus from the 'house of bondage' in Exodus 12. The same point can be made for the wilderness theme and the conquest theme. Each has its particular structure, organized around a particular leitmotif. The conclusion means rather that no evidence exists that proves the independence of the themes from each other.

76. In more recent publications, the suggestion that all four themes must have been originally interdependent, combined under the shadow of the Moses figure, does appear. See Herrmann, pp. 321, 327.

77. Von Rad, *Theology*, I, p. 291.

78. Von Rad, *Theology*, I, p. 291.

79. Von Rad, *Theology*, I, p. 292.

80. Von Rad, *Theology*, I, pp. 292-93.

81. Von Rad, *Theology*, I, pp. 293-94.

82. Von Rad, *Theology*, I, p. 294.

83. Von Rad, *Theology*, I, p. 296.

84. Gerhard von Rad, *Moses*, World Christian Books 32 (London: Lutterworth Press, 1960), p. 10.

85. Von Rad, *Moses*, pp. 8-9.

86. Schnutenhaus, p. 6.

87. Schnutenhaus, p. 180.

88. Vater, p. 130.

89. Vater, p. 139.

90. Vater, p. 149.

91. Vater, pp. 151-52. For a more recent treatment of the messenger traditions, see Ann M. Vater, 'Narrative Patterns for the Story of Commissioned Communication in the Old Testament', *JBL* 99 (1980), pp. 365-82.

92. Robert M. Polzin, *Moses and the Deuteronomist: A Literary Study of the Deuteronomic History* (New York: Seabury Press, 1980).

93. Polzin, 'Gerhard von Rad', pp. 150-73.

94. George W. Coats, *From Canaan to Egypt; Structural and Theological Context for the Joseph Story*, CBQMS 4 (Washington: Catholic Biblical Association, 1976), pp. 55-60.

95. Rolf Rendtorff, *Das überlieferungsgeschichtliche Problem des Pentateuch*, BZAW 147 (Berlin: de Gruyter, 1977), pp. 80-146; 'The "Yahwist" as Theologian? The Dilemma of Pentateuchal Criticism', *JSOT* 3 (1977), pp. 2-10; Hans Heinrich Schmid, *Der sogenannte Jahwist. Beobachtungen und Fragen zur Pentateuchforschung* (Zürich: Theologischer Verlag, 1976); John van Seters, *Abraham in History and Tradition* (New Haven: Yale University Press, 1975), pp. 148-53.

96. Hermann Gunkel, 'Mose', in *Die Religion in Geschichte und Gegenwart* (2nd edn; Tübingen: Mohr, 1930). Gunkel's analysis of Moses traditions stands at the head of a long series of treatments exploring the traditions of the Old Testament in order to uncover the historical kernel (so, p. 233). Yet Gunkel sets the pace for the analysis by recognizing that the tradition does not give us immediate access to the historical Moses, but rather a *Sagenkranz* (p. 232). And the character of the narratives as '*Sagen*' influences the shape of the portrait projected by the narratives. That shape is the concern of the exploration that follows.

97. Elements in this chapter were presented as a Fulbright lecture at Oxford and Cambridge, May, 1977. My suggestion that the Moses traditions should properly be understood as heroic appears in two essays: 'Moses Versus Amalek: Aetiology and Legend in Exod. 17.8-16', in *Congress Volume Edinburgh. Supplement to Vetus Testamentum 28* (Leiden: Brill, 1975), pp. 29-41; 'The King's Loyal Opposition: Obedience and Revolution in the Moses Traditions', in *Canon and Authority in the Old Testament*, ed. George

W. Coats and Burke O. Long (Philadelphia: Fortress, 1977), pp. 91-109. For a more recent proposal that the Moses traditions can be defined as heroic, see James Nohrnberg, 'Moses', in *Images of Man and God. Old Testament Short Stories in Literary Focus*, ed. Burke O. Long (Sheffield: Almond, 1981), pp. 35-57.

98. Martin Noth, *A History of Pentateuchal Traditions*, trans. Bernhard W. Anderson (Englewood Cliffs: Prentice Hall, 1972), p. 161.

99. It would seem to me to be a clearly established fact that precise units of tradition with marked beginnings and an explicitly conceived structure that moves to marked endings constitute the themes of tradition in the Moses narratives: (1) the exodus theme, structured around a leitmotif about redemption from Egyptian oppression, and (2) the wilderness theme, structured around a wilderness itinerary and introduced by a leitmotif about aid to the people in the face of wilderness crises. (3) A Sinai theme may have been an original third item in the series. But in the present structure of the Pentateuch, it is one among several elements in the wilderness itinerary and thus a (secondary?) part of the wilderness theme. (4) The conquest theme, structured around a series of battle reports and introduced by a leitmotif about fear among the Canaanites of the approaching army of the Lord would represent a fourth theme. But for the Moses traditions the conquest is not a distinct element with a marked beginning.

100. Noth, p. 162.

101. See the comments about this problem in Chapter 2 below.

102. My seminar address to the 1983 convention of the Society of Biblical Literature entitled 'The Form-Critical Problem of the Pentateuch' dealt with these issues.

103. Bernhard W. Anderson, *Understanding the Old Testament* (3rd edn; Englewood Cliffs: Prentice-Hall, 1975), p. 48. See also Gerhard von Rad, *Moses*, World Christian Books 32 (London: Lutterworth, 1960), p. 10.

104. Lord Raglan, 'The Hero of Tradition', in *The Study of Folklore*, ed. Alan Dundee (Englewood Cliffs: Prentice-Hall, 1965), pp. 142-57.

105. Jan de Vries, *Heroic Song and Heroic Legend*. trans. B.J. Timmer (New York: Oxford University Press, 1963), pp. 210-26.

106. Joseph Campbell, *The Hero with a Thousand Faces*, Ballingen Series 17 (Princeton: Princeton University Press, 1949), p. 30. See also Carl Edwin Armerding, 'The Heroic Ages of Greece and Israel: A Literary-Historical Comparison' (Boston: Unpublished dissertation [Brandeis], 1968), pp. 262-79.

107. James L. Crenshaw, *Samson. A Secret Betrayed; a Vow Ignored* (Atlanta: John Knox, 1978).

108. Crenshaw, p. 126.

109. See de Vries, pp. 235-41.

110. R.F. Johnson, 'Moses', in *The Interpreter's Dictionary of the Bible* (Nashville: Abingdon, 1962), p. 448.

111. John van Seters, *Abraham in History and Tradition* (New Haven: Yale University Press, 1975), pp. 131-37.

112. Van Seters, p. 131, n. 19. I would agree completely with his objections to current translations of the German term *Sage*. I would also include in the objections his own term. Legend can be simply something read or spoken, thus *Sage*. But it can also have a more precise, generic meaning. See Ron Hals, 'Legend: A Case Study in OT Form-Critical Terminology', *CBQ* 34 (1972), pp. 166-76; reprinted in *Saga, Legend, Tale, Novella, Fable. Narrative Genres in Old Testament Literature*, ed. George W. Coats; JSOTS 34 (Sheffield: JSOT, 1984). If objections against using legend for this kind of narrative nonetheless arise, then some other term must be proposed, for Hals and others have correctly distinguished a genre of narrative material. I would think that until a more workable term acceptable to a larger range of members in the field appears, 'legend' should be reserved for the genre Hals defines. *Sage* might be represented with a more neutral term such as narrative or story, or perhaps even better, account.

113. Robert W. Neff, 'Saga', in *Saga, Legend, Tale, Novella, Fable. Narrative Genres in Old Testament Literature*, ed. George W. Coats; JSOTS 34 (Sheffield: JSOT, 1984).

114. So, Neff.

Notes to Chapter 2

1. George W. Coats, 'Legendary Motifs in the Moses Death Reports', *CBQ* 39 (1977), pp. 34-44.

2. James S. Ackerman, 'The Literary Context of the Moses Birth Story (Exodus 1-2)', in *Literary Interpretations of Biblical Narratives*, ed. Kenneth R.R. Gros Louis, James S. Ackerman, Thayer S. Warshaw (Nashville: Abingdon, 1974), pp. 89-96. 'Scholars have pointed out that the foundling child motif appears in many hero birth stories throughout the ancient near East.' See also D.B. Redford, 'The Literary Motif of the Exposed Child', *Numen* 14 (1967), pp. 209-28.

3. Brevard S. Childs, 'The Birth of Moses', *JBL* 84 (1965), pp. 109-122.

4. See the form analysis by Childs, 'The Birth of Moses'.

5. On the Egyptian name of Moses, see Childs, *The Book of Exodus, A Critical, Theological Commentary*, Old Testament Library (Philadelphia: Westminster, 1974), p. 19. Childs observes that while the name is obviously Egyptian, the storyteller does not reveal any awareness of that fact. The story sets up an irony. This point is suggested by James Plastaras, *The God of Exodus. The Theology of the Exodus Narratives* (Milwaukee: Bruce, 1966), p. 42. 'The Egyptian name sounded just like the present participle of the Hebrew verb *mashah*, meaning "to draw out" . . . Moses, the future savior of

Israel, must himself first be saved. Before he can be God's instrument in "drawing out", he must himself be drawn out. His very life is a prophetic sign of the exodus'.

6. Childs (*The Book of Exodus*, p. 11) concludes that the midwives tale functions as introduction for the birth tale. It does not reflect ancient tradition. But see the comments of Plastaras, p. 40.

7. This intention would obtain regardless of the position about the dependence or independence of the midwives tale.

8. Childs, *The Book of Exodus*, p. 11.

9. James B. Pritchard, ed., *Ancient Near Eastern Texts* (Princeton: Princeton University Press, 1955), p. 119.

10. For the significance of the designation of Sargon's mother as a 'changeling' who could not keep her baby; see Childs, *The Book of Exodus*, pp. 8-9. Childs cites a possible argument: 'One could argue that Sargon's claim of an *entu* as a mother automatically implied that his father was a king'. In that case, the parallel with the Moses story would be closer, since then the parentage of both would be known and, indeed, important for the intention of the tale. But Childs does not embrace this possibility.

11. So, Childs, *The Book of Exodus*, p. 9.

12. Childs, *The Book of Exodus*, pp. 10-11. Childs attributes both 1.15-21 and 2.1-10 to E. For an alternative position, see Martin Noth, *Exodus, a Commentary*, trans. J.S. Bowden; Old Testament Library (Philadelphia: Westminster, 1962), pp. 23-25. Noth attributes 1.15-21 to E and 2.1-10 to J.

13. Hans Walter Wolff, 'Elohistic Fragments in the Pentateuch', in *The Vitality of Old Testament Traditions*, ed. Walter Brueggemann & Hans Walter Wolff (Atlanta: John Knox, 1975), pp. 67-82.

14. See the comments on this motif in my essay, 'Abraham's Sacrifice of Faith. A Form-Critical Study of Genesis 22', *Interp* 27 (1973), p. 396 n. 7.

15. Trent C. Butler, 'An Anti-Moses Tradition', *JSOT* 12 (1979), p. 10. 'The section begins with the typical temporal clause. Tension is built through imperfect consecutives describing the murderous act of Moses...' Butler depicts this narrative as a description of the *guilt* of Moses, the presumptuous pretender. I cannot, however, detect any explicit element in the text that suggests the intention as a picture of guilt. To be sure, he looks this way and that before he acts. But that element arises out of self-defense in the face of his enemies, not out of guilt for killing one of them. See the discussion of this interpretation in Childs, *The Book of Exodus*, pp. 41-42.

16. See the discussion of this question in Childs, *The Book of Exodus*, p. 41.

17. Noth, *Exodus*, pp. 30-31.

18. George W. Coats, 'Moses in Midian', *JBL* 92 (1973), pp. 3-10.

19. So, my argument in 'Moses in Midian'.

20. On the name of the father-in-law, see W.F. Albright, 'Jethro, Hobab and Reuel in Early Hebrew Tradition', *CBQ* 25 (1963), pp. 1-11; J. Philip

Hyatt, *Commentary on Exodus*, New Century Bible (London: Oliphants, 1971), pp. 67-68.

21. Noth, *Exodus*, p. 37.

22. Childs, *The Book of Exodus*, p. 31. 'The writer is extremely restrained in his description of this intervention. He is obviously not interested in portraying Moses as a folk hero. (Contrast this reservation with the description of Samson or Jonathan in action.)' Yet, some critical question would be in order. The description in v. 17b may be restrained. But it uses a key verb to describe Moses' action: *wayyôsi'ān*. Compare Judg. 3.31; 6.15; 10.1; 1 Sam. 10.27; Hos. 13.10; Jer. 14.9. The verb in the daughters' speech to their father, v. 19, might also be relevant: *hiṣṣîlanû*. Compare the use of the verb in the exodus story: Exod. 5.23; 12.27; 18.8. These occasions refer to Yahweh's act in the event. But they do show the importance of the word.

23. Butler, p. 11, suggests that this story is anti-Moses because it features a marriage between an Israelite and a Midianite in contradiction to Numbers 25. Yet, the Numbers text is so explicitly focused on the apostasy of Baal Peor that it serves only with difficulty as a general principle; at least it does not serve as a principle at the center of the text in Exodus 2. There is no intrinsic element of polemic there, no notion that marriage to a Midianite is wrong.

24. See my definition of transition in 'A Structural Transition in Exodus', *VT* 22 (1972), pp. 129-42. Verses 23-25 fit the structural pattern for transition by tying into the preceding pericope. This function is fulfilled by the allusion to the death of the king of Egypt, an allusion that picks up the tradition, but not the source formulation of 2.15. Then the transition looks ahead to the commission of Moses, with reference to a cry from the people of Israel which God heard. The reference alludes to both Exodus 3, although the verb is *zā'aq* rather than *ṣā'aq*, and to Exodus 6, where the noun is *na*ᵃ*qâ*.

25. Plastaras, pp. 58-59.

26. Albright, pp. 1-11. Albright offers a reconstruction of the tradition in order to explain the shift in name for the father-in-law of Moses from Reuel to Jethro. According to his thesis, the name of the priest was Jethro, member of a tribe named Reuel.

27. Roland de Vaux, *The Early History of Israel*, trans. David Smith (Philadelphia: Westminster, 1978), pp. 330-38. De Vaux reviews the broad discussion. For this particular point, see p. 333.

28. Rolf Knierim, 'Exodus 18 und die Neuordnung der mosaischen Gerichtsbarkeit', *ZAW* 73 (1961), pp. 146-71.

29. De Vaux, pp. 813-14. De Vaux attributes Numbers 31 to a later level of P. On the story in Numbers 25, see Noth, *A History*, pp. 78-79.

Notes to Chapter 3

1. Norman Habel, 'The Form and Significance of the Call Narratives', *ZAW* 77 (1965), pp. 297-323. See also Kutsch, 'Gideons Berufung und Altarbau Jdc. 6, 11-24', *TLZ* 81 (1956), pp. 75-84; Walther Zimmerli, 'Zur Form- und Traditionsgeschichte der prophetischen Berufungsgeschichte', *Ezechiel*, BKAT 13/1 (Neukirchen-Vluyn: Neukirchener Verlag, 1969), pp. 16-21.

2. Jörg Jeremias, *Theophanie. Die Geschichte einer alttestamentlichen Gattung*, WMANT 10 (Neukirchen-Vluyn: Neukirchener Verlag, 1965). On the importance of fire for such narratives, see Hugo Gressmann, *Mose und seine Zeit. Ein Kommentar zu den Mose-Sagen*, FRLANT 18 (Göttingen: Vandenhoeck & Ruprecht, 1913), pp. 28-29.

3. Childs, *The Book of Exodus*, pp. 68-69. 'Whereas the J tradition identifies Yahweh with the God of the Father, the E tradition, followed by P, marks a discontinuity in the tradition... The E tradition has Moses approaching the people with the claim of being sent to them by the God of their father... Verse 15 supplies the answer. *Yahweh* is the God of the fathers'. For the basic study of this traditio-historical problem, see Albrecht Alt, 'The God of the Fathers', in *Essays on Old Testament History and Religion*, trans. R.A. Wilson (Garden City: Doubleday, 1968), pp. 14-18.

4. Noth, *Exodus*, p. 41.

5. George W. Coats, 'Self-Abasement and Insult Formulas', *JBL* 89 (1970), pp. 14-26.

6. Childs, *The Book of Exodus*, pp. 56-60

7. Childs, *The Book of Exodus*, pp. 57-58.

8. See the review of the argument by E.W. Nicholson, *Exodus and Sinai in History and Tradition*, Growing Points in Theology (Oxford: Blackwell, 1973).

9. Nicholson's conclusions are summarized on pp. 53-84. See esp. p. 82. 'What conclusions may be drawn concerning the relationship between the Sinai tradition embodied in the JE narrative in Exodus 19 and the Exodus tradition? Here surely the evidence is that those traditions were interrelated from the beginning. For the figure of Moses which, as we have seen, was integral to the Exodus tradition from the beginning, is likewise integral to the tradition in Exodus 19 and cannot be regarded as having been only secondarily inserted or associated with it. There are no sound reasons—whether from a literary-critical, form-critical, or traditio-historical point of view—for believing that the Sinai tradition embodied in the old JE narrative in Exodus 19 either originated or developed independently of the Exodus tradition in early Israel'.

10. Martin Buber, *Moses. The Revelation and the Covenant*, Harper Torchbooks 27 (New York: Harper, 1958), pp. 51-55. See also Plastaras, pp. 94-100.

11. See the review of this discussion by Childs, *The Book of Exodus*, pp. 61-64.

12. This complex may reflect a relatively late stage in the history of the tradition. But it is significant to see that the stage here is a pre-literary, pre-Yahwistic one.

13. George W. Coats, 'Despoiling the Egyptians', *VT* 18 (1968), pp. 450-57.

14. See Gerhard von Rad, 'Faith Reckoned as Righteousness', in *The Problem of the Hexateuch and other essays*, trans. E.W. Trueman Dicken (London: Oliver and Boyd, 1965), pp. 125-30.

15. Heinrich Gross, 'Der Glaube an Mose nach Exodus (4.14, 19)', in *Wort-Gebot-Glaube: Beiträge zur Theologie des Alten Testaments*, ed. Johann Jakob Stamm, Ernst Jenni, Hans Joachim Stoebe (Zürich: Zwingli, 1970), pp. 57-65.

16. Horst Seebass, *Mose und Aaron, Sinai und Gottesberg*, Abhandlungen zur evangelischen Theologie 2 (Bonn: Bouvier, 1962), pp. 28-31.

17. Martin Noth, *Numbers, a Commentary*, trans. James D. Martin (Philadelphia: Westminster, 1968), p. 130. 'Here Aaron, in the list of Israelite tribes, is simply the representative of the tribe of Levi as if, besides the Aaronites, there were no other "Levites".'

18. See Michael Mulhall, 'Aaron and Moses. Their Relationship in the Oldest Sources of the Pentateuch' (Washington: Unpublished dissertation, 1973).

19. Dewey M. Beegle, *Moses, The Servant of Yahweh* (Grand Rapids: Eerdmans, 1972), p. 79: 'Whatever the signs were which Yahweh gave to Moses, they did not overcome his reluctance, and so finally he comes to one of his deep-seated fears. "Oh, my Lord, I am not eloquent. . . " He could not speak well before Yahweh appeared to him, and his condition has not improved during the burning bush experience. . . Yahweh knows that he has made Moses a stammerer, but he is going to use him anyway.' Auerbach, p. 34, makes a similar observation: 'Moses raises the objection that . . . for him the formulation of the right words is difficult'.

20. De Vries, pp. 227-41.

21. Childs, *The Book of Exodus*, pp. 95-101.

22. Gressmann, *Mose und seine Zeit*, pp. 30-31.

23. Noth, *A History of Pentateuchal Traditions*, p. 202.

24. Childs, *The Book of Exodus*, p. 55.

25. Childs, *The Book of Exodus*, pp. 55-56.

26. Childs, *The Book of Exodus*, p. 56.

27. Habel, pp. 297-323.

28. Vater, pp. 136-37.

29. Childs, *The Book of Exodus*, p. 55.

30. Noth, *A History of Pentateuchal Traditions*, p. 36.

31. Noth, *A History of Pentateuchal Traditions*, p. 36.

32. For details, see Childs, *The Book of Exodus*, pp. 111-14.

33. Norbert Lohfink, 'Die priesterschriftliche Abwertung der Tradition von der Offenbarung des Jahwenamens an Mose', *Bibl* (1968), pp. 1-8.

34. Noth, *A History*, p. 178.

35. Noth, *A History*, pp. 180-81.

36. Heinrich Valentin, *Aaron. Eine Studie der vor-priesterschriftlichen Aaron-Überlieferung*, Orbis Biblicus et Orientalia 18 (Göttingen: Vandenhoeck & Ruprecht, 1978), pp. 412-18.

37. Noth, *A History*, pp. 182-83.

Notes to Chapter 4

1. See the effective analysis of structure in Exodus 3-11 by Moshe Greenberg, *Understanding Exodus. The Heritage of Biblical Israel II/1* (New York: Behrman House, 1969). A shorter version of the same material appears in 'The Thematic Unity of Exodus iii-xi', in *Fourth World Congress of Jewish Studies* (Jerusalem: World Union of Jewish Studies, 1967), I, pp. 151-54.

2. Noth, *A History*, p. 71.

3. Coats, 'Self-Abasement and Insult Formulas'.

4. Coats, *Rebellion*, pp. 29-36.

5. Noth, *A History*, p. 71.

6. Rudolf Smend, *Yahweh War and Tribal Confederation. Reflections upon Israel's Earliest History*, trans. Max Gray Rogers (Nashville: Abingdon, 1970), pp. 125-27.

7. Noth, *A History*, p. 30.

8. Noth, *A History*, p. 66.

9. Greenberg, 'Thematic Unity', p. 153.

10. Dennis J. McCarthy, 'Moses' Dealings with Pharaoh: Ex 7, 8-10, 27', *CBQ* 27 (1965), pp. 336-45. The abbreviations in the following outlines refer to patterns in each scene: M—Moses; A—Aaron; Ph—Pharaoh; NL—the Pharaoh would 'not listen'; AYS—as the Lord said; NLPG—he would 'not let the people go'; KF—knowledge formula: 'you shall know that I am the Lord'; DLPG—he did not let the people go.

11. Childs, *The Book of Exodus*, p. 151.

12. Noth, *A History*, p. 71.

13. H.J. Kraus, *Worship in Israel. A Cultic History of the Old Testament*, trans. Geoffrey Buswell (Richmond: John Knox, 1965), pp. 45-55.

14. George W. Coats, 'Despoiling the Egyptians', *VT* 18 (1968), pp. 450-57.

15. Julian Morgenstern, 'The Despoiling of the Egyptians', *JBL* 68 (1949), pp. 2-3.

16. David Daube, *The Exodus Pattern in the Bible. All Souls Studies* (London: Faber and Faber, 1963), pp. 55-57. See also Georg Fohrer, *Überlieferung und Geschichte des Exodus. Eine Analyse von Ex 1-15*, BZAW

91 (Berlin: Töpelmann, 1964), p. 82 n. 7.

17. In contrast, see Dennis J. McCarthy, 'Plagues and Sea of Reeds: Exodus 5-14', *JBL* 85 (1966), pp. 137-58.

18. Gerhard von Rad, *Old Testament Theology. The Theology of Israel's Prophetic Traditions*, trans. D.M.G. Stalker (New York: Harper & Row, 1965), II, pp. 95-96.

19. It is clear here that the two facets are complementary. The rod of God is the rod of Moses. The point thus supports the thesis formulated above.

20. Noth, *Exodus*, p. 70.

21. Childs, *Book of Exodus*, p. 131 Childs notes his dependency on the source analysis of Fohrer. See Fohrer, p. 70.

22. Childs, *Book of Exodus*, p. 137.

23. Childs, *Book of Exodus*, p. 137.

24. Childs, *Book of Exodus*, p. 131.

25. Fohrer, pp. 62-70.

26. Fohrer, p. 63.

27. Fohrer, p. 63.

28. Fohrer, p. 70. The synopsis of the three sources appears here.

29. George W. Coats, 'The Failure of the Hero: Moses as a Model for Ministry', *ATJ* 41 (1986), pp. 15-22.

Notes to Chapter 5

1. George W. Coats, *Rebellion in the Wilderness. The Murmuring Motif in the Wilderness Traditions of the Old Testament* (Nashville: Abingdon, 1968).

2. Coats, *Rebellion*, pp. 156-84.

3. James Muilenburg, 'Intercession of the Covenant Mediator', in *Word and Meanings*; *Essays Presented to David Winton Thomas* (Cambridge: Cambridge University Press, 1968), pp. 159-83; L. Dunlop, 'The Intercession of Moses. A Study of the Pentateuchal Traditions' (Rome: Pontifical Biblical Institute [dissertation], 1970); George W. Coats, 'The Kings's Loyal Opposition: Obedience and Authority in Exodus 32-34' in *Canon and Authority; Essays in Old Testament Religion and Theology*, ed. G.W. Coats, B.O. Long (Philadelphia: Fortress, 1977), pp. 91-109.

4. Coats, 'The King's Loyal Opposition', pp. 105-109.

5. Coats, *Rebellion*, pp. 209-16.

6. George W. Coats, 'The Sea Tradition in the Wilderness Theme: A Review', *JSOT* 12 (1979), pp. 2-8.

7. 2 Kgs 18.4 makes the point explicitly that the bronze serpent was an object in the paraphernalia of the cult which could be traced directly to Moses. It is clear that the serpent symbolizes God's protection for his people, indeed, his ability to heal his people in the face of physical threat to their

lives. It is therefore significant that the symbol of God's protection/healing, rooted in the wilderness period, is tied directly to Moses. The connection may, however, be secondary. See H.H. Rowley, 'Zadok and Nehushtan', *JBL* 58 (1939), pp. 113-41; K.R. Joines, 'The Bronze Serpent in the Israelite Cult', *JBL* 87 (1968), pp. 245-56.

8. Cf. Noth, *A History*, p. 269. These suggestions are only slightly different.

9. Norbert Lohfink, 'Die Ursünde in der priesterlichen Geschichtserzählung', in *Die Zeit Jesus*, ed. G. Bornkamm, K. Rahner (Freiburg: Herder, 1970), p. 46 n. 32.

10. Coats, *Rebellion*, pp. 47-53.

11. Martin Noth, *Exodus, a Commentary*, trans. J.S. Bowden (Philadelphia: Westminster, 1962), p. 114.

12. Coats, *Rebellion*, pp. 71-82.

13. Aaron Wildavsky, *The Nursing Father: Moses as a Political Leader* (Tuscaloosa: University of Alabama Press, 1984). The author emphasizes Moses' identity with his people. See pp. 92, 102, 113, 118.

14. Coats, *Rebellion*, pp. 140-41.

15. Coats, *Rebellion*, pp. 140-41; W.L. Moran, 'The End of the Unholy War and the Anti-Exodus', *Bibl* 44 (1963), pp. 333-42.

16. Noth, *A History*, p. 273.

17. Eduard Meyer, *Die Israeliten und ihre Nachbarstämme* (Halle: Niemeyer, 1906), pp. 51-70.

18. Noth, *A History*, p. 164.

Notes to Chapter 6

1. Ron M. Hals, 'Legend: A Case Study in Old Testament Form-Critical Terminology', *CBQ* 34 (1972), pp. 166-76. Reprinted in *Saga, Legend, Tale, Novella, Fable*, ed. George W. Coats, JSOTS 34 (Sheffield: JSOT, 1984). The form by definition would not permit an argument that the narrative really intends to describe the virtue of God or any other third person behind the scene. To the contrary, the form requires that the interpreter recognize the hero as the principal focus. See also George W. Coats, 'Tale', in *Saga, Legend, Tale, Novella, Fable* (Sheffield: JSOT Press, 1984).

2. Jan de Vries, *Heroic Song and Heroic Legend*, trans. B.J. Timmer (London: Oxford, 1963).

3. George W. Coats, 'Moses Versus Amalek: Aetiology and Legend in Exodus xvii 8-16', in *Congress Volume Edinburgh*. *VTSup 28* (Leiden: Brill, 1975), pp. 29-41.

4. George W. Coats, 'Humility and Honor: A Moses Legend in Numbers 12', in *Art and Meaning. Rhetoric in Biblical Literature*, ed. David J.A.

Clines, David M. Gunn & Alan J. Hauser; JSOTS 19 (Sheffield: JSOT, 1982), pp. 97-107.

5. Noth, *A History*, pp. 30-32. In n. 120, Noth observes: 'Chapter 12, which is in itself very broken, is one of the hopeless cases of Pentateuchal analysis and therefore I shall not even attempt source analysis. Since the divine name occurs throughout, it might be basic J material with all kinds of proliferations, alterations and, in this case, losses too'.

Notes to Chapter 7

1. George W. Coats, 'The Wilderness Itinerary', *CBQ* 34 (1972), pp. 135-52.

2. Walter Beyerlin, *Origins and History of the Oldest Sinaitic Traditions*, trans. S. Rudman (Oxford: Blackwell, 1965). See also Otto Eissfeldt, 'Die älteste Erzählung vom Sinaibund', *ZAW* 73 (1961), pp. 137-46.

3. Brevard S. Childs, *The Book of Exodus. A Critical, Theological Commentary*, OTL (Philadelphia: Westminster, 1974), pp. 349-50.

4. Childs, *Book of Exodus*, pp. 349-50.

5. See Dennis J. McCarthy, *Treaty and Covenant. A Study in Form in the Ancient Oriental Documents and in the Old Testament*, AB 21 (Rome: Biblical Institute Press, 1978)

6. Childs, *Book of Exodus*, p. 348.

7. Childs, *Book of Exodus*, p. 348

8. Childs, *Book of Exodus*, p. 355.

9. Thomas Dozeman, 'Divine Servant and Israelite Hero', *Hebrew Annual Review* 8 (1985). Dozeman highlights the double character of the Moses image as it appears in Exodus 32 in order to show that Moses appears here as 'ideal mediator'. He defends the thesis in a concluding statement: 'The contradictory functions of Moses pleading to Yahweh for Israel's survival and purging Israel for Yahweh are not the result of separate narratives. On the contrary, Exodus 32 accentuates these conflicting roles by presenting the devotion of Moses for Yahweh and for Israel with equal intensity through the qualities of justice, violence, and prudence. The structure of the narrative suggests that these conflicting loyalties are at the very core of mediation in ancient Israel and necessarily unreconcilable'.

10. Childs, *The Book of Exodus*, p. 351.

11. James Muilenburg, 'The Intercession of the Covenant Mediator (Exodus 33.1a, 12-17)', in *Words and Meanings*, ed. Peter R. Ackroyd & Barnabas Lindars (Cambridge: Cambridge University Press, 1968), pp. 159-81. Muilenburg offers no argument for the existence of 'covenant mediator' as an established office.

12. Childs, *The Book of Exodus*, p. 355.

13. James Muilenburg, 'The "Office" of the Prophet in Ancient Israel', in

The Bible in Modern Scholarship, ed. J. Philip Hyatt (Nashville: Abingdon, 1965), pp. 74-97.

14. Aubrey R. Johnson, *The Cultic Prophet in Ancient Israel* (Cardiff: University of Wales Press, 1962), p. 48.

15. It is well known that the act of 'intercession' has commonly been attributed to the cultic prophet (Gerhard von Rad, *Old Testament Theology*, trans. D.M.G. Stalker [New York: Harper, 1962], II, pp. 51-52). But the act of intercession is not peculiar to the cultic prophet. Cf. 2 Sam. 12.16. Norman K. Gottwald, *The Tribes of Yahweh. A Sociology of the Religion of Liberated Israel, 1250-1050 B.C.E.* (Maryknoll: Orbis, 1979), p. 690. Gottwald points to the diverse elements in this office: 'There was probably even a priestly or lay figure who played the mediator role of Moses in cultic-ideological covenant renewal ceremonies'. His view of the office sets up an analogy with the minor judge. He avers, p. 38, that 'it seems fully as logical an inference, and in the end more convincing, to attribute the primacy of the role of Moses to the impact of the Yahweh cult in Canaan in which there existed a central office (or offices) occupied by one (or more) who articulated the traditions and instructions of the faith and who was (were) conceived in the august role of Moses, "the covenant mediator" or "law proclaimer".' See also Frank M. Cross, *Canaanite Myth and Hebrew Epic. Essays in the History of the Religion of Israel* (Cambridge, Mass.: Harvard University Press, 1973), p. 197. Cross sees the association of Moses with the Tent as evidence of a dominant priestly cast for the image.

16. Childs, *The Book of Exodus*, pp. 355-58.

17. A. Jirku, 'Die Geschichtsmaske des Mose', *ZDPV* (1974), pp. 43-45.

18. George W. Coats, 'The King's Loyal Opposition: Obedience and Authority in Exodus 32-34', in *Canon and Authority. Essays in Old Testament Religion and Theology*, ed. George W. Coats & Burke O. Long (Philadelphia: Fortress, 1977), pp. 91-109.

19. Noth, *A History*, pp. 158-59.

20. Noth, *A History*, p. 121.

21. Cross (p. 197) appparently agrees with Wellhausen's opinion that an allusion to Moses in an archaic poem in Deut. 33.8 ties Moses to the tribe of Levi and offers evidence of an early identification of Moses as a priest. The interpretation of the poem, however, seems to me to be weak. The lines in the two halves of v. 8 are synonymous in parallel, as Wellhausen observes. The context defines the subject of v. 8 as Levi. What, then, supports an identification of 'the faithful one' as Moses rather than Levi? Contrast the interpretation of Moses in the Tent by Childs.

22. See Gottwald, p. 749 n. 254.

23. Coats, *Rebellion, passim*.

24. Jay A. Wilcoxen, 'Some Anthropocentric Aspects of Israel's Sacred History', *JR* 48 (1968), pp. 333-50.

Notes to Chapter 8

1. Hans Walter Wolff, 'The Kerygma of the Yahwist', *Interp* 20 (1966), pp. 131-58.

2. George W. Coats, 'Structural Transition in Exodus', *VT* 22 (1972), pp. 129-42.

3. George W. Coats, 'An Exposition for the Wilderness Theme', *VT* 22 (1972), pp. 288-95.

4. George W. Coats, 'The Wilderness Itinerary', *CBQ* 34 (1972), pp. 135-52.

5. George W. Coats, 'Conquest Traditions in the Wilderness Theme', *JBL* 95 (1976), pp. 177-90; 'An Exposition for the Conquest Theme', *CBQ* 47 (1985).

6. Coats, 'Conquest Traditions', pp. 180-90.

7. Noth, *A History*, pp. 170-71.

8. Coats, 'Conquest Traditions', pp. 177-90.

9. Noth, *A History*, p. 16.

10. George W. Coats, 'Legendary Motifs in the Moses Death Reports', *CBQ* 39 (1977), pp. 34-44.

11. Wayne A. Meeks, *The Prophet-King. Moses Traditions and the Johannine Christology*, NTSup 14 (Leiden: Brill, 1967), pp. 311-13.

12. Coats, 'Legendary Motifs', pp. 34-44.

13. Hillel Barzel, 'Moses: Tragedy and Sublimity', in *Literary Interpretations of Biblical Narratives*, ed. Kenneth R.R. Gros Louis, James S. Ackerman, Thayer S. Warshaw (Nashville: Abingdon, 1974), pp. 120-40.

14. Thomas W. Mann, 'Theological Reflections on the Denial of Moses', *JBL* 98 (1979), pp. 481-94.

Notes to Chapter 9

1. Gerhard von Rad, 'The Form-Critical Problem of the Hexateuch', in *The Problem of the Hexateuch and Other Essays*.

2. Von Rad, 'Problem'.

3. J. Wijngaards, 'הוצא and העלה: A Twofold Approach to the Exodus', *VT* 15 (1965), pp. 91-102. See also Brevard Childs, 'Deuteronomical Formulae of the Exodus Traditions', in *Hebräische Wortforschung* (Leiden: Brill, 1967), pp. 30-39; von Rad, *Theology*, I, pp. 175-86.

4. Childs, 'Deuteronomic Formulae'.

5. Martin Noth, *A History of Pentateuchal Traditions*, trans. Bernhard W. Anderson (Englewood Cliffs: Prentice-Hall, 1972), pp. 58-59.

6. George W. Coats 'The Traditio-Historical Character of the Reed Sea Motif', *VT* 17 (1967), pp. 253-65; Brevard S. Childs, 'A Traditio-Historical Study of the Reed Sea Tradition', *VT* 20 (1970), pp. 406-18. In the later

tradition, the sea event loses its firm contact with the wilderness theme. I am convinced nonetheless that it remains a wilderness topic even for the priestly source. See my comments in 'The Sea Tradition in the Wilderness Theme: A Review', *JSOT* 12 (1979), pp. 2-8.

7. Brevard S. Childs, *The Book of Exodus: A Critical, Theological Commentary*, OTL (Philadelphia: Westminster, 1974), pp. 243-53. A Lauha, 'Das Schilfmeermotiv im Alten Testament', in *Congress Volume Bonn*. *VTSup* 9 (Leiden: Brill, 1963), pp. 32-46. Frank M. Cross, 'The Divine Warrior in Israel's Early Cult', in *Biblical Motifs*, ed. A. Altman (Cambridge, Mass.: Harvard University Press, 1966), pp. 11-30.

8. F.M. Cross, 'The Song of the Sea and Canaanite Myth', in *Journal for Theology and the Church* 5 (1968), pp. 1-25; George W. Coats, 'The Song of the Sea', *CBQ* 31 (1969), pp. 1-17.

9. Robert Bach, 'Die Erwählung Israels in der Wüste' (Bonn: Unpublished dissertation, 1950).

10. Wildavsky, pp. 92, 99-106.

11. George W. Coats, 'Conquest Traditions in the Wilderness Theme', *JBL* 95 (1976), pp. 177-90.

12. One should note the implication of this position for the analysis of the Pentateuch. To recognize that structure in the Pentateuch embraces four distinct themes, elements that compose the whole, does not require a conclusion that the four elements were originally distinct and independent units. The Moses heroic saga increases the weight of an argument that suggests that while the four elements of structure in the Pentateuch obviously exist, they do not obviously disintegrate the apparent unity of the whole. To the contrary, the structure of the heroic saga argues for unity among the elements of structure represented by the themes of tradition. Contrast the evaluation of this analysis by Robert M. Polzin, 'Martin Noth's *A History of Pentateuchal Traditions*', in *Biblical Structuralism. Method and Subjectivity in the Study of Ancient Texts* (Philadelphia: Fortress, 1977), pp. 174-201.

13. See the description of the typical narrative display of theophany by Jörg Jeremias, *Theophanie. Die Geschichte einer alttestamentlichen Gattung*, WMANT 10 (Neukirchen-Vluyn: Neukirchener Verlag, 1965), pp. 7-19.

14. Gerhard von Rad, *Old Testament Theology*, trans. D.M.G. Stalker (New York: Harper & Row, 1962), p. 188.

15. Coats, *Rebellion*, pp. 184-96

16. J.M. Sasson, 'Bovine Symbolism in the Exodus Narrative', *VT* 18 (1968), pp. 380-87.

17. Sasson, pp. 380-87. See also Moses Aberbach and Leivy Smolar, 'Aaron, Jeroboam, and the Golden Calves', *JBL* 86 (1967), pp. 129-40; George W. Coats, 'The Golden Galf in Ps 22: A Hermeneutic of Change', *Horizons in Biblical Theology* 9/1 (1987).

18. George W. Coats, 'History and Theology in the Sea Tradition', *ST* 29 (1975), pp. 53-62.

19. Walther Zimmerli and Joachim Jeremias, *The Servant of God*, SBT 20 (London: SCM, 1952), p. 24. Zimmerli observes that the title can be pre-exilic, although he does not mention this text.

20. Werner E. Lemke, 'The Way of Obedience: 1 Kings 13 and the Structure of the Deuteronomistic History', in *Magnalia Dei. The Mighty Acts of God*, ed. Frank M. Cross, Werner E. Lemke & Patrick D. Miller (Garden City: Doubleday, 1976), pp. 301-26.

21. Zimmerli and Jeremias, pp. 21-22.

22. Zimmerli and Jeremias, pp. 21-22.

23. G.J. Wenham, 'Aaron's Rod (Num. 17.16-28)', *ZAW* 93 (1981), pp. 280-81.

24. George W. Coats, *Rebellion in the Wilderness. The Murmuring Motif in the Wilderness Traditions of the Old Testament* (Nashville: Abingdon, 1968), p. 49.

25. George W. Coats, 'History and Theology in the Sea Tradition', *ST* 29 (1975), pp. 53-62.

26. H.H. Rowley, 'Zadok and Nehushtan', *JBL* 58 (1939), pp. 113-41. Rowley suggests that the Nehushtan came into the Temple, along with Zadok, the priest, from the cult practiced in pre-Davidic Jerusalem. This argument contends to the contrary that the attribution of the Nehushtan to Moses should be taken seriously. And it points to the heroic responsibility of Moses to meet the needs of his people for healing.

27. It is interesting to note that entwined serpents on a pole function even to this day as the symbol of the healing profession.

28. George W. Coats, 'The King's Loyal Opposition: Obedience and Authority in the Moses Traditions', in *Canon and Authority in the Old Testament*, ed. George W. Coats & Burke O. Long (Philadelphia: Fortress, 1977), pp. 91-109.

29. Coats, 'The Golden Calf...'

30. George W. Coats, 'The Ark of the Covenant: A Probe into the History of a Tradition', *HAR* 9 (1985), pp. 137-57.

31. George W. Coats, 'Healing: A Probe into the History of the Moses Traditions', forthcoming in the Childs Festschrift.

Notes to Chapter 10

1. Gerhard von Rad, *Old Testament Theology*, trans. D.M.G. Stalker (New York: Harper, 1962), I, pp. 77-84.

2. Robert Polzin, *Moses and the Deuteronomist. A Literary Study of the Deuteronomic History* (New York: Seabury, 1980). See also von Rad, *Theology*, I, pp. 219-31.

3. Polzin, pp. 205-12.

4. H. Munro Chadwick, *The Heroic Age* (Cambridge: Cambridge University Press, 1926), pp. 227-28. See also Carl Edwin Armerding, 'The Heroic Ages of Greece and Israel: A Literary-Historical Comparison', (Boston: Brandeis University unpublished dissertation, 1968), pp. 109-261.

5. Bernhard W. Anderson, *Understanding the Old Testament* (3rd edn; Englewood Cliffs: Prentice-Hall, 1975), pp. 199-225.

6. George W. Coats, *Rebellion in the Wilderness. The Murmuring Motif in the Wilderness Traditions of the Old Testament* (Nashville: Abingdon, 1968), pp. 199-224.

7. George W. Coats, 'The God of Death: Power and Obedience in the Primeval History', *Interp* 29 (1975), pp. 227-39.

8. Walther Zimmerli, *Ezekiel*, trans. James D. Martin; Hermeneia (Philadelphia: Fortress, 1969), II, pp. 203-23. Zimmerli calls attention to the common use of the term 'shepherd' for king in the larger context of ancient near eastern literature, pp. 213-15. But the dominant item in this description of the shepherds of Israel is not office but activity. The shepherds are judged negatively for failure in a specific series of responsibilities. In the Old Testament, that series belongs more properly with the Moses traditions than with the Davidic traditions. The new David will match office with responsibility.

9. See also Otto Eissfeldt, *The Old Testament. An Introduction*, trans. Peter R. Ackroyd (New York: Harper, 1965), p. 228. 'The similarity of this psalm to Judg. v shows that taken for itself it could be old and even very ancient indeed'. One should note, however, that textual difficulties make the reading uncertain. I.L. Seeligmann, 'A Psalm from Pre-regal Times', *VT* 14 (1964), p. 79: 'The whole conception of Moses as a lawgiver to the congregation of Jacob is hardly in harmony with an ancient poem. Accordingly, one cannot help maintaining that vs 4 is an interpolation betraying a midrashic exegesis'. But whether an old image of Moses or a later midrashic interpretation, the point remains that the image of Moses as lawgiver is fundamental to the tradition. I cannot agree that the allusion to Moses as lawgiver, simply because it is an allusion to him as lawgiver, must be late, a reflection of 'the part played by the Thorah in the life of the Jewish congregations in the Diaspora'.

10. My point must be precise. I am not asserting that the origin of the Moses tradition is in the Sinai theme, originally independent of the other themes of tradition in the Pentateuch. I am suggesting that the image of Moses as lawgiver is implicit in all of the themes about God's mighty acts relevant for the Moses traditions. The most fundamental image for the Moses saga is Moses, the lawgiver. Reference to Moses as lawgiver cannot be taken as distinct from the action of redemption for Israel effected in some manner by Moses. The image of lawgiver cannot be cut away from the image of liberator or shepherd. The point does not deny an original role in the

Moses traditions for the image of Moses as liberator or shepherd or even warrior. But these images do not derail the significance of the picture that casts Moses as lawgiver, even for the earliest tradition.

Notes to Chapter 11

1. Robert Polzin, *Moses and the Deuteronomist. A Literary Study of the Deuteronomic History* (New York: Seabury, 1980).

2. Polzin, *Moses*, p. 10.

3. Trent Butler, 'An Anti-Moses Tradition', *JSOT* 12 (1979), pp. 9-15. See also Polzin, p. 35.

4. If the Deuteronomistic Historian speaks with the authority of Moses, why would he condemn as apostasy an act of reform designed to restore Mosaic tradition? Perhaps the Deuteronomistic Historian appeals to Mosaic authority only when that does not interfere with his primary loyalty to David and Zion. But the problem also points to the difficult mixing between Moses tradition and David tradition. The traditions, at times at war with each other, at times serve a common goal.

5. Does the complaint in 50.8 not mirror the complaint in the Meribah tradition, Exod. 17.1-7 and Num. 20.1-13?

6. Aage Bentzen, *Messias; Moses redivivus; Menschensohn*, ATANT 17 (Zürich: Zwingli, 1948), pp. 42-71.

7. Charles E. Hambrick-Stowe, 'Ruth, the New Abraham; Esther, the New Moses', *Christian Century* 100 (1983), pp. 1130-34.

8. On the connection between Abraham and David, see Ronald Clements, *Abraham and David. Genesis 15 and its Meaning for Israelite Tradition*, Studies in Biblical Theology 2/5 (London: SCM, 1967).

9. Jack Dean Kingsbury, *Matthew: Structure, Christology, Kingdom* (Philadelphia: Fortress, 1975), pp. 99-103.

10. Kingsbury, p. 89.

11. Kingsbury, p. 91.

12. It seems to me to be clear that Matthew's Christology also does not treat Jesus simply as New David, a figure that displaces New Moses in the same way that the Gospel might displace the Law. But the tradition is explicit. In Jesus, the law is not displaced. It is fulfilled. And Jesus is not simply Son of God, a New David. That would leave Matthew with a docetic image that would have no contact with the world of human beings. Combined with images of New Moses, this New David appears in the forms of human being, one who suffers, weeps, bleeds, dies. But he is an authentic human being, obedient to God, compassionate for his people. He is more than New David. He is also New Moses, who with the roles of the New David fulfills the order of creation. In the union, he is New Adam.

BIBLIOGRAPHY

Aberbach, M., & L. Smolar, 'Aaron, Jeroboam, and the Golden Calves', *JBL* 86 (1967), pp. 129-40.

Ackerman, J.S., 'The Literary Context of the Moses Birth Story (Exodus 1-2)', in K.R.R. Gros Louis, *et al.*, eds., *Literary Interpretations of Biblical Narratives* (Nashville: Abingdon, 1974).

Albright, W.F., 'From the Patriarchs to Moses. II. Moses out of Egypt', *BA* 36 (1973), pp. 48-76.

—'Jethro, Hobab and Reuel in Early Hebrew Tradition', *CBQ* 25 (1963), pp. 1-11.

—'Moses in Historical and Theological Perspective', in F.M. Cross, *et al.*, eds., *Magnalia Dei. The Mighty Acts of God* (Garden City: Doubleday, 1976).

Alt, A., The God of the Fathers', in *Essays on Old Testament History and Religion*, trans. R.A. Wilson (Garden City: Doubleday, 1968).

Anderson, B.W., *Understanding the Old Testament* (3rd edn; Englewood Cliffs: Prentice-Hall, 1975).

Armerding, C.E., 'The Heroic Ages of Greece and Israel: A Literary-Historical Comparison' (Boston: Unpublished dissertation [Brandeis], 1968).

Auerbach, E., *Moses* (Detroit: Wayne State University, 1975).

Bach, R., 'Die Erwählung Israels in der Wüste' (Bonn: Unpublished dissertation, 1950).

Barzel, H., 'Moses: Tragedy and Sublimity', in K.R.R. Gros Louis, *et al.*, eds., *Literary Interpretations of Biblical Narratives* (Nashville: Abingdon, 1974), pp. 120-40.

Baumgärtel, F., 'Der Tod des Religionsstifters', *KuD* 9 (1963), pp. 223-33.

Beegle, D.M., *Moses, the Servant of Yahweh* (Grand Rapids: Eerdmans, 1972).

Bentzen, A., *Messias; Moses redivivus; Menschensohn*, ATANT, 17 (Zürich: Zwingli, 1948).

Beyerlin, W., *Origins and History of the Oldest Sinaitic Traditions*, trans. S. Rudman (Oxford: Blackwell, 1965).

Bright, J., *A History of Israel* (Philadelphia: Westminster, 1972).

Brueggemann, W., *The Prophetic Imagination* (Philadelphia: Fortress, 1978).

Buber, M., *Moses. The Revelation and the Covenant*, Harper Torchbooks, 27 (New York: Harper, 1958).

Butler, T.C., 'An Anti-Moses Tradition', *JSOT* 12 (1979), pp. 9-15.

Campbell, E.F., 'Moses and the Foundation of Israel', *Interp* 29 (1975), pp. 141-54.

Campbell, J., *The Hero with a Thousand Faces*, Ballingen Series, 17 (Princeton: Princeton University Press, 1949).

Chadwick, H.M., *The Heroic Age* (Cambridge: Cambridge University Press, 1926).

Childs, B.S., 'The Birth of Moses', *JBL* 84 (1965), pp. 109-22.

—*The Book of Exodus. A Critical, Theological Commentary*, OTL (Philadelphia: Westminster, 1974.

—'Deuteronomical Formulae of the Exodus Traditions', in *Hebräische Wortforschung* (Leiden: Brill, 1967), pp. 30-39.

—'A Traditio-Historical Study of the Reed Sea Tradition', *VT* 20 (1970), pp. 406-18.

Clements, R., *Abraham and David. Genesis 15 and its Meaning for Israelite Tradition*, Studies in Biblical Theology, 2/5 (London: SCM, 1967).

Coats, G.W., 'Abraham's Sacrifice of Faith. A Form-Critical Study of Genesis 2', *Interp* 27 (1973), pp. 389-400.

—'The Ark of the Covenant: A Probe into the History of a Tradition', *HAR* 9 (1985), pp. 137-57.

—'Conquest Traditions in the Wilderness Theme', *JBL* 95 (1976), pp. 177-90.

—'Despoiling the Egyptians', *VT* 18 (1968), pp. 450-57.

—'An Exposition for the Conquest Theme', *CBQ* 47 (1985), pp. 47-54

—'An Exposition for the Wilderness Theme', *VT* 22 (1972), pp. 288-95.

—*From Canaan to Egypt: Structural and Theological Context for the Joseph Story*, CBQMS, 4 (Washington: Catholic Biblical Association, 1976).

—'The Failure of the Hero: Moses as a Model for Ministry', *ATJ* 41 (1986), pp. 15-22.

—'The God of Death': Power and Obedience in the Primeval History', *Interp* 29 (1975), pp. 227-39.

—'The Golden Calf in Ps 22: A Hermeneutic of Change', *Horizons in Biblical Theology* 9/1 (1987).

—'Healing: A Probe into the History of the Moses Traditions', forthcoming in the Childs Festschrift.

—'History and Theology in the Sea Tradition', *ST* 29 (1975), pp. 53-62.

—'Humility and Honor; A Moses Legend in Numbers 12', in *Art and Meaning: Rhetoric in Biblical Literature*, JSOTS, 19 (Sheffield: JSOT, 1982), pp. 97-107.

—'The King's Loyal Opposition: Obedience and Revolution in the Moses Traditions', in G.W. Coats & B.O. Long, eds., *Canon and Authority in the Old Testament*, pp. 91-109.

—'Legendary Motifs in the Moses Death Reports', *CBQ* 39 (1977), pp. 34-44.

—'Moses in Midian', *JBL* 92 (1973), pp. 3-10.

—'Moses Versus Amalek: Aetiology and Legend in Exod. 17.8-16', *VTSup* 28 (1975), pp. 29-41.

—*Rebellion in the Wilderness. The Murmuring Motif in the Wilderness Traditions of the Old Testament* (Nashville: Abingdon, 1968).

—'The Sea Tradition in the Wilderness Theme: A Review', *JSOT* 12 (1979), pp. 2-8.

—'Self-Abasement and Insult Formulas', *JBL* 89 (1970), pp. 14-26.

—'A Structural Transition in Exodus', *VT* 22 (1972), pp. 129-42.

—'The Traditio-Historical Character of the Reed Sea Motif', *VT* 17 (1967), pp. 235-65.

—'What Do We Know of Moses?', *Interp* 28 (1974), pp. 91-94.

—'The Wilderness Itinerary', *CBQ* 34 (1972), pp. 135-52.

Crenshaw, J.L., *Samson. A Secret Betrayed; a Vow Ignored* (Atlanta: John Knox, 1978).

Cross, F.M. *Canaanite Myth and Hebrew Epic. Essays in the History of the Religion of Israel* (Cambridge, Mass.: Harvard University Press, 1973).

—'The Divine Warrior in Israel's Early Cult', in A. Altman, ed., *Biblical Motifs* (Cambridge, Mass.: Harvard University Press, 1966), pp. 11-30.

—'The Song of the Sea and Canaanite Myth', *Journal for Theology and the Church* 5 (1968), pp. 1-25.

Daube, D., *The Exodus Pattern in the Bible. All Souls Studies* (London: Faber & Faber, 1963).

Dozeman, T., 'Divine Servant and Israelite Hero', *Hebrew Annual Review* (1985).

Dunlop, L. 'The Intercession of Moses. A Study of the Pentateuchal Traditions' (Rome: Dissertation, Pontifical Biblical Institute, 1970).

Eakins, J.K., 'Moses', *RevEx* 74 (1977), pp. 461-71.

Eichrodt, W., *Theology of the Old Testament*, trans. J.A. Baker (Philadelphia: Westminster, 1961).

Eissfeldt, O., 'Die älteste Erzählung vom Sinaibund', *ZAW* 73 (1961), pp. 137-46.

Engnell, I., *A Rigid Scrutiny. Critical Essays on the Old Testament*, trans. J.T. Willis (Nashville: Vanderbilt, 1969).

Fohrer, G., *Überlieferung und Geschichte des Exodus. Eine Analyse von Ex 1-15*, BZAW, 91 (Berlin: Töpelmann, 1964).

Gerlin, A., *The Poor of Yahweh*, trans. Mother K. Sullivan (Collegeville: Liturgical Press, 1964).

Gottwald, N.K., *The Tribes of Yahweh. A Sociology of the Religion of Liberated Israel, 1250-1050 BCE* (Maryknoll: Orbis, 1979).

Greenberg, M., *Understanding Exodus. The Heritage of Biblical Israel*, II/1 (New York: Behrman House, 1969).

—'The Thematic Unity of Exodus iii-xi', *Fourth World Congress of Jewish Studies* (Jerusalem: World Union of Jewish Studies, 1967), I, pp. 51-54.

Gressmann, H., *Mose und seine Zeit. Ein Kommentar zu den Mose Sagen*, FRLANT, 18 (Göttingen: Vandenhoeck & Ruprecht, 1918).

Gross, H., 'Der Glaube an Mose nach Exodus (4.14, 19)', in J.J. Stamm, *et al.*, eds., *Wort-Gebot-Glaube: Beiträge zur Theologie des Alten Testaments* (Zürich: Zwingli, 1970), pp. 57-65

Gunkel, H., 'Mose', in *Die Religion in Geschichte und Gegenwart* (2nd edn; Tübingen: Mohr, 1930).

Gunneweg, A.H.J., *Leviten und Priester. Hauptlinien der Traditionsbildung und Geschichte des israelitisch-jüdischen Kultpersonals*, FRLANT, 89 (Göttingen: Vandenhoeck & Ruprecht, 1965).

Habel, N., 'The Form and Significance of the Call Narratives', *ZAW* 77 (1965), pp. 297-323.

Hals, R., 'Legend: A Case Study in Old Testament Form-Critical Terminology', *CBQ* 34 (1972), pp. 166-76; reprinted in G.W. Coats, ed., *Saga, Legend, Tale, Novella, Fable. Narrative Genres in Old Testament Literature*, JSOTS, 34 (Sheffield: JSOT, 1984), pp. 45-55.

Hambrick-Stowe, C.E., 'Ruth, the New Abraham; Esther, the New Moses', *Christian Century* 100 (1983), pp. 1130-34.

Herrmann, S., 'Mose', *EvT* 28 (1968), pp. 301-28.

Hesse, F., 'Kerygma oder geschichtliche Wirklichkeit? Kritische Fragen zu Gerhard von Rads "Theologie des Alten Testaments", I. Teil', *ZThK* 57 (1960).

Hort, G., 'The Plagues of Egypt', *ZAW* 69 (1957), pp. 84-102.

Hyatt, J.P., *Commentary on Exodus*, New Century Bible (London: Oliphants, 1971).

Jeremias, J., *Moses und Hammurabi* (Leipzig: Hinrichs, 1903).

Jeremias, Jörg, *Theophanie. Die Geschichte einer alttestamentlichen Gattung*, WMANT, 10 (Neukirchen-Vluyn: Neukirchener Verlag, 1965).

Jirku, A., 'Die Geschichtsmaske des Mose', *ZDPV* (1974), pp. 43-45.

Johnson, A.R., *The Cultic Prophet in Ancient Israel* (Cardiff: University of Wales Press, 1962) III, pp. 441-50.

Johnson, R.F., 'Moses', in *The Interpreter's Dictionary of the Bible* (Nashville: Abingdon, 1962).

Joines, K.R., 'The Bronze Serpent in the Israelite Cult', *JBL* 87 (1968), pp. 245-56.

Kaiser, W.C., Jr, *Towards an Old Testament Theology* (Grand Rapids: Zondervan, 1978.

Keller, C.A., 'Von Stand und Aufgabe der Moseforschung', *ThZ* 13 (1957), pp. 430-41.

Kingsbury, J.D., *Matthew: Structure, Christology, Kingdom* (Philadelphia: Fortress, 1975).

Knierim, R., 'Exodus 18 und die Neuordnung der mosaischen Gerichtsbarkeit', *ZAW* 73 (1962), pp. 146-71.

Koch, K., 'Der Tod des Religionsstifters', *KuD* 8 (1962), p. 105.

Kraus, H.J., *Worship in Israel. A Cultic History of the Old Testament*, trans. G. Buswell (Richmond: John Knox, 1965).

Kutsch, 'Gideons Berufung und Altarbau Jdc. 6,11-24', *TLZ* 81 (1956), pp. 75-84.

Lauha, A., 'Das Schilfmeermotiv im Alten Testament', in *Congress Volume Bonn. VTSup* 9 (Leiden: Brill, 1963), pp. 32-36.

Lemke, W.E., 'The Way of Obedience: 1 Kings 13 and the Structure of the Deuteronomistic History', in F.M. Cross, *et al.*, eds., *Magnalia Dei. The Mighty Acts of God* (Garden City: Doubleday, 1976), pp. 301-26.

Lohfink, N., 'Die priesterschriftliche Abwertung der Tradition von der Offenbarung des Jahwenamens an Mose', *Bibl* (1968), pp. 1-8.

—'Die Ursünde in der priesterlichen Geschichtserzählung', in G. Bornkamm & K. Rahner, eds., *Die Zeit Jesu* (Freiburg: Herder, 1970).

—'Plagues and Sea of Reeds: Exodus 5-14', *JBL* 85 (1966), pp. 137-58.

Luker, M., 'The Figure of Moses in the Plague Traditions' (Madison: Unpublished dissertation, 1968).

Mann, T.W., 'Theological Reflections on the Denial of Moses', *JBL* 98 (1979), pp. 481-94.

McCarthy, D.J., 'Moses' Dealings with Pharaoh: Ex 7, 8-10, 27', *CBQ* 27 (1965), pp. 336-45.

—*Treaty and Covenant. A Study in Form in the Ancient Oriental Documents and in the Old Testament*, AB, 21 (Rome: Biblical Institute Press, 1978).

Meeks, W.A., *The Prophet-King. Moses Traditions and the Johannine Christology*, NTSup 14 (Leiden: Brill, 1967).

Meyer, E., *Die Israeliten und ihre Nachbarstämme* (Halle: Niemeyer, 1906).

Moran, W.L., 'The End of the Unholy War and the Anti-Exodus', *Bibl* 44 (1963), pp. 333-42.

Morgenstern, J., 'The Despoiling of the Egyptians', *JBL* 68 (1949), pp. 2-3.

Mowinckel, S., *Psalms in Israel's Worship*, trans. D.R. Ap-Thomas (Nashville: Abingdon, 1962).

Muilenburg, J., 'The Form and Structure of the Covenantal Formulations', *VT* 9 (1959), pp. 347-65.

—'Intercession of the Covenant Mediator', in *Word and Meanings: Essays Presented to David Winton Thomas* (Cambridge: Cambridge University Press, 1968), pp. 159-83.

—'The "Office" of the Prophet in Ancient Israel', in J.P. Hyatt, ed., *The Bible in Modern Scholarship* (Nashville: Abingdon, 1965).

Mulhall, M., 'Aaron and Moses. Their Relationship in the Oldest Sources of the Pentateuch' (Washington: Unpublished dissertation, 1973).

Neff, R.W., 'Saga', in G.W. Coats, ed., *Saga, Legend, Tale, Novella, Fable. Narrative Genres in Old Testament Literature*, JSOTS, 34 (Sheffield: JSOT, 1984), pp. 17-32.

Newman, M.L., *The People of the Covenant. A Study of Israel from Moses to the Monarchy* (Nashville: Abingdon, 1962).

Nicholson, E.W., *Exodus and Sinai in History and Tradition*, Growing Points in Theology (Oxford: Blackwell, 1973).

Nohrnberg, J., 'Moses', in B.O. Long, ed., *Images of Man and God. Old Testament Short Stories in Literary Focus* (Sheffield: Almond, 1981), pp. 35-57.

Noth, M., *Exodus, a Commentary*, trans. J.S. Bowden; Old Testament Library (Philadelphia: Westminster, 1962).

—*A History of Pentateuchal Traditions*, trans. B.W. Anderson (Englewood Cliffs: Prentice-Hall, 1972).

—*Numbers, a Commentary*, trans. J.D. Martin (Philadelphia: Westminster, 1968).

Osswald, E., *Das Bild des Mose in der kritischen alttestamentlichen Wissenschaft seit Julius Wellhausen*, Theologische Arbeiten, 18 (Berlin: Evangelische Verlagsanstalt, 1962).

Perlitt, L., 'Moses als Prophet', *EvT* 31 (1971).

Plastaras, J., *The God of Exodus. The Theology of the Exodus Narratives* (Milwaukee: Bruce, 1966).

Polzin, R.M., 'Gerhard von Rad's *The Form-Critical Problem of the Hexateuch*', in *Biblical Structuralism. Method and Subjectivity in the Study of Ancient Texts* (Philadelphia: Fortress, 1977), pp. 150-73.

—'Martin Noth's *A History of Pentateuchal Traditions*', in *Biblical Structuralism. Method and Subjectivity in the Study of Ancient Texts* (Philadelphia: Fortress, 1977), pp. 174-201.

—*Moses and the Deuteronomist: A Literary Study of the Deuteronomic History* (New York: Seabury, 1980).

Porter, J.R., *Moses and the Monarchy. A Study in the Biblical Tradition of Moses* (Oxford: Blackwell, 1963).

Pritchard, J.B., ed., *Ancient Near Eastern Texts* (Princeton: Princeton University Press, 1955).

Rad, G. von, 'Faith Reckoned as Righteousness', in *The Problem of the Hexateuch and Other Essays*, trans. E.W. Trueman Dicken (London: Oliver & Boyd, 1965), pp. 125-30.

—'The Form-Critical Problem of the Hexateuch', in *The Problem of the Hexateuch and Other Essays*, pp. 1-78.

—*Moses*, World Christian Books, 32 (London: Lutterworth, 1960).

—*Old Testament Theology. The Theology of Israel's Prophetic Traditions*, trans. D.M.G. Stalker (New York: Harper & Row, 1965).

Raglan, Lord, 'The Hero of Tradition', in A. Dundee, ed., *The Study of Folklore* (Englewood Cliffs: Prentice-Hall, 1965).

Redford, D.B., 'The Literary Motif of the Exposed Child', *Numen* 14 (1967), pp. 209-28.

Rendtorff, R., *Das überlieferungsgeschichtliche Problem des Pentateuch*, BZAW, 147 (Berlin: De Gruyter, 1977).

—'Moses als Religionsstifter? Ein Beitrag zur Diskussion über die Anfänge der israelitischen Religion', in *Gesammelte Studien zum Alten Testament* (München: Kaiser, 1975), pp. 152-71.

—'The "Yahwist" as a Theologian? The Dilemma of Pentateuchal Criticism', *JSOT* 3 (1977), pp. 2-10.

Rowley, H.H., 'Zadok and Nehushtan', *JBL* 58 (1939), pp. 113-41.

Sasson, J.M., 'Bovine Symbolism in the Exodus Narrative', *VT* 18 (1968), pp. 380-87.

Schmid, H., *Mose. Überlieferung und Geschichte*, BZAW, 110 (Berlin: Töpelmann, 1968).

—*Der sogenannte Jahwist. Beobachtungen und Fragen zur Pentateuchforschung* (Zürich: Theologischer Verlag, 1976).

—'Der Stand der Moseforschung', *Judaica* 21 (1965), pp. 194-221.

Schnutenhaus, F., 'Die Entstehung der Mosetraditionen' (Heidelberg: Unpublished dissertation, 1958).

Seebass, H., *Mose und Aaron, Sinai und Gottesberg*, Abhandlungen zur evangelischen Theologie, 2 (Bonn: Bouvier, 1962).

Seeligmann, I.L., 'A Psalm from Pre-regal Times', *VT* 14 (1964), pp. 75-92.

Smend, R., *Das Mosebild von Heinrich Ewald bis Martin Noth*, Beiträge zur Geschichte der biblischen Exegese, 3 (Tübingen: Mohr, 1959).

—*Yahweh War and Tribal Confederation. Reflections upon Israel's Earliest History*, trans. M. Rogers (Nashville: Abingdon, 1970).

Söderblom, W., *Werden des Gottesglaubens. Untersuchungen über die Anfänge der Religion* (Leipzig: Hinrichs, 1915).

Thompson, T.L., 'The Joseph and Moses Narratives', in J.H. Hayes & J.M. Miller, eds., *Israelite and Judean History* (Philadelphia: Westminster, 1977).

Valentin, H., *Aaron. Eine Studie der vor-priesterschriftlichen Aaron-Überlieferung*, Orbis Biblicus et Orientalia, 18 (Göttingen: Vandenhoeck & Ruprecht, 1978).

Van Seters, J., *Abraham in History and Tradition* (New Haven: Yale University Press, 1975).

Vater, A.M., 'The Communication of Messages and Oracles as a Narration Medium in the Old Testament' (New Haven: Unpublished dissertation, 1976).

—'Narrative Patterns for the Story of Commissioned Communication in the Old Testament', *JBL* 99 (1980), pp. 365-82.

Vaux, R. de, *The Early History of Israel*, trans. D. Smith (Philadelphia: Westminster, 1978).

Vries, J. de, *Heroic Song and Heroic Legend*, trans. B.J. Timmer (New York: Oxford University Press, 1963).

Wenham, G.J., 'Aaron's Rod (Num. 17.16-28)', *ZAW* 93 (1981), pp. 280-81.

Widengren, G., 'What Do We Know About Moses?', in J.I. Durham & J.R. Porter, eds., *Proclamation and Presence. Old Testament Essays in honour of Gwynne Henton Davies* (Richmond: John Knox, 1970), pp. 21-47.

Wijngaards, J., 'הוצא and העלה: A Twofold Approach to the Exodus', *VT* 15 (1965), pp. 91-102.

Wilcoxen, J.A., 'Some Anthropocentric Aspects of Israel's Sacred History', *JR* 48 (1968), pp. 333-50.

Wildavsky, A., *The Nursing Father: Moses as a Political leader* (Tuscaloosa: University of Alabama Press, 1984).

—'The Kerygma of the Yahwist', *Interp* 20 (1966), pp. 131-58.

Zimmerli, W., *Ezekiel*, trans. J.D. Martin; Hermeneia (Philadelphia: Fortress, 1969).

—'Zur Form- und Traditionsgeschichte der prophetischen Berufungsgeschichte', *Ezechiel*, BKAT 13/1 (Neukirchen-Vluyn: Neukirchener Verlag, 1969).

—& Joachim Jeremias, *The Servant of God*, SBT, 20 (London: SCM, 1952).

INDEX

INDEX OF BIBLICAL REFERENCES

INDEX OF AUTHORS

JOURNAL FOR THE STUDY OF THE OLD TESTAMENT

Supplement Series

* Out of print